BRISÉES:

BROKEN BRANCHES

by Michel Leiris

translated by Lydia Davis

NORTH POINT PRESS
San Francisco *1989*

LIBRARY OF CONGRESS
CATALOGING-IN-PUBLICATION DATA
Leiris, Michel, 1901–
   Brisées: Broken branches / by Michel Leiris ; translated by
   Lydia Davis.
     p.   cm.
   ISBN 0-86547-375-7
   I. Title.   II. Title: Broken branches.
PQ2623.E424B74   1989
844'.912—dc19   89-2870

Contents

Author's Note

Back in 1949, Maurice Saillet and I conceived the plan of collecting in a single volume a number of texts I had written that were not strictly literary. The title—*Brisées*—had been decided upon, Mercure de France had agreed to publish it, and I had even drafted a provisional synopsis. Why did I delay so long in carrying out this plan, which goes back more than fifteen years now? The reason is simple: I had gone ahead with the work a little too fast; I needed to have more texts to choose from, texts that would accumulate over time. Now I can say that in any case I have the material not for a pure "collection" but for a fairly complete picture of what has preoccupied me, in very different fields, since the distant period at which I hoped that a certain way of pulverizing words would allow me to grasp the last word in all things.

Despite favorable circumstances, I probably would still have avoided putting this panorama together if I had had to take on the task alone or find help of a more or less mechanical sort. My thanks, therefore, to Denis and Elisabeth Hollier, Alexandra Darkowska, and Louis Yvert for having very kindly spared me the library searches and other small drudgeries involved in the preparation of these *Brisées*.

[March, 1966]

Brisées (bri-zée), s. f. plur.
1. Branches cassées par le veneur
pour reconnaître l'endroit où est la
bête. . . . 3. Marques faites aux
arbres par le passage d'une bête.
4. Branches taillées pour marquer
les bornes d'une coupe de bois.
*"Chaque coupe forme un carré dont les
quatre angles sont marqués par des fossés,
des brisées."* P. L. Cour. I, 239.

E. LITTRÉ, *Dictionnaire de la langue
française* (Paris: Librairie Hachette et
Cie, 1878).

BRISÉES:

BROKEN BRANCHES

Glossary: My Glosses' Ossuary (1925)

A monstrous aberration causes people to believe that language came into being to facilitate their relations with one another. It is with this end in mind, of usefulness, that they make dictionaries in which words are catalogued and given a well-defined meaning (they believe), based on usage and etymology. Now, etymology is a perfectly ineffectual science that is not at all informative about the *true* meaning of a word, that is, the particular, personal signification that each individual ought to assign to it, as his mind pleases. As for usage, it is superfluous to say that that is the lowest criterion to which one could refer.

The everyday meaning and the etymological meaning of a word can teach us nothing about ourselves, since they represent the collective part of language, which was made for all people and not for each of us individually.

By dissecting the words we like, without bothering about conforming either to their etymologies or to their accepted significa-

First published in *La Révolution surréaliste* 1, no. 3 (1925). This note, preceded by a poetic interpretation of seventy-five French words, the first fragments of *Glossary* . . . , was followed by these lines from Antonin Artaud: "Yes, this is all that language is good for from now on, a means of going mad, eliminating thought, rupturing; a labyrinth of foolishness, not a DICTIONARY into which certain pedants from the environs of the Seine may channel their spiritual narrownesses."

tions, we discover their most hidden qualities and the secret ramifications that are propagated through the whole language, channeled
by associations of sounds, forms, and ideas. Then language changes
into an oracle, and there we have a thread (however slender it may be)
to guide us through the Babel of our minds.

Jean-Arthur Rimbaud's Adventurous Life

I cannot imagine what poetry might be, if not a manifestation of a person's essential revolt against the absurd laws of this universe he finds himself thrust into despite himself. Some people will exhaust themselves in jeremiads over the sadness of life, but this is not true revolt: the melancholy that gnaws at them does not bring with it any desire for destruction. Others will make a systematic attempt to destroy every notion in their minds that might push them to act: since any action, they believe, presupposes a minimum of optimism, a certain pragmatism by which a thing is judged according to its results, one must rebel against this as well as against the rest, for to reconcile oneself to taking this path would be to *accept*. These people will remain eternally motionless, sad stylites fed upon by mosquitoes and all the other insects of compromising with one's conscience, defeated in advance by all of life's "hopeless battles," because they did not understand that one must choose this minimal defeat (if one can even call it *defeat*), that which involves the least shame because it is capable of engendering the most destruction, if one is not to be subjected to many other, even more severe, defeats.

A man may believe for a certain time that poetry is the most *real* way he has to show his revolt. He is separating himself from the physical world, he thinks, remaining in communication with it

This review of Jean-Marie Carré's *Vie aventureuse de Jean-Arthur Rimbaud* (Jean-Arthur Rimbaud's Adventurous Life) (Paris: Librairie Plon, 1926) first appeared in *Clarté* 5, n.s., no. 2 (1926).

only through the vague magic link of words, upsetting relations by agitating these same words, sometimes building a new world in his own image . . . He thinks he has broken all his chains, spurned all forms of acceptance. Yet he is forgetting that his system is still subject to the convention of language (one of the most crushing) and that the physical world is still there, in the multiple splendor of its garbage.

But this blindness doesn't usually last long. The poet's quarrels with ideas, sentences, and words soon show him what hard compromises he was accepting and how derisory and unreal was the hold he claimed to have over the world through the intermediary of words. Poetry will no longer be enough to assuage his revolt, and he will turn to the world and look for a way to breach its detested laws.

If the time or the country he lives in allows him still to believe in the power of magic, he will become a sorcerer or a necromancer, will conclude a pact with the forces of hell so that he can dominate the earthly world. If, on the other hand, the "lights" of his time prevent him from relying seriously on these resources, he will draw up a rational plan of his prison, then try to find out to what extent he can control it.

He will first discover that the laws of physics can't be changed. Hallucination at one time might have given him the illusion that they were metamorphosing, but he knows well that when he wakes up the weight is still there, along with the beating of his heart and the flux of his blood. He will then fall back on the second series of laws he is slave to: the laws of society. An enormous drive will raise him against the idiotic laws that men have invented to constrain one another; he will become a lycanthrope, an anarchist, a rebel against all social relations imposed on his person. He will think he can shake off this yoke and smash it—another utopian fantasy, for he is the one who will be fatally smashed by the laws, without his having been able to make a breach in their severity.

Giving up individual revolt when he realizes that it can only lead him to destroy himself without changing, that is, destroying, anything in the world, this man will turn to social revolution, the only way to carry out his revolt, the one method of transmuting values. He will understand in what way he can help create an upheaval in the world, in his sphere at least, by allying himself with the oppressed majority in its implacable struggle against the oppressive minority. Whether this upheaval is great or not, in absolute terms, it is in any case the greatest a man can produce, and this is certainly enough for the feeling of revolt to find a concrete manifestation in it and change from being vague and abstract to being precise, tangible, and for this very reason capable of transforming at least a wrinkle in the face of the universe.

Only Revolution can deliver us from the ignoble dead weight of holdovers. A total renewal of relations between man and man will arise from it. It will cause the whole rotten armature of contemporary thinking to crumble. More than sufficient reasons, I think, for any true poet to devote himself to it body and soul.

Perhaps all this hasn't much to do with Jean-Marie Carré's book on the life of Rimbaud.

Arthur Rimbaud, "French poet and traveler," say the Larousse Dictionary. Let me add: and revolutionary . . .

All true poetry is inseparable from Revolution.

The Hieroglyphic Monad

> The magic alphabet, the mysterious hieroglyphic
> come to us incomplete and falsified either by time
> or by those very beings whose interest is to keep
> us ignorant; let us retrieve the lost letter or the
> obliterated sign, let us recompose the dissonant scale,
> and we will become strong in the world of the spirits.
>
> GÉRARD DE NERVAL

*I*t was inevitable that man, inventor of writing and language, would fall into this trap, which he had built with his own hands. He hypostatized words and signs and then believed some god had revealed them to him. "I am Alpha and Omega," says the Word incarnate in Apocalypse, thus showing, even more than tradition and the cabala would have it, that if God is the beginning and end of all things, he is at the same time a mere sign, a combination of letters and words. Nowadays, when Science reigns supreme everywhere, man is reverting to his old mistake and, though he often claims the opposite, tends to view the laws he has forged to explain phenomena not as a way of describing the universe, a convenient notation invented by him for his personal use, but as the true omnipotent God who commands all things, arranging them as he likes. Now that he has delimited the area of his knowledge, carefully denying it every-

This review of *La Monade hiéroglyphique* by John Dee, of London, translated from the Latin by Grillot de Givry (Paris: Bibliothèque Chacornac, 1925), first appeared in *La Révolution surréaliste* 3, nos. 9–10 (1927).

thing that could make it noble, denying it incursions into the Absolute, he heaps every sort of scorn on those who believed in the possibility of a transcendent science, one not enslaved to utilitarian ends but capable of truly giving "the place and the formula." At the very most, contemporary scholars and philosophers condescend to regard occultists and alchemists as their precursors, deigning to note that the search for the Philosophers' Stone, for example, fortuitously led to the discovery of many substances; that the idea of the transmutation of metals is not, in any case, in disagreement with current hypotheses about the structure of matter and that a start was made recently at verifying it experimentally in certain radioactive phenomena; observing also that magic has always had an influence on philosophy and that it is possible, among other things, to make a connection between Hegel and the German Philosophers of Nature, on the one hand, and Jakob Böhme, Paracelsus, and the Alexandrian mystics on the other. These modern scholars and philosophers, so concerned about being sure, so alien to conjecture, and so unambitious, seeking to satisfy only a very lame curiosity, have reduced everything to their own measure. They pretend to regard alchemists merely as vulgar fabricators, motivated by a banal cupidity or lost in sorry research projects in which they had neither the intelligence nor the means to be successful. Even more often, they accuse them of pure and simple bad faith. They forget that many were inspired men primarily pursuing the construction of a palpable absolute, the development of a concrete substance containing all secrets and capable of yielding to them the hidden forces of the universe, an admirable claim to freedom . . .

Written by John Dee (1537–1607), astrologer and geographer to Elizabeth I of England, and dedicated to Maximilian, "King of the Romans, of Bohemia, and of Hungary," *Monas hieroglyphica* is a brief, abstruse treatise composed of twenty-four theorems (whose contents, at least in the case of the most important ones, seem to stand in symbolic relation to the number designating the place they occupy in the sequence of the work), along with many figures and pictures.

> The first mystical letters of the Hebrews, Greeks, and Romans formed by God alone and transmitted to mortals (something man's arrogance may object to), as well as all the signs that represent them, were produced with dots, straight lines, and peripheries of circles. . . . *First Theorem*: It was with a straight line and a circle that the first and simplest demonstration and representation of things was made, both of those that did not exist and those hidden under the veils of nature.[1]

Such are the principles on which the cabalistic method of John Dee is based, a method which, combined with the mystical interpretation of numbers and of the hieroglyphics of the stars, will allow him to establish that a figure he calls a "hieroglyphic monad," composed of certain astrological signs (of which the main one is the hieroglyph of Mercury derived from the central dot or generating IOD) arranged according to a predetermined order and predetermined measurements, is truly "the felt Unity of Images," the "most unique monad" in which all the diversity of the universe is condensed: Man's metaphysical destiny, the motion and influence of the stars, the formula for burning mirrors, the germination and death of creatures, the formation of the terrible Stone, called DARR in the language of the angels.[2]

In this strange work, punctuated here and there by the obscure outcropping of some myth relating to the Great Work of alchemy (the Egg and the Scarab, the Phoenix, the garden of the Hesperides, the Man-of-Every-Hour), the cross, sign of the four elements, both

---

[1] See, in Dionysius the Areopagite (*The Divine Names*, chapter 4), the passage relating to the analogy between the movements of celestial intelligences and the movements of the soul: *circular, oblique, direct.*

[2] The angels' name for the Stone was revealed by an apparition to John Dee and his medium Edward Kelly, as he tells us in an account published in 1659, *A True and Faithful Relation of What Passed for Many Years between Dr. John Dee and Some Spirits.*

ternary and quaternary (two intersecting lines and their point of in-
tersection—four straight lines constituting four right angles), is the
site of the metamorphoses. It is from the cross that one deduces the
number 252, which symbolizes the Stone; the letter L, which is pronounced like the Hebrew name EL, meaning God; and the Latin
word LUX, Light, formed of the three letters v = 5, x = 10, and
L = 50, "Word that is final and magisterial (through the union and
conjunction of the Ternary in the Unity of the Word)." Nevertheless, the primordial role reverts to the phallic IOD, the generating
point that marks the center of the cross.

Beyond this theurgy (constantly and closely tied, in fact, to the
search for the Philosophers' Stone, which John Dee correlates with
Christ), the author—still using a method of thought entirely different from modern Western logic—describes how particles of matter move, what chemical operations govern the formation of the
Stone and the appropriate form for the vessels[3] and instruments that
will be employed, all of this rigorously deduced from the figure of
the monad, whose precise geometrical construction he also teaches
us. The whole book centers on philosophical research, and the following passage from Khunrath (1560–1605), in the *Amphitheatrum
sapientiae aeternae*, defines the scope of it for us:

> What is, in the cabala, UNION with GOD by man reduced to the sim-
> plicity of a Monad, is the same thing, in Physical Chemistry, as the
> FERMENTATION of our glorious, supremely perfect Stone with the
> Macrocosm in its parts. —And: just as man joined to GOD is, because
> of GOD, almost a human god or a divine man, that is, almost DEI-
> FIED, and for this reason can do anything he wants, since it is what
> GOD HIMSELF wants; so the PHILOSOPHERS' STONE having fer-
> mented with the larger World in its parts transforms itself by reason
> of this ferment into whatever it likes and diversely changes every-
> thing into everything, according to the diverse nature of each thing;
> and it will coequalize all things totally, singularly, and universally.

[3]One will represent an alpha, the other an omega.

True Stone of scandal and sacrilege for the modern logician and theologian (if indeed these moles deign to take seriously into account the existence of such a book), John Dee's little work, because of its subject, its language, the mysteriously premeditated arrangement of its parts, constitutes a profoundly troubling object. The almost magical action it exercises on the spirit causes one to be able to see it as creating, in the domain of writing, something analogous to that concretized absolute, that vehicle of secret capacities that the ancient alchemists and the author himself hunted, in the domain of Nature, in the form of the Philosophers' Stone. The schemata that illustrate it, far from remaining fixed, become filled with a disturbing life through the numerous changes in their interpretation.

"Horizon of Time." "Horizon of Eternity." "Shadows. Crystalline Serenity. Citrinity. Anthrax." Each of these terms loosens a slab of rock that walled a phantom into one of the caves of understanding, but this book remains obstinately closed . . .

"*Intellectus iudicat veritatem. Contactus ad punctum.* —Here the Vulgar Eye will see only darkness and will greatly despair." John Dee, *Monas hieroglyphica*. Antwerp, 1564.

The Case of
Arnold Schoenberg

*For Georges Limbour, whose works are haunted
by the spirits of marvellous musicians.*

No one had ever before torn asunder rhythm and the magma
of sound except in the completely relative manner in which one cuts
up an animal: there remained, always, a spinal column with regu-
lated intervals to serve as a guide to the timid across the auditory pit
in which various orchestral monsters roared at a certain distance
from one another; the brasses being a head that was capable, at most,
of taking the bit in its teeth now and then; the violins a foot better
than a hare's foot for coating faces with a sentimental makeup. Harmony was in fairly good health, despite alleged licenses, and the
greatest indiscretions never consisted of more than upsetting the
flowerpot in order to make the petals drop off in a more directly intoxicating way. All in all, then, people were very well behaved, despite some acts of violence, and when they grew tired of games and
the smell of flowers, they liked nothing better than to invoke the
Great Discipline, the severe grace of the mathematical divinities, as
calmly beautiful as pictures in their sharp-edged showcases.

This article, inspired by a concert devoted to Arnold Schoenberg and conducted by
him (Paris, December 15, 1927), was written in 1929 for *Documents*, which did not
take it, and then published (with a small cut noted here) in the program of the Festival de Musique Contemporaine dedicated to Arnold Schoenberg (two concerts
conducted by René Leibowitz, January 25 and 29, 1947, at the Ecole Normale de
Musique).

They did not think, or dare, however, to take this logic as far as it could go, to push it to its cruelest limits of frenzy, to the point where the last veil would drop from this divinity, so very sympathetic, and it would be revealed, in its terribly dazzling height, as more fit to cause fear than even the most desperate pleasure. It was Arnold Schoenberg who dared perform the sacrilege, and for this, as is only right, his reward has been the derisive laughter of idiots everywhere.

A magician from the tales of Hoffmann could not be dressed otherwise than in these skimpy-looking suits, could have no other face than this hairless mask surmounted by a bald skull and adorned with huge glasses that must offer his eyes the spectacle of a vitrified world. But it is precisely this glaucous vision that he reconstructs in his music, when he builds up this great space, almost deserted and almost dead—foliated like a harmonica—whose few elements (though they are connected) seem destined to remain forever separate, isolated in a pure state by the ravines surrounding them—a world at once unified and broken, each constituent part of which retains its particular virtue, independent of any relation to another—as happens in the world of classical magic, where stones, plants, and animals are small individual worlds, each one endowed with its own life, though closely bound together by the mysterious link of correspondence, whose power always works, despite the interstices.

Such a "scandalous" dissociation—which does not allow for the creation of unity except by virtue of relations quite different from the relations ordinarily allowed—seems unprecedented in the field of music and in other fields can only be compared to the poetic revolution caused by Arthur Rimbaud, for instance, in his *Illuminations* or (no doubt more exactly) those created after him by Mallarmé, for one, in *Un Coup de dés jamais n'abolira le hasard*, and Picasso, for another—when both were the first coolly to turn the kaleidoscope of invention to achieve their disconcerting reconstructions . . .

Arnold Schoenberg, musician and aesthetician, is also a painter, and we know of several extraordinary *visions* of his, among more mediocre pictures. Yet it is profoundly significant that such a man should have thought of painting a portrait of himself viewed from the back, he who mercilessly denudes the corridors of the world of sound, shows the other side of things—the reverse of more than one medal with a profile that is altogether too pleasant—and does not allow any framework to remain, no matter how vague, not even a skeletal sort of background.

When the human voice is reduced to being no longer a song, a word, or a cry, but the articulation of the unnamable itself, it is natural that there should be no other sound than the grinding of ice in polar regions, the light, intermittent crackling of silk in the highest zones of the atmosphere, at the moment when the aurora borealis unfurls its strange, cold spangles. Majesty does not tolerate other eyes than these hard crystals; but in fact is there majesty here?

A description, of whatever kind it may be, always consists of discovering something human in its object, of bringing down to our human height the inordinately large size that objects acquire from the fact that they are separate from us. Art criticism, too, has its arsenal of weapons, but how many of its harquebuses and halberds are rusty . . .

Viridity, purity, majesty, cruelty, and even if one were to add *miraculous intimacy*—a wretched rubble of words, ridiculous pebbles we drop one by one behind us, ever fearful as we are, dismayed at being thrown into this simple, new world, the world of Schoenberg, where our lightest footstep echoes like the clanking of a bunch of keys!

It is no more worthwhile to use the vocabulary of Wagnerian "depth," Russian "sensuality," or French "clear architecture" than it would be to quote one of those absurd, all-purpose commonplaces tossed haphazardly into the conversation as soon as it bears on music—like Thomas Browne's famous remark, that "even that vulgar and Tavern-Music, which makes one man merry, another mad, strikes me into a deep fit of devotion," or Baudelaire's even more famous remark, that "music carves out the sky."

Indeed, it would be just as grotesque to say that *every note of Schoenberg's is the physical conjuring of a spirit* . . .

If it makes sense, however, to observe the rule of not applying to such an amazingly closed object the least qualifier (bound to have no more value than a mere—and fatally deceptive—label or ordinary scrap of paper), one thing still remains to be said, which, though it is a truism, will nevertheless never be proclaimed loud enough: *that at last one must get used to not seeking everywhere only what is pleasant.*

Music is not made to charm the ears, even austerely, any more than painting is made to enchant the eyes. At the very most, one can say that it is necessarily addressed to the sense of hearing, as painting is addressed to sight. And possibly, even so, it strikes the ear only in an imaginary way.[1]

Let us be rid, once and for all, of the hedonistic principle that can basically be found—in a form that is more or less disguised—at the root of almost every attack against innovation! Enough of those overly facile, weak, and fastidious "voluptuaries" . . . In truth, everything takes place well beyond pain or pleasure.

And let us, especially, not speak of something as beautiful or ugly, "consonant" or "dissonant"—or classical or romantic, ancient or modern, retrograde or progressive!

What is more important than anything else is the battle we have been obliged to wage from time immemorial against the outside world, thwarting its barbarous tricks with tricks that are even more barbarous. Despite the apparent variety of different processes that one of these tricks has taught for centuries past (the one that was not

[1]As though music were something to read more than something to hear. But Schoenberg's music seems to me, in 1966, to be one of the most *direct* there can be, as habit has its effect and taste changes! [At this point in the main body of the text some material from the unpublished original essay was cut.]

so long ago still known as the "fine arts"), it is one single process that is being judged today: that of reality. When music and painting attack respectively time and space (which form the canvas of reality), this struggle is their highest reason for existing.

Going far beyond the solutions proposed by his fellows, who are infatuated with Reason, Humor, or Brutality, Arnold Schoenberg genially takes part in this process, because—abandoning himself entirely to this "inner constraint" whose slave he declares himself to have been—he is not afraid to place music on a point that is steeper and more at risk than any other: vertigo's very crest, bristling with saw teeth.

Metaphor

*M**etaphor* (from the Greek μεταφορά, transfer) is a figure
by which the mind applies the name of one object to another object,
because of a shared characteristic that allows them to be put side by
side and compared" (Darmesteter). And yet it is hard to know where
metaphor begins and where it ends. An abstract word is formed by
the sublimation of a concrete word. A concrete word, which never
designates an object by more than one of its qualities, is itself hardly
more than a metaphor, or at the very least a figurative expression.
Moreover, to designate an object by an expression that corresponds
to it not figuratively but literally, one would need to know the very
essence of that object, which is impossible, since we can know only
phenomena, not things in themselves.

Not only language but the whole of intellectual life is based on a
play of transpositions, a play of symbols, which can be described as
metaphorical. Then again, knowledge always proceeds by comparison, so that all known objects are connected to one another by relations of interdependency. With any two of them, it is impossible to
determine which is designated by the name proper to it and is not a
metaphor of the other, and vice versa. A man is a moving tree, just
as much as a tree is a rooted man. In the same way, the sky is a rarefied
earth, the earth a denser sky. And if I see a dog running, it is just as
much *the run that is dogging*.

. . . Even this article is metaphorical.

This text and the seven that follow were written for and published in *Documents* 1,
nos. 3–7 (1929). "Metaphor," "Talkie," "Mouth Water," and "Debacle" appeared
under the heading "Dictionary." "Hans Arp" is the review of an exhibition of Arp's
sculptures at the Galerie Goemans.

Civilization

*H*owever little taste one might have for proposing metaphors as explanations, civilization may be compared without too much inexactness to the thin greenish layer—the living magma and the odd detritus—that forms on the surface of calm water and sometimes solidifies into a crust, until an eddy comes to break it up. All our moral practices and our polite customs, that radiantly colored cloak that hides the coarseness of our dangerous instincts, all those lovely forms of culture we are so proud of—since it is thanks to them that we can call ourselves "civilized"—are ready to disappear at the slightest turbulence, to shatter at the slightest impact (like the thin mirror on a fingernail whose polish cracks or roughens), allowing our horrifying *primitiveness* to appear in the interstices, revealed by the fissures just as hell might be revealed by earthquakes, when these cosmic revolutions burst the fragile skin of the earth's circumference and for a moment lay bare the fire at the center, whose wicked and violent heat keeps even the stones molten. Not a day goes by that we don't notice some premonitory sign of such a catastrophe, so that we can truly say not that we are dancing or standing on a volcano but that our whole life, our very breathing, is in touch with lava flows, craters, geysers, and everything else to do with volcanoes and that as a consequence, if we hold up to it a mirror with suitably thick silvering and with a sufficiently sensitive surface, it must be capable of painting long sulfur-colored lines thereon.

A woman's fingernail, as red and as pointed as a ruby dagger (amazing that the blood has remained in the middle and not run to

[For source information, see p. 18.]

the tip), and the wounds cut in precious stones by keen, hard tools that murder the mineral and reduce it to a constellation of angles in turn murderous; a bodily attitude that abruptly relaxes; a fleeting gesture as touching as the sudden swell of a sail on a rising sea— these are precious signs that help us understand how close we are to savages, our various finery of dark or bright cloth being in no way different from skin-and-feather costumes over tattoos depicting mysterious adventures on the body, like the writing of the stars, which in the air forecasts human events . . .

We're tired of all-too-insipid shows that aren't inflated by any potential or actual revolt against sacred "politeness"—the politeness of the arts, which we call "taste"; the politeness of the brain, which we call "intelligence"; the politeness of life, which we designate by a word that smells as dusty as the bottom of an old bureau drawer: "morality." It would be wrong to characterize us as blasé, but the fact is we're sick of plots that are always the same, derived from our living habits, which are further discredited every day, and it isn't enough for us to act in a way that might be equivalent, for example, to the behavior of certain savages who think the best possible use for a telegraph pole is to turn it into a poison arrow (because isn't that more or less what we're doing when we take a mask or a statue that was made for complicated, precise ritual purposes and turn it into a vulgar art object—an infinitely more deadly insult than that paid to European inventions by the savages I just mentioned, since it attacks a fateful, serious mystical theology rather than mere telegraphy, which is the fruit of a science that can never receive too much scorn?). We've had enough of all that, which is why we would so much like to get closer to our primitive ancestry, why we have so little esteem left for anything that doesn't wipe out the succession of centuries in one stroke and put us, stripped of everything, naked, in a more immediate and newer world.

Over the past few years we have seen many signs of this rebellion in literature and painting, we have seen them in all the arts, but in theater there have so far been very few capable of giving us such distinct satisfaction as the following note, which appears in the program of a show everyone will recognize as soon as they read it and is intended as an explanation of one scene in the revue:

PORGY
The subject of the scene is as follows:
"In the Southern states, the land is at sea level and when a Negro dies, if he is not rich enough to be buried in the mountains, he is buried in the swamps, where his body floats to the surface again. When a Negro dies and he is poor, all the other Negroes in the village gather around his coffin and with their singing create a sort of hysteria that induces the men to steal and the women to sell themselves to white men, to raise enough money to bury the dead man. The scene takes place in a barn."

Pedants tend to be disdainful about everything to do with American Negro jazz and art, seeing the current taste for these works as nothing more than a fashion, a passing infatuation with certain exotic forms similar to an earlier infatuation with Hungarian gypsies—in short, a simple matter of wanting to keep up with the latest trend. Others, who are more sentimental and drip with romanticism, can talk about nothing but slavery, nostalgia, primitive violence, pathetic Garden of Eden stammerings, or the melancholy of big cities, which are like vast sugarcane plantations with their stands of pipes and chimneys. Now that we have seen the *Black Birds* show, we have to put an end to all this nonsense.

What is beautiful about such art is not its exotic aspect nor the highly modern elements in it (this modernism is pure coincidence), but primarily the fact that it doesn't really constitute an Art. Actually, it seems quite absurd to take such bright, spontaneous productions and stick them with this awful capitalized word that we should write only with a pen full of spiderwebs. Obviously, jazz and whatever derives from jazz have their own rules and their own logic, but that doesn't mean we can talk about "Art," about Great Art, as though we were talking about a particular work by someone who knew he was (or thought he was) inspired . . . Shows like the *Black Birds* revue take us back to a point very far this side of art, to a point of human development at which that bastard conception, issue of the illegitimate loves of magic and free play, has not yet been hypertrophied.

Furthermore, all this is as remote as it could be from gypsy sentimentality. Negro music does not sing about "the eternal regrets that stab our hearts," as they say; what we can say about it is just the opposite, that as we listen to it we feel a terrible regret, the regret that we are so painfully incapable of this sort of simple and beautiful expression, the regret that we are so mediocre, living such a mediocre life, that we are so dull and ugly compared to these creatures, who are as touching as trees.

And so this music and this dancing don't stop at our skin but put down deep, organic roots in us, roots whose thousand ramifications penetrate us; and though this surgery is painful, it gives us stronger blood.

Yet what we may feel sorry about in such shows is that, however powerfully they move us, they still don't completely manage to overcome our spinelessness and create a hysteria as enormous as the hysteria described in the "Porgy" account, a hysteria so intense that it would be capable of immediately driving the audience to commit sordid acts or indulge in extravagant debauches. For this reason it seems the sculptor Giacometti was entirely correct when he said one day that he thought the only possible theater piece would be the following: the curtain rises, a fireman comes on stage and shouts "Fire!," the curtain falls, everyone panics, and the theater empties in wild disorder.

Perhaps circus acts, like the unforgettable scene in the Gleich Circus when a whole crowd of acrobats performed far above us, go a little further than other spectacles, because something real is happening here and because here, just as on the spot where a murder has been committed or in the vicinity of a slaughterhouse, we breathe in the disgusting odor of death, suspending the threat of danger above our passive spectators' heads. We're not really very far away from the Stone Age, and the thick blood of the ancient mammoths killed by our grandfathers often rushes to our heads again in billows of dark malice.

This viewpoint is borne out by the following passage taken from the *Journal* of August 15, 1929:

THE ZOOLOGICAL GARDENS
Mlle Claryse (Diavolina), the new attraction in the Zoological Gardens' free circus, will make her debut today, August 15, at 4 P.M. Her leap from one springboard to another will be 8 meters long and 4 meters high.

Diavolina will perform her leap of death again at 10 P.M. She has been engaged by the Gardens until the end of August, *so that all of Paris will be able to admire this beautiful young woman as she risks her life in each of the performances of the free circus*, which take place every day at 4 P.M. and 10 P.M.

And so we enjoy seeing other people take risks as we sit comfortably back in our chairs and give ourselves up to the maddening exhilaration of danger, while never actually exposing ourselves to the slightest hazard likely to destroy our flesh, so enamored of lazy tranquillity. This is perhaps the only difference that exists between our period and the period of the cavemen: today we hire a multitude of scapegoats who take it upon themselves to perform for us everything we wouldn't be brave enough to perform ourselves. This is the very reason, I think, that murderers are so popular: a good crime is no doubt horrible, but at the same time it unconsciously satisfies everyone, and the murderer becomes a kind of sorcerer who has ritually performed the most terrifying of sacrifices.

The time we are living in, the second quarter of the twentieth century, clearly fails to live up to the hopes of the naive optimists. There really is great boredom, despite these few glimmers of madness. The worst misfortune is that even though we live in the midst of magic, we are no longer openly mystical enough to be entitled, every day, to sign a pact with the devil!

Joan Miró

*Born April 20, 1893, in Barcelona, Joan Miró entered his native city's
School of Fine Arts at a very early age; there he proved to be very awkward
and a very bad student. After several fights with his family he dropped painting and went to work in an office. But he had a habit of covering the account
books with sketches and naturally enough was soon shown the door . . .
When he was nineteen, Miró entered the Gali Academy in order to devote
himself entirely to painting. During this period he was, in his own words, a
"phenomenon of awkwardness." "I am a colorist, but when it comes to form,
I am a nonentity. I can't distinguish a straight line from a curve. I manage
to attain a strong sense of form by drawing from touch, with my eyes closed."
After three years, Miró left the Academy and worked by himself. "I have no
plastic means of expressing myself," he wrote; "this makes me suffer atro-
ciously and I sometimes bang my head against the wall in despair . . ." In
March 1920 he moved to Paris, and his first show in France was at the Galerie La Licorne from April 29 to May 14, 1921. Nothing was sold. A period
of poverty and hard times followed . . . At last a show at the Galerie Pierre
from June 12 to 27, 1925, caused a considerable stir.*

*"I am always guided by passion and faith," Miró writes about himself
as he is now. "I often change the way I paint, looking for ways of expressing
myself; always I am guided by this burning passion, which makes me walk
from right to left."*

Today it certainly seems that before writing, painting,
sculpting, or composing anything worthwhile, one has to have accustomed oneself to an exercise analogous to that performed by cer-

[For source information, see p. 18.]

tain Tibetan ascetics for the purpose of acquiring what they call, more or less (I say "more or less" because here the language of the West, which presents everything in a dramatic form, must very probably turn out to be inadequate), the *understanding of emptiness*. This technique—one of the most astonishing that has ever been invented in regard to the alchemy of the spirit—consists, approximately, of this: You look at a garden, for instance, and you examine its every detail (studying the most infinitesimal particularities of each), until your memory of it is so exact and intense that you can continue seeing it, with equal clarity, even with your eyes closed. Once you are in perfect possession of this image, you subject it to a strange treatment. The idea is to subtract, one by one, all the elements that make up the garden, without the image losing anything of its force or ceasing to fascinate you, however weakly. Leaf by leaf you mentally strip the trees, stone by stone you bare the ground. You remove a wall from one spot, from another a stream, farther off a living creature, somewhere else a flower-covered gate. Soon nothing remains but the sky purified of all its clouds, the air washed of its rains, the ground reduced to arable land and a few thin trees raising their trunks and desiccated branches. You eliminate these last plants in their turn, so that only the sky and the earth remain face to face. But now the earth and the sky too must disappear, the sky first, abandoning the earth to a terrible soliloquy, then the earth itself, which is not replaced by anything, this last absence allowing the spirit really to see and contemplate *emptiness*. Only then do you reconstruct the garden piece by piece, traveling the same route in the opposite direction; then you begin again, performing this series of successive destructions and reconstructions in a quicker and quicker rhythm, until you have acquired a total understanding of physical emptiness, the first step toward an understanding of true emptiness—of moral and metaphysical emptiness, which is not, as one might be tempted to believe, the negative notion of nothingness but the positive understanding of a term at once identical and contrary to nothingness, one designated by a name as cold as a marble pedestal and as hard as a bell clapper, the *absolute*, more elusive than a tiny vein of bronze in the interstices of an imaginary stone.

The Catalan Joan Miró must in all fairness be included among the contemporary painters who have gone furthest in this sort of endeavor.

It may at first seem strange to speak of asceticism in Miró's case. The burlesque aspect of his canvases, the astonishing joy that emanates from them seem to belie this view of him. And yet when we look at him closely, we can understand that this painter must have achieved an emptiness in himself that was quite complete for him to have rediscovered such a childhood, at once so serious and so clownish, stitched in such a primitive mythology, based on the metamorphoses of stones, plants, animals, somewhat as in tales of primitive tribes, where all the elements in the world go through such unlikely transformations.

If there was a time when Miró's painting posed and resolved, without any difficulty, all sorts of small equations (sun = potato, slug = small bird, gentleman = moustache, spider = sex, man = soles of the feet), it seems that today things have changed and this painter is no longer satisfied by overly simple solutions. It was possible to believe he gave a very faithful picture of our sky eternally filled with bitter antics, in canvases where hordes of strange will-o'-the-wisps made merry, along with dogs whose hindquarters were lemon halves, trees with newspapers for branches, toes like tentacles . . . In the same way one can justly consider the picture composed uniquely of a small hole made with a pin near one of the upper corners of a more or less uniformly colored surface to be the very portrait of humor . . . Of the same sort, too, were those immense canvases that seemed not so much painted as soiled, murky as ruined buildings, alluring as faded walls on which generations of poster-plasterers, together with centuries of drizzle, have inscribed mysterious poems, long spots with evil configurations, as uncertain as alluvial deposits that have come from some unknown place, sands carried along by rivers with perpetually changing courses, subject as they are to the motion of the wind and rain.

Now it seems that Miró has broken away from this sorcery. His pictures are still exciting mysteries, but mysteries that do not fear the noon light, and all the more disconcerting because no cock's crow will put them to flight. The specters he brings on stage will not vanish when the smugly happy clocks strike twelve. After looking at them, one's eyes will no longer bulge to the very outer limit of their sockets. Hats will raise solid scaffoldings on heads, themselves mounted on necks as resistant and monstrous as the necks of ducks. And the very beautiful lady, still with her beautiful wasp's waist, the very beautiful lady whose charms buzz around our childish dreams, will not turn to cigar smoke when the North Star appears.

If, however, the bedroom of the queen of Prussia consists of no more than a floor and some bare walls, the reason for this is very simple: the furniture has dissolved in water, the way my table does sometimes, when I'm tired and my books and cigarettes turn out to be incapable of beguiling my boredom. (At these times I leave my house, I walk through the streets, my eyes wide, trying to adopt toward my surroundings the attitude of a wonder-struck child, which is Miró's attitude. All these organisms have set out from their points of origin and flow by, pools of brilliant colors, yet enclosed within clearly delimited contours; here I am back at Miró's pictures. I blow my nose; and for the second time that nasal trumpet takes me back to Miró's pictures. I quicken my step, I look at a shop window in which some superb ties are bursting into flame; and for the third time . . .). It is Miró who has expressed this liquefaction, this relentless evaporation of structures—as relentless as any of the other vicious circles in which I, and all of creation, turn round and round—this soft leakage of the substance that makes all things—us, our thoughts, and the setting we live in—like jellyfish or octopi; he has been the one to express this so satisfactorily in several of his old canvases and especially in his current series of *Portraits*. As beautiful as sarcastic laughter or graffiti showing human architecture in its particularly grotesque and horrible aspect, each of these works is a mocking pebble sending out vicious, circular ripples when cast into the swamp of understanding, where for so many years already, so many traps and nets have been moldering . . .

But since an individual, when he finds himself suddenly put up against the wall or tragically locked in the labyrinth of such a vicious circle, cannot tolerate being a prisoner any longer and consequently seeks to escape at any cost from this enchanted circus, using a rope ladder that happens to be a quite ordinary conclusion, here is that conclusion:

The only legitimate end to an article on an artist as close to life as Miró is, endowed with such a feeling for nature and (whether or not he suspects it) tied to folklore by so many points of contact, must be a proverb or a moralizing apologue. Everyone stands to gain from it, the reader as well as the author . . .

Here, then, is that proverb:

Man, in his match with the world, employs a deck of cards of five different colors, which are the five senses; but naturally he comes up against a Greek who always cheats. To get the better of this enemy, with whom it would be useless to try cunning, one can only resort to a simplicity such as Miró's (not the simplicity of an idiot or an innocent, exactly, but perhaps more that of a somewhat sly and artful peasant) or a simplicity such as one finds among people less rotten with intellectuality than we are, ignorant of the crude processes of writing and capable of using, as letters and signs, the aide-mémoire notches used by certain Negroes, the Mexican *quippos*, the knotted cords Lao-Tse speaks of, and the famous knot in the handkerchief that I will perhaps take one day (what do I know?) as a slip knot, but never—and I mean never!—as a means to avoid forgetting, as ought to happen more, the existence of logic and the outside world.

Talkie

After a number of films with sound, at least one of which, *Our Dancing Daughters*, will certainly mark an epoch in the history of cinema, not so much for technical reasons as because it signals the appearance of a totally new form of sentimentality in films, with the charm of an easy life, unspoiled by any concern other than to show protagonists of a sparkling youth and grace, we have now been given a real talkie, with retorts bouncing back and forth that sometimes add a sort of vocal close-up to the visual close-up.

The English language is the language of *love*—such is the great lesson taught by *Weary River*, and this is enough to make us forget a scenario of idiotic puritanism, illuminated only by great gleams of passion now and then pouring out their marvelous reds.

The narrow-minded have not failed to perform their nasty work with respect to talkies, warning of disaster, as they always do, in this case the end of cinema. Such a film gives the lie to them peremptorily because of its very weaknesses, since what saves it is not so much a visual image here or there as the role played by the voices in it. Which shows why talkies are interesting.

Thanks, then, to these talking films, from which we should expect everything (as *Weary River* has shown), we can at last allow ourselves to be taken body and soul by scenes of a burning sensuality, cast adrift on the raft of voices while everything collapses around us except, perhaps, an amazing movement of lip or throat, a trembling of fingertips, an oracular speech issuing from the mouth of a woman

[For source information, see p. 18.]

in love, with the heartrending accent of the mountains, the sea, dimly lit taverns and prison bars at midnight, a beautiful voice, at once harsh and sweet, which has been crossed by every road, every furrow, every path, in a region where we know no more about the sun than about the moving barriers of rain.

Hans Arp

*L*ong-bearded gnomes descending in a flow of earth, korrigans of sculpted wood, sylphs with airy hands, naiads with legs tangled in folds of water, salamanders with flaming lips, everything that is situated between crude matter and person, independent of the four kingdoms but also connected to all of them, neither boulder nor stream, neither shadow nor metal, neither idea nor framework, neither gaseous nor solid, half fig half grape, neither flesh nor fish, everything whose fate it is to be forever caught between bark and tree, unlicked cubs, caterpillars struggling to change into butterflies, anthropoid monkeys, sphinxes, sirens, performing animals, chimeras, hermaphrodites, griffins, everything that hesitates between a pail of water and a measure of oats, Buridan's asses, Newton's apples and Condillac's statues, Vaucanson's automatons, the amazing phenomenon of osmosis through so-called semipermeable walls, mineral salts in a state of superfusion, the amalgams of snow and mud with which the Eskimos coat the runners of their sleds, five-legged calves, lion-men in funfairs, homunculi, pygmies, palotins,* amphibians, mandrakes, withered trees with ghost branches, seawater containing an indiscriminate mix of blood serum, scraps of filth and living corpuscles, bovine clouds, vermicular rains, hailstorms of bloodclots, thieving mockingbirds, meteorites simulating old medals, brooms of houndstooth grass—all this can be found in the poems and the other works of Hans Arp, who is hurled into his

[For source information, see p. 18.]
*[Word invented by Alfred Jarry and used in his *Ubu roi* to signify "minor characters."]

most extreme intensity by the force of the eruption of this volcano of humor.

Hans Arp takes the universe and transforms it into a piece of corrugated iron—he who is so well acquainted with cabinetmaking and all that one can derive from matter. He causes forms to double over and, making everything almost like everything else, systematically overturns illusory classifications and the very scale of created things. He plays with the world like an elf escaped from a forest and conducts himself, in the midst of various relationships, in the magnificent manner of a dog in a game of ninepins (I will even go so far as to say *a Scotch terrier*). His painted wood reliefs and his recent rope reliefs could be the "remains" of some extravagant meal—a theophagic or anthropophagic ritual—during which a family of giants, not yet very clearly differentiated from the mountainous masses that engendered them, and a string of dwarves as charming as plant lice have been fraternizing, gulping down what some call divinity and cutting up naturing nature and natured nature into wildly bleeding slices seasoned with a parsley capable of instantly ridding heaven and earth of all the doddering and indigent parrots of eternity.

Mouth Water

We are so used to the sight of our fellow human beings that we don't usually notice what is monstrous about each of the elements that constitute our structure. Only rarely does eroticism hurl great revelatory flashes of lightning that sometimes make us understand the true nature of a certain organ, suddenly restoring its integral reality and its stunning force while also establishing as supreme goddess the abolition of hierarchies, those hierarchies on whose different levels we normally file as best we can the different parts of the body, placing some high, others low (according to the value we attach to the different activities they are responsible for), the eyes at the very top—because they are evidently wonderful beacons—but the organs of excretion as remotely far down as possible, quite below any watermark, in the wet caves of a sea stagnant with grief, poisoned by a million sewers . . .

Just below the eyes, the mouth occupies a privileged position, because it is the site of speech, the orifice of respiration, the den where the pact of a kiss is sealed, much more, we think, than an oily factory of mastication. On the one hand *love* is needed to restore to the mouth all of its mythological function (it is no more than a warm, damp grotto, though the teeth ornament it with hard stalactites, and within its folds the tongue lies hidden, a dragon guarding God knows what treasures!); on the other hand *spit* is needed to make it tumble, all at once, to the bottom rung of the organic ladder, by endowing it with a function of ejection, even more repugnant than its role as doorway to be stuffed with food.

[For source information, see p. 18.]

Spit is very close to manifestations of eroticism, because like love it "sweeps away" the classification of the organs. Like the sexual act performed in broad daylight, it is the epitome of scandal, since it relegates the mouth—which is the visible sign of intelligence—to the rank of the most shameful organs and, as a consequence, man in his entirety to the level of those primitive animals that, possessing only a single opening for all their needs and being therefore exempt from that elementary separation of the organ of nutrition from that of excretion to which would correspond the differentiation of noble from ignoble, are still completely plunged in a sort of diabolical chaos in which nothing has yet been disentangled.

Because of this, spit represents the height of sacrilege. The divinity of the mouth is soiled by it every day. What value can we really give to reason, or to speech, or, hence, to man's so-called dignity, if we think that every philosophical oration, thanks to the fact that language and spit come from one and the same source, can legitimately be represented by the incongruous image of a sputtering orator?

Finally, spit, because of its lack of consistency, its indefinite contours, the relative imprecision of its color, and its wetness, is the very symbol of *formlessness*, of what is unverifiable, of what can't be put into a hierarchy, the soft and sticky stumbling block that, better than any sort of rock, trips up the steps of everyone who imagines a human being to be something—*something other* than an unmuscled, hairless animal, the spit of a delirious demiurge who roars with laughter at having expectorated this conceited larva, this comical tadpole who swells up into a demigod's puffy meat . . .

Debacle

The phenomena of nature form a vast alphabet of symbols upon which we draw in forging a number of our expressions. Who hasn't heard of "a bolt from the blue," "a silver lining," "a tempest in a teapot," or "a rain of abuse"?

However worn most of these images are, one of them is still capable of moving us because it is so brutally, implacably concise, one that is, in fact, *bâclé* [bungled], with the very haste that characterizes disasters—and this is the word *débâcle*.*

Used to describe the war of 1870 in the work by Zola that takes the word as its title and popularized especially to designate monetary collapses and financial crashes, this term is still very powerful today, all the more so since, given the current situation, it can appear to be prophetic.

The fact is that life today is bound and frozen in the thick ice of industry that would like to turn us into cadavers. The rivers of truly human relations are motionless and dead, the cold is spreading, the air is solidifying, and just as during the winter of 1870–1871, which the most dreadful old people love to recall, the solidified Seine offered its back, its spine of hardened water, for the passage of trucks, cars, and people on foot, our rivers of sentiment are changing into arteries full of chilly, congealing blood, avenues for the stubborn animalcules of a state of things in which nothing has any other

---

[For source information, see p. 18.]

*[The primary, concrete meaning of *débâcle* (as well as the English *debacle*) is "the breakup of drifting ice"; hence the ice and water imagery that follows. The related *bâclé* means "blocked," "botched," or "bungled."]

reason for existing except an economic one, wretched social relations as dirty as lice, more difficult to support with our vertebral columns than entire loads of market-gardening trucks or buses full to bursting with men whose faces are necessarily ignoble. Prisoners of the cold, just as mummies are prisoners of their stiffened bandages, in grimacing poses like shameful paralytics, we do not budge, we remain inert, we do not even feel that we are, so to speak, "pieces of wood" any longer, and yet we hope for nothing so much as a *débâcle* . . .

If the river were to thaw, that would be the end of the traffic that binds us up, this grotesque circulation of tiny calculations that bend us under the yoke and make us worse than domestic servants. In order to emerge from this dusty storeroom in which we are moldering, we and our tarnished ex-priests—as rusty as the old sabers of Reichshoffen cuirassiers—the waters of our hearts, muscles, and skin would have to return to their natural state, at the same time regaining all their primitive violence, the violence of the time of floods, glacial cataclysms, and tidal waves, to break apart all the countryside, whether it be fallow lands, fields, towns, or hamlets, drowning everything that has nothing human about it as they pass through and finally evaporating, so that this resurrection is immediately transformed into a defeat, and its ultimate result, after it has first shattered what was hostile and foreign to it and then destroyed itself by turning into a chimerical vapor, is to annihilate *absolutely everything*.

The 1929 Fox
Movietone Follies

*S*o then, Oxford Street, stony-hearted stepmother, thou that listenest to the sighs of orphans, and drinkest the tears of children, at length I was dismissed from thee! The time was come that I no more should pace in anguish thy never-ending terraces; no more should wake and dream in captivity to the pangs of hunger. Successors too many to myself and Ann have, doubtless, since then trodden in our footsteps, inheritors of our calamities. Other orphans than Ann have sighed; tears have been shed by other children; and thou, Oxford Street, hast since those days echoed to the groans of innumerable hearts. For myself, however, the storm which I had outlived seemed to have been the pledge of a long fair weather.

This passage from *Confessions of an English Opium-Eater* immediately follows Thomas de Quincey's tale of the poor child he met in an all-but-abandoned house where he had rented lodgings, a child terrorized by ghosts and suffering from hunger and cold, who at night would huddle against him for comfort and warmth; then comes the moving story of Ann, the little London prostitute with whom de Quincey, in his darkest days, would mournfully roam the sidewalks of Oxford Street and who may once have saved him from starving to death by buying him a glass of spiced port with her own meager funds.

The most brilliant scenes in the *Fox Follies*, however attractive they may be, are outdone by two much more unexpected tableaux in

[For source information, see p. 18.]

which this magic of the street appears, glittering or dark but always a marvelous velvet casket in which, whether one suspects it or not, gleam the intoxicating tears of a young girl . . . The one who stands lamenting, pretty but too modestly dressed, before a sumptuous store window, until the wax figures inside come to life, draw her to them in a dream, and dress her in the most beautiful clothes; the one who sobs in the falling snow, while a dubious-looking crowd of multicolored people flashes by, with gestures of an inexpressible absurdity—those two little match sellers from a child's story or orphans from a melodrama, and even those who are not crying: the sirens who, during an underwater ballet, descend and slowly float back up along endless strands of seaweed, like the mysterious bottle-imps turning majestically in the aquarium scene in *Locus Solus*, Raymond Roussel's inspired play, the short-skirted chorus girls and mischievous, bare-legged schoolgirls, the whole lovely "nursery" side, the turbid childishness that oscillates between laughter and tears, fresh candor and perverse senility, the beauties that sing a scale and then replace their "do, re, mi, fa, sol . . ." by the enumeration of different parts of the body: "Eyes, lips, hair, legs, etc. . . ." while on the screen appear the same eyes, the same smile, the same silky hair, the same shaking leg multiplied innumerable times, all the cheap eroticism, the easy sensuality, the sentimentality that "drives one to tears," the music one walks out humming, the absolute deficiency of any idea, the unimaginable puerility of the scenario, the tawdry luxuriousness, the almanac jokes, a quality reminiscent of old phonographs, provincial Folies-Bergère, sham virginity—all of this is resolved into the primary beauty of those two major scenes, in which the falling snowflakes mingling with falling tears as large as eyes, and the grand finale of the moaning girl whose double, as though enchanted, crosses through the windowpane and dons a luxurious evening dress, carry everything else along in the wake of a touching atmosphere that also encompasses even the apparently very cheery scenes, even the explosions of rippling laughter.

There is not the slightest suspicion of an aesthetic in this spectacle. Despite certain appearances, everything here is popular, admirably cheap. The women alone dominate it because they are very beautiful and consequently as touching in their gaiety as in their sentimentality, as pleasant as old drawing-room ballads, despite the black background of the street and that ancient horror one does not forget, society, "stony-hearted stepmother" who hears still different sobs than those of the orphans and drinks tears that are a hundred thousand times bloodier and more bitter than those of children cudgeled by a brutal father to teach them how one should behave in the world, live to be bored, and scorn others, from the heights of what he calls: seriousness, nobility, morality . . .

But the superb *first names* of *Sue* Caroll, *Sharon* Lynn blur every species of verbiage under their adorable makeup, and no further questions, serious or not, occur to the heart or the mind, except those a child might ask himself, when one very simply takes him to a fairy play.

Note: *The* Fox Movietone Follies, *shown at the Moulin-Rouge, ran for only a short time. The public's xenophobia had a good deal to do with its lack of success. What is more, intellectual circles could feel only contempt for such a simple, unpretentious spectacle. It is not so easy to recapture the freshness of childhood . . . Even less easy than to learn English.*

Man and His Insides

*I*n a popular nineteenth-century book (Emile Colombey's *Les Originaux de la dernière heure* [Paris: E. Dentu, Hetzel Collection, 1862], p. 105), I read the following anecdote:

AN EXCESS OF CLEANLINESS
Seeing an open side of beef being gutted in a butcher's stall, a woman experienced such profound disgust that she nearly fainted. When questioned about the attack she was suffering, she asked:
"Do we have so many nasty things inside our bodies too?"
The answer she was given convinced her to let herself starve to death.

If the sight of animal or human viscera is almost always unpleasant, the same is not necessarily true of their figurative representation, and one would be wrong to regard the anatomical plates that embellish old treatises on medicine from a strictly medical point of view, without concerning oneself overmuch with the extraordinary beauty that marks many of them, a beauty that has to do not with the greater or lesser purity of the forms but rather with the fact that here the human body is revealed in its most intimate mystery, along with its secret places and the subterranean reactions for which it is the theater, accompanied, in sum, by everything that confers on it the magical value of a scaled-down universe.

Of all plastic representations, that of the human body is without question the most directly moving. I am speaking not of the conventional nude of official painting—scrubbed clean and in some

Commentary on three plates from *Nouvelles Tables anatomiques*, by Amé Bourdon (Paris, 1678); first published in *Documents* 2, no. 5 (1930).

sense *dehumanized*, with nothing about it to evoke even a shadow of the disturbance that the sight of a body really engenders—nor of those nudes that are meant to be naturalistic, in which only the apparent structure of bodies is studied, to the exclusion of everything that could suggest to us something about their real signification, the role they play as *palpable links* between us and the outside world, the only bridges by which we can attach ourselves, however tenuously, to the gigantic, remote universe over the abyss that separates us—we who are limited in time and space—from nature, which appears to be unlimited and immortal.

If we had to stand alone, confined to the use only of our own bodies in the face of external nature, this position would perhaps be grand—that of a god or a hero—but more dreadful than any other, for we would never understand what was that *other thing*, so distinct from our being, so indifferent to us, strange with a strangeness so very distant and glacial. What gives us the possibility of connecting ourselves with it is the existence of human creatures other than ourselves, who then act as mediators, because on the one hand they participate in nature (since, like it, they are exterior to us), while on the other hand they participate in us (since their constitution is more or less similar to our own constitution). Thus, society becomes the link between us and nature, and our human relations immediately become the most important of the many relations existing between us and the world, so that the sight of human bodies, whether we consider them friend or foe, is what touches us the most by far, since they are in any case the living signs of the alliance that nature has consented to sign with us, the magical seals that consecrate this imaginary pact.

This symbolic description of our situation in the world is connected to the great religious myths in which there is a mediator—an incarnated god or a man made divine—such as Orpheus or Christ, heroes one adores but who always die in the end, victims of some holocaust. Love can also be connected to it, since it gives us—beyond all the malice it may include—the illusion of conjuring the forces of the universe because we possess one of its parts, which allows us, in some way, to enchant it, even to cast a spell over it.

Think of the films of Adolphe Menjou, in which we are shown the sinister decadence of a man-about-town who is still quite handsome but tired and blasé, or the wonderful film *La Femme de quarante ans*, in which Pauline Frederick plays the most stunning role of the mature woman who is still very desirable but is reduced to "preserving herself" (here I am thinking of the marvelous photographs in advertisements for Elizabeth Arden beauty products that appear regularly in *Vogue* and show a woman's pale face wrapped in linen bandages and offered up to the massage of two delicate hands); compare the images we retain of these to the anatomical plates in which one sees flayed people, for instance, or a man holding either a head under his arm or an ear between his thumb and index finger, or a half-flayed woman standing before half a nervous sytem, her head open like a Minerva, her hair tumbling down, while an abundant circulation of vapors flows between her mouth and feet and a multitude of drops of sweat beads almost the entire surface of her naked skin, barely distinct from the tears that spring from her eyes, and you will understand why such representations of the human body, which show us either its secret mechanisms—at once fascinating and dreadful—or its aging, one of the most critical stages in its history, are truly more beautiful and more erotically moving than any of the representations painting may claim to give us when devoted to the production of nudes that are either academic or unnatural but never teach us anything whatsoever about the real arcana of human nature.

Masochism, sadism, and almost all the vices are in the end only ways of feeling more human—because one is engaged in deeper and more sudden relations with bodies—in the same way that the sight of wrinkles and viscera, terrible for some people, causes us to take

one more step in the direction of intensifying our human consciousness. "Not to know what to do with oneself,"* a magnificent popular
idiom that expresses all the boredom very well and already contains,
for anyone who knows how to understand it, more than a simple sug-
gestion of how to remedy it! A primitive man who has his body tat-
tooed with signs that give him a magical relation to various different
parts of the Universe, a person whose skin becomes an arsenal of ci-
catrices, swellings, scarifications, burns, etc., either for religious
reasons (in the case of a so-called savage) or because of some vice (in
the case of a civilized person who loves "unusual sensations," as they
say), is only yielding half-consciously to a need to increase what is already most human in him. The same is true of modern cosmetics,
whose object is to preserve or repair what is for us the bodily norm
(here two images appear: the dazzling poster for Palmolive soap that
shows a gypsy talking to a gentle, blonde Englishwoman . . . "Protect that youthful complexion," she says as she hands her a bar of
Palmolive soap; then, an exciting, nude wax figure, her blonde hair
flowing down from her head, crowned with a complicated apparatus
for "permanent waving" that haloes her with a murderous luster like
that of a sword of Damocles and illustrates an identical threat: the
threat of age, which no adornment or care will succeed in eluding),
modern cosmetics, as I say, and all the paraphernalia it involves
(which is eternal, moreover)—rouges, powders, dyes, perfumes—
have a terribly erotic, human character, fascinating symbols that
they are of the fight against aging either through a pure and simple
obliteration of the signs of decrepitude or through an attempt, even
in youth, to replace the face, victim of withering, by a kind of mask
that is fixed and separate from time, as attractive as the most gracious
of all statues but as sacrosanct as an idol.

"Humanity" in fact has no more to do with happiness than with good-
ness: the most atrocious visions, as well as the cruelest pleasures, are

*[The French expression, literally, is "not to know what to do with one's skin."]

entirely legitimate if they contribute to the development of such a humanity. Only puritans will be able to contradict me, because they see the body as nothing more than crude matter, a contemptible magma of viscera, and not the mysterious theater in which all exchanges take place, as much physical as intellectual or sentient, between what is inside and what is outside: the X and the Y that look each other in the whites of the eyes, a beautiful pair of mirrors that, for lack of a cudgel to make them fly into a thousand splinters, might well each be cut in two by an exceedingly vulgar diamond . . . Unless it were to draw upon them—symbol of a love capable of resolving their duality in its own way—a very strange and very distantly soft name whose calligraphy would cross out a peculiar graffito representing a contemporary Orestes in top hat and well-cut suit fleeing from the bewitching Furies, their fingers freighted with rings, snakes, and whips, which, eternally incapable as he is of amusing himself in ways considered to be moral, he has caused to appear fully armed from his Jupiter's brain, in a grand finale of anvils of battered flesh and loathsome sparks the color of violet bruises or drops of blood.

Phantom Africa

*T*ired of the life he was leading in Paris, seeing the trip as a poetic adventure, a method of acquiring concrete knowledge, a test, a symbolic means of arresting the process of aging by traveling through space in order to negate time, the author, who is interested in ethnography because of the importance he attributes to this science in clarifying human relations, takes part in a scientific expedition that crosses Africa.

What does he find there?

Few adventures, studies that excite him at first but soon reveal themselves to be too inhuman to satisfy him, a growing erotic obsession, a greater and greater emotional emptiness. Despite his disgust with civilized people and life in the big cities, toward the end of the trip he is looking forward to going back.

His attempt at escape has been only a failure, and he also no longer believes in the value of escape: despite the fact that capitalism tends more and more to make all true human relations impossible, is it not within his own civilization that a Westerner has some chance of fulfilling himself where his passions are concerned? Once again, however, he will learn that here as elsewhere, man cannot escape his isolation; so that one day he will set off again, in the grip of new phantoms—though without illusions this time!

Such was the general plan for the work the author would perhaps have written had he not been anxious above all to produce as objec-

Insert for *L'Afrique fantôme* (Paris: Gallimard, 1934), a journal kept from May 19, 1931, to February 16, 1933, during an ethnographic and linguistic expedition headed by Marcel Griaule.

tive and sincere a document as possible, preferring to confine himself to his logbook and simply publish that.

Throughout this journal, in which events, observations, feelings, dreams, and ideas are noted down without any order, that plan is perceptible, at least latently.

It is up to the reader to discover the germs of a sudden awareness achieved only well after the return from the trip, as he follows along after the author, encountering men, sites, changes of fortune, from the Atlantic to the Red Sea.

Fred Astaire

*F*red Astaire in a black suit and a top hat, Fred Astaire bareheaded in a tuxedo, Fred Astaire in Prince of Wales check and a boater, Fred Astaire in a bowler with an umbrella, Fred Astaire gloveless in a fedora, Fred Astaire in a double-breasted suit wearing gloves, Fred Astaire in shirtsleeves, Fred Astaire in a sweater, Fred Astaire in a travel overcoat with a suitcase, Fred Astaire knotting his cravat, Fred Astaire pulling at his suspenders, going into a restaurant, waiting in the rain, juggling with his cigarette lighter, taking a walk in the country, courting a woman—there is a whole gallery of Fred Astaires, we see him at night and in the daytime, in winter and in spring, in comfortable furnished rooms or on the pavement, in convulsions, humming, stretching or jumping, his face consumptive but his eyes laughing, his smile wide between the tense features of an alcoholic, and with his look of a harebrained nice guy and that inimitable distinction which only certain regally dressed hooligans can aspire to. "We had to adopt a manner that was, you might say, rather dry," said Vaché. "A cemetery of uniforms and liveries," said Marcel Duchamp. And Rimbaud spoke of "the cruel bearing of tawdry finery," while occupying himself with quite other matters and obviously never doubting that one day there would exist this severe jacket that suddenly becomes delirious, these shoes of beautiful

First published in *La Bête noire*, no. 1 (1935). The trip during which I saw a performance of *The Gay Divorcée* (which was made into the film that inspired this article) was the immediate source of the poem *Les Veilleurs de Londres* (*Haut Mal* [Paris: Gallimard, 1943], pp. 99–106), which is haunted by the figure of the now-famous dancer. A picture of his sister Adele—his first partner—was reproduced in *Documents* 1, no. 4 (1929): 227.

quality leather that suddenly go into a trance and strike the floor as though they wanted to defy it or enrage it, this fine silk handkerchief lying over a heart that suddenly begins to bleed—for this store window mannequin, this automaton, this sylph, is also a man, and all his luxury, his multifarious outfit of costly odds and ends, his little idiosyncrasies, will not prevent him from falling in love sometimes or becoming bored.

One of the most intense aspects of the modern malaise is embodied in Fred Astaire, this marvelous dancer and slightly macabre clown who is so well dressed (whose clothes are just skimpy enough to make him look a little shabby, but at the same time ample enough to make him look like an emaciated starveling and for him to become heartrending, if the song falls apart), and when I saw him dance in London in *The Gay Divorcée* about a year and a half ago, he reminded me irresistibly of the drawings that one of my friends and I used to scribble in our notebooks during the war and that all depicted perfectly elegant skeletons, some civilian, others military—the expression of a very special brand of *frivolity*.

How I Wrote
Certain of My Books

*A*s he promised a few months before his death, Raymond
Roussel has just revealed to us, in a posthumous collection he took
pains to prepare himself, the process he employed in composing his
prose works, including his theater pieces.

From the opening, title essay and from what we know from other
sources about the way Roussel worked, for him, literary creation
could be broken down into three phases: first, the fabrication of puns
or phrases with double meanings (taking off from "anything at all,"
he writes), these chance formal aspects inciting the different elements to confront one another and start things going; next, the establishment of a logical network joining these elements, however
peculiar and disparate they might be; finally, the formulation of
these relations, on as realistic a level as possible, into a text written
with as much rigor as possible, with no concern about form for form's
sake but simply obeying the customary rules of grammar and style.
Several different thoughts about this method come to mind.

First of all, the process as a whole reveals that Roussel exploited
the creative power of words more than anyone had up to then. What
was involved here was a magic nominalism such that the word summoned the thing, and the dislocation ("a little as though it were a

This review of Raymond Roussel's *Comment j'ai écrit certains de mes livres* (How I
Wrote Certain of My Books) (Paris: A. Lemerre, 1935) was first published in *La
Nouvelle Revue française* 24, no. 268 (1936).

matter of extracting rebus drawings from it") of a succession of ordinary sentences entailed the re-creation of the universe, the construction of a special world that took the place of the ordinary world.
The final result being a description, or a narrative, of imaginary objects or events; in sum, a series of mythical inventions substituted for
wordplays—one may think that here Roussel rediscovered one of
mankind's oldest and most widespread mental habits: the formation
of myths from words, that is (as though one proposed to illustrate
Max Müller's theory that myths were born of a sort of "illness of language"), the transposition into dramatic action of what was at first
only a simple language event.

One may wonder if Roussel—who tells how, in his preliminary
work, he went from word to word, taking each "in a sense other than
that which offered itself first"—was not actually obsessed by the
idea of double meanings. A passage from *Nouvelles Impressions d'Afrique* (the footnote on pages 2 1 3–2 1 7: words whose meaning
"jumps" to another meaning) seems revealing in this respect. One
can assume that the wordplay generating the myth imposed itself on
his mind with a coercive force, that it was impossible for him to avoid
the hallucinatory power contained in language, so that he could have
applied to his own case Rimbaud's remark, "A mere vaudeville title
would summon fearful specters before me."

What seems interesting about the method employed by Roussel
is that his voluntary submission to a complicated, difficult rule (and
especially the fact of having to focus his attention on solving a problem whose givens are as foreign, detached, futile as possible) is accompanied, as a corollary, by a *distraction* from all the rest, which results, through this indirect method, in a much more effective lifting
of censorship than a process such as automatic writing can achieve,
whereby one sets out to abolish it directly through passivity, self-
abandonment, the will to create a void within oneself. Manipulat-
ing elements that were apparently gratuitous and that he himself

did not distrust, he created myths that were true in the sense that they were all authentically symbolic, expressed as clearly as possible the author's deep layers of emotion, as is attested by the striking frequency of certain themes in his work as a whole: control over the universe or the fusion of the microcosm with the macrocosm, ecstasy, paradise, hidden treasure, the obsession with death, enigma, fetishistic or sadomasochistic sorts of themes, etc.

One can also say, on the other hand, that this process (correctly regarded by Roussel as related to rhyme, since "in both cases there is unexpected creation due to phonetic combinations") corresponds to what a technique always ought to be: a method of inspiration, a way of rousing the imagination, something essentially active and not—as a confusion that is all too common would have it—a fixed rule of fabrication, even an aesthetic canon.

Roussel's results prove the excellence of his method, at least as far as he is concerned: the obtainment—by means of a chain of words coming together through puns or simple associations—of elements that appeal to one another and echo one another, forming an underlying network analogous, on an intellectual level, to rhymes, to that "filling-in" Mallarmé supposedly sought when he was working on *Igitur*, or perhaps, for painters, to plastic relations; the action of that subterranean web on the reader's unconscious, giving him a secret intuition of the harmony of the work; in a crystalline language (so concise as to be funny sometimes), *pure* poetry, that is, the creation of interplay among concrete elements beyond any sentimental or didactic preoccupation, the formation of those "equations of facts" that Robert de Montesquiou spoke of and that one could call "constellations," to borrow a term from the part of *How I Wrote Certain of My Books* that is devoted to the game of chess.

It appears, then, that Roussel was able—ingeniously—to find the most effective way to create a work that would conform to all that was represented by his constant aspiration to "euphoria," to ecstasy, to that "universal glory" (connected much more to a notion of magical force, chance, plenitude, than to any vulgar idea of vanity) of which he spoke to Dr. Pierre Janet when the latter was caring for him—a sort of divine state, a sort of isolation within a universe he had built from the ground up and over whose fate he presided.

Spain, 1934–1936

A bull's head into the neck of which (not far from a banderilla with frills as light as flames, and close to the furious eye under the frame of horns enclosing the skull) plunges the peremptory verticality of a sword: one might think that by marking his invitation cards with such a tragic inaugural sign, André Masson has attempted to condense, as in a coat of arms, all the burning intensity that Spain has represented for him during these past two years and all it suffers today under the swords of the old soldiers, who manage the final thrust only with great difficulty.

Masquerades of insects; the hoarse cries of roosters; blood-red lands in which fire smolders and sometimes bursts into actual flames; Don Quixotes lunging at uncertain creatures—miasmas or clownish concretions—then keeping watch, lances in their fists, as thin as the long splinters continually rising from the centers of their hearts; human bodies mangled by Roman legionnaires; a cosmic delirium illuminating the nights around the Montserrat monastery; ghosts of asses wandering under the walls of Avila; parish priests pursued by dubious thoughts that have changed into lobsters' claws; the hysteria of dead bodies that endeavor to veto, by force, what is only the natural flux of life—this whole world, teeming, wounded, greedy, desirous, clashing, is summed up in the dizzying and severe beauty of the best "tauromachies."

This review of an exhibition by André Masson at the Galerie Simon was first published in *La Nouvelle Revue française* 25, no. 280 (1937), and reprinted in *André Masson et son univers*, by Michel Leiris and Georges Limbour (Geneva and Paris: Editions des Trois Collines, 1947).

A painter as in love with nature as André Masson—I mean loving it enough to study it, look at it from the inside, bare its inner workings with the same patient ardor as though some alchemical transmutation were involved—was especially well endowed to broach the subject of tauromachy, in itself already almost mythical.

A hostile gravitation of man and beast, a murder and a fusion at the same time, a geometry whose theorems admit only active proofs through iron and blood, the coinciding of a smooth arabesque and a dark mass of frenzy, the corrida, a sacrificial festival and a major art, well illustrates the artist's duel with the outside world when, tearing off his own skin and standing flayed before the work to be created, he attempts to subdue nature by catching it in the palpitating folds of that cape and, another Damocles, tries to abolish death by creating for himself a sparkling weapon out of the menace that has always hung over him.

By way of the bullfights, André Masson leads us to art's crucial point: the inexpiable war between the creator and his work, between the creator and himself, and between the subject and the object; a fecund dichotomy, a bloody joust in which the entire individual is engaged, a last chance for man—if he is willing to risk his very bones for it—to give form to something *sacred*.

Erik Satie's Humor

Of course the evening devoted to Satie's humor by Marcel Herrand and Jean Marchat's Rideau de Paris last November 29 seemed dated and even outmoded. The fact is that nowadays we are quite far removed from the time when, without being too naive, one could believe in certain possibilities of freedom. Since the blossoming and astonishing growth of so-called modernism, circumstances have changed; in these new, cruder prewar years, it is impossible to speak that simple word "freedom" without irony, anger, or bitterness. It is in some sense normal, therefore, that these days works as airy and transparent as those of Satie should readily assume the antiquated guise of a childhood with sailor hat, Scottish kilt, and hoop. Yet one can feel the opposite, too—that everything that inclines or has inclined toward a greater freedom is now more valuable than ever, that there is no such thing as old age for inventors, and that anything that at some given moment signified the rejection of some restraint keeps intact the freshness of its response to one of our most vital needs. From this point of view, the Rideau de Paris evening seems quite timely.

During a period when all of poetry was dying of boredom under the too-costly drapes and jewels of an arrogant aestheticism, there were a few people who boldly started from the ground up and deliberately chose to work with the poorest materials. Picasso's packets of tobacco, bottles, playing cards; Max Jacob's table talk, spontaneous dreams, grumblings; Erik Satie's comic songs, farces, witticisms—

First published in *La Nouvelle Revue française* 26, no. 292 (1938).

all correspond, on different levels, to the same hygienic desire to eliminate grandiloquence, preciosity, and pedantry.

Although there are musical works by Satie that in themselves constitute more than mere indications as to the nature of the system (for instance, *La Belle Excentrique* or the songs recited the other night by Agnès Capri, who seems to be an incarnation of Satie's poetry: at once automatic and distraught, a Sylvie from the outskirts of Paris just as there was a Sylvie from Ile-de-France for Gérard de Nerval), although the composer has expressed himself very clearly in his *Cahiers d'un mammifère* and other series of aphorisms, it is still true that in *Le Piège de Méduse*, a one-act comedy with "music by the same Gentleman," one perceives most distinctly what this system really is.

Lighthearted buffoonery built on a framework so tenuous that it seems almost nonexistent, *Le Piège de Méduse* is presented as a succession of family playlets with musical interludes sustaining the graceful choreographic maneuvers of a "beautiful giant monkey stuffed with straw by the master's hand," who is the good spirit of the house. From the midst of a dialogue that is stunningly banal emerge, now and then, overhanging locutions, sorts of bifurcations of language that are not true wordplays but give thought an absurd turn: "a little telephone call in the ears"; "you leave now, go off like a rifle!"; "I ask myself out loud." The constant use of devices of this kind (tending to insinuate snares everywhere, verbal or not, over which the intelligence hesitates, trips, and sometimes even breaks its nose) constitutes a real "trap" [*piège*]—a booby trap and also a poetry trap, since poetry's favorite moment is when one loses one's footing because of a landslide or a seismic shaking of thought. Thus, the most vulgar material (which we think we know best) will also be the most poetic, through the deflection it undergoes, the dislocation inflicted upon it, the way in which it is torn apart or imperceptibly altered.

The fairground charm of *Parade* and even the limpidity of *Socrate* arise from a similar method: to start with a few elements of a total simplicity but, through a subtle maneuver, to draw them from their natural context and situate them distinctly. True, it is here that the game becomes complicated, here that one must—obviously!— prove to be a great strategist, here that Satie-Medusa laughs softly into his beard.

Rafaelillo at
Nîmes on October 9

*P*icasso used to draw and paint sickly boys like these. Dressed in faded harlequin costumes or meager tights glued to flesh that was itself threadbare, sometimes perched on balls or occupied with indefinite tasks, these slender-faced circus troupers were endowed with mouths whose ambiguous lines hesitated between the fixedness of ecstasy and the wince of pain. This was how the young Rafaelillo from Valencia appeared to me the other Sunday when he was fighting in the Nîmes bullring, at the corrida that many people had certainly believed they would never be able to witness, wondering whether incalculable thousands of men might be killed in early October, instead of six bulls.

A good many current stars of tauromachy are no more than vain stylists, concerned above all about the purity of their attitudes, of the art, to the detriment of the tragedy. With Rafaelillo, the corrida regains all its meaning. One has to see this little man with his serious expression moving about only a hairbreadth away from the horns, as though some secret magnetism always kept his body an indiscernible distance from their tips, in order to understand the reality of fighting a bull.

Without pointless flourishes—only what it takes to show that

First published in *La Nouvelle Revue française* 27, no. 304 (1939).

Originally scheduled for October 2, 1938, this corrida (six bulls from Domecq to be fought by Vicente Barrera, Luis Gómez El Estudiante, and Rafael Ponce Rafaelillo) had been delayed a week because of the international crisis resulting in the Munich Pact.

one is the master of one's art and does not hesitate to take a few additional risks—without swaggering gestures, without theatrical tricks, Rafaelillo fights only with all his attention, all his passion and courage, allowing no other signature to his work as a whole but a rip in his costume from getting too close to the animal or a bloody right hand from plunging his sword in with total frankness.

Thus, the frail boy who resembled the circus troupers and other wretched creatures of the early periods of Picasso's painting, the slender boy with eyes like knife blades and the benign smile of an ill man, teaches a lesson in greatness to anyone who cares to watch him: nothing can have any value except what is done without trickery, what one does of one's own free will and with all one's heart, subduing the material to be worked just as the bull must be subdued before the final thrust.

Glossary: My Glosses' Ossuary (1939)

 *B*etween its utilitarian floorboards and its religious rigging lofts, however befouled the stage may be, the world could never become so closed that there would not remain a little room for play. "Poetic archaisms," grimaces, blasphemies, logomachy, mirages, cabala: at man's height the mouth utters its cries, tosses forth its oracles, gives vent to its puns. To allow words to come to life, bare themselves, and show us by chance, for the space of a lightning bolt bony with dice, a few of our reasons for living and dying—such is the convention of the game. Midway between the too-soiled ground and the too-sublime vaults, at the level of the air, entering the skin of the role, poetry plays its game.

Insert for *Glossaire: J'y serre mes gloses*, illustrated by André Masson (Paris: Editions de la Galerie Simon, 1939).

Epilepsy

*I*n our daily life we feel, move, speak, without paying much attention to what is strange about speech, the fact that it is at once a mode of shared understanding and a conducting wire for our private meditations.

Oriented toward the outside, on the one hand, this same language through which the daily exchanges that our social existence requires of us are effected is, on the other hand, the thoroughfare along which we glide, far from the din of the street, in search of our most particular and profound possessions.

Added to the current value of words, to the exchange value that the various elements of discourse possess as coins for commerce with others, there is the personal value assigned to them in the usage each of us may make of them for our most interior, least public ends, when we prospect and transmute into poetry our most secret sediments.

This twofold nature of language—like this pair of antagonistic needs, one pushing them toward the bright sunlight of a complete communication with men, the other inducing them to descend ever farther into their night—is, in large part, the source of the torment characteristic of a number of poets. Seeing that they are thus divided, we should not be surprised that one of them will sometimes unbosom himself in a tumultuous flood of words, like a drunkard or the Pythia in her trance, and at other times disappear behind an inhuman mask, like an epileptic falling down with clenched teeth and foaming mouth.

Insert for *Haut Mal* (Epilepsy) (Paris: Gallimard, 1943).

Mallarmé, Teacher of Morality

*L*ately people have been loudly attacking Mallarmé as a "champion of the ivory tower," a "teacher whose whole 'life' was spent within the four walls of a lycée and those of a dining room—office," in addition to describing him as "a canker" and "the source of all our ills."

It is quite significant that in this era of shameless prostitution—when corrupt scribblers are pullulating more than ever, when so many of our great men (whose lives, presented as exemplary, once served as illustrations in books on morality) are regarded as only good enough to be featured on signs for the Casino-State when it puts into operation the expedient of the national lottery—it is certainly in keeping with this period of official demoralization that representatives of the *young* should come to reproach a poet for having been too "pure" and for not having made any concessions, throughout his life, to the desire for success or the need for money.

Even if Mallarmé were no more than this negative figure of a man who refused all compromise and chose to teach English in a lycée rather than see the most subtle products of his thought turn into a commodity, if Mallarmé were no more than this gentleman, this petty bourgeois of rather ordinary appearance at first sight but unsullied, he would deserve all our respect.

Certain of the most elementary virtues—one would hardly have believed, even recently, that the day would come when it was im-

First published in *Les Lettres françaises*, no. 9 (1943). In this multiauthor publication with unsigned texts, the article was entitled "Mallarmé proffesseur [*sic*] de morale."

portant to praise them—certain quiet virtues such as a minimum of probity in the conduct of one's life and the exercise of one's intelligence, a love of finished work, a disdain for *arrivisme*, and a constant fidelity to what one believes to be true have nowadays been so degraded, despite the show of morality marking official phraseology, that one hesitates to qualify as "aestheticism" the attitude of a poet who shrinks, quite simply, from dirtying himself and for whom the practice of these aforementioned virtues was taken for granted, like the rules of a very general *savoir vivre* that people of all classes apply without even thinking about them because they are the alphabet of all moral behavior in our civilized societies.

No one will deny that Mallarmé is a poet difficult to penetrate. We should keep in mind that if he is disconnected to so great an extent, it is because he has succeeded in doing what few poets could pride themselves on having done: he has created for himself a language perfectly suited to his object, a language whose aim is not so much to describe or recount as to spark certain motions of the spirit. We should also keep in mind the absolute integrity he displayed during this enterprise, which demanded not only the highest power of invention but the efforts of an entire lifetime. In these times when, for the requirements of a propaganda everyone is familiar with, so many men—not content to live on their knees—pass off as gospel truth the most deceptive words, we can only profit from the lesson of the teacher Mallarmé.

Orestes and the City

The flies—and here I mean the real ones, the police flies, the ones that proliferate in the mercenary newspapers—buzzed very loud last summer against the other *Flies*, a play whose subject is that of Aeschylus's *Oresteia* and which has just been revived at the Théâtre de la Cité.

This was actually an excellent godsend, for in the work—of a force unequaled in France for many years—a crucial problem is broached: freedom as the very basis of man's existence or the sine qua non for his retaining his humanity, in the strictest sense of the term.

There is no need to say more than a few words here about the *Oresteia*'s subject: after the murder of Agamemnon, king of Argos and Mycenae, by his wife, Clytemnestra, with the help of her lover Aegisthus, Orestes, Agamemnon's son, helped by his sister Electra, whom the two murderers have thrown into bondage, kills them and at the same time frees Argos from their tyranny; having taken refuge in Athens, Orestes, protected by Apollo and Minerva, makes his peace with the Erinyes, who had been pursuing him as agents sent by the gods to avenge his mother's blood.

The Flies retains the *Oresteia*'s central theme: Clytemnestra's and Aegisthus's punishment by the young Orestes, who must then confront the Erinyes, here represented in the form of flies, insects as obsessive, in fact, as the pangs of remorse. But the orientation of the

First published in a slightly abridged form in *Les Lettres françaises*, no. 12 (1943), this unsigned review of a revival of Jean-Paul Sartre's *Les Mouches* (The Flies) at the Théâtre de la Cité (Théâtre Sarah Bernhardt renamed) was attributed to Jean Leseure in *Les Lettres françaises clandestines* (Paris, 1947).

contemporary drama is entirely different from that of the ancient tragedy: Orestes has changed from a victim of fate to a champion of freedom. If he kills, it is no longer in the thrall of obscure forces but in full knowledge of his act, in order to do justice and, through that deliberate choice, to exist as a man at last, instead of remaining the ill-defined adolescent whom the flowers of the finest culture had freed from common prejudices without having provided him the means to accede to manhood (one is almost reminded here of the initiatory murder in certain so-called primitive societies that a young man is obliged to perform before taking his place among the adults). If he respects the Erinyes, it is no longer because of the effect of a ritual and a procedure but because, having assumed complete responsibility for his act, he does not have to experience remorse and can confront these sirens boldly, though they are portrayed to us as both terrifying and charged with all the seductiveness the weak find in morose delectation and self-accusation.

Contrasting to the rigor of Orestes' attitude is the inconsistency of that of Electra, who is vehement and sacrilegious but, because she is incapable of leaving the circle of passions, of escaping the cycle of family resentments, appears stuck between eroticism and a sort of counterreligiosity that is, in the end, only a reversed piety and is consequently still situated on a religious plane. Consumed by hatred, as the people of Argos are consumed by fear, Electra, who, for lack of perceptivity and courage, did not act freely—in this resembling her mother Clytemnestra, just as she resembles her physically—will be prey to remorse and will not escape the Erinyes except through repentance, going so far as to repudiate the fury that filled her when she goaded her brother to take revenge.

Besides these new contributions to the classical theme of the *Oresteia*, in *The Flies* there is also Orestes' conduct toward the people whom he has rid of their tyrants. Whereas at the end of the *Oresteia*, Orestes returns to Mycenae to resume possession of his father's heritage, in *The Flies*, Orestes refuses to rule and leaves his native city without any intention of returning, taking along with him the flies, or Erinyes, that were infesting the place.

Young Orestes' activity is as different from the passivity of Aegisthus (so tired of his power, so crushed by repugnance, that he offers himself, like a sacrificial victim, to the murderer's knife) as a living thing is from a thing already dead. Tyranny, in fact, has locked Aegisthus into a vicious circle: he turned to murder out of a love of order, so that order would reign *through him*; but that order soon proves to be merely the web of beliefs and rituals he himself must create to make others fear him, to make them share his bad conscience; in the end, as he says, he is the victim of the image of himself that he imposes on his subjects. At that point there is nothing left in him but fear: fear of the specters he himself has invented to terrify others through these personifications of their remorse; his fear that a day will come when he will not cause enough fear in others; fear of the emptiness he feels in himself.

Unlike Aegisthus, Orestes commits a murder that leaves him feeling no remorse and confers on him a sense of fulfillment, because what is involved here is not vengeance or personal ambition but an act freely performed to punish the couple who were humiliating the community in which he wanted to be included. Instead of crushing others, as had Aegisthus, under the weight of a remorse by which he was the first to be crushed, instead of embodying hatred of himself and therefore of others too, he delivers them and finds his place and his function in taking upon himself all the latent guilt of the society, along with the blood with which he has not hesitated to soil himself. In this way he frees them twice over: once by eliminating their tyrant and teaching them that human nature is freedom; a second time by playing the part of a scapegoat on whom others can unload their sins (in the very horror with which they invest the image of this remorseless murderer) or, rather, the part of a healing shaman whose power relies on the fact that he alone is large enough to take upon himself, without succumbing to it, the demon who caused the illness.

Opposing the spiritual power represented by a cunning god and the temporal power represented by the old soldier Aegisthus, Orestes' act of self-affirmation assumes the form of a revolution. As far removed from the comfortable skepticism he imbibed from his humanist and liberal culture as he is from Electra's crude act of rebellion, which was no more than a blind outburst, equally disdainful of the too-easy life people lead in a city like Corinth and of the tremulous devotion to the dead in which the inhabitants of Argos delight, Orestes has broken the fatal circle, opened the path that leads from the rule of necessity to the rule of freedom. But for him there can be no question of taking power: now free, Orestes has broken the circle and therefore does not have to dominate others, treat others like things; because he has no chains, he does not need to chain others. Moreover, isn't a leader necessarily bound to his people by bonds of reciprocal dependence, and within the framework of relations involving slavery can there be any question of freedom for anyone? The consequence of his own freedom is the freedom he allows others, since he could not impose laws on them without at the same time being the dupe of those laws himself.

After delivering them from the great fear that one must have because "that is how one becomes an honest man," Orestes confines himself to bequeathing his own example to the people of Argos: let each person do as he did and make the leap, dangerously and by his own decision entering upon the arid road thus opened, in search of a Good that is actually *"their* Good," that of men alienated from themselves by respect for the established order. "I am neither the master nor the slave, Jupiter. I *am* my freedom," says Orestes, who declares shortly afterward that "every man must invent his own path." It is quite possible that the city of Argos, revealed for what it is by Orestes' act, will change from an aggregate of masters and slaves into an association of men who have become aware of their responsibilities and who, freed from their religious yoke as from their political one, stand at their own height, beyond happiness and despair.

This is, briefly, the great moral lesson about the city that should be drawn, it seems, from *The Flies*.

Michel Fardoulis-Lagrange and the Poetic Novel

*I*n 1942, *Sébastien, l'enfant et l'orange*, a small but brilliant book published by René Debresse, attracted a few people's attention to Michel Fardoulis-Lagrange.

What we have here is not so much a "poetic novel"—as people too hastily tend to call any novel more or less tinged (but only tinged) with poetry—as what could be called a "poetry novel": a novel in which the speech appears as an essential motivating force, in keeping with what is normal in *poetry*, a literary genre that, it seems, takes language as the primary element and is first and foremost a matter of words and phrasings, in contrast to the *novel*, where writing plays a role that is most often secondary, principally oriented as it is toward characters and situations and kept, by this fact, at the level of a simple tool for for exposition.

In Fardoulis-Lagrange's work, the two poles of properly literary creation came together in a striking balance: as in the most naturalistic of novels, there was continual reference to the everyday; as in the most subjectively lyrical poem, reality was at every moment transfigured or fragmented.

From one sentence to the next, the tale told in *Sébastien* moves forward, conjuring up for the reader a world that is torn apart, but into pieces that are almost all quite real despite the fact that none of them could truly be described as "a slice of life." What we have here is not

Preface (dated December 1943) to *Volonté d'impuissance* (The Will to Powerlessness), by Michel Fardoulis-Lagrange, illustrated by Raoul Ubac (Paris: Messages, 1944).

painting, nor even dreaming or meditating: it is the pure emission, not so much melodic as by fits and starts, of a voice that churns up ideas and realities (makes them appear and dissolves them); the doling out of a series of concrete facts alternating with notions established—peremptorily—by the unconditional authority of the speech, a sort of lyrical proliferation operating on these various elements so that at each instant the tale is thrown into confusion; a perpetual encroachment of the act of narration on the thing narrated; a constant interference of the sign with the signified, the themes presented and the language that expresses them being continuously in osmosis, as though the thing to be expressed were constantly subjected to the ascendancy of the expression (which works it, transforms it, prolongs it to the point that what might originally have been there to be expressed is devoured), indeed as though the expression, there from the start, tended to find an object for itself by becoming the maker of the very thing it should have had the function of expressing.

To the extent that the speech immerses itself again and again, second after second, in everyday reality, instead of purely and simply digging the bed of something supernatural that would be connected with life in only the most fortuitous and cowardly way (as is the case, too frequently, with texts obtained by means of such procedures as automatic writing), it seems that a piece of writing of this order, not unrelated to certain surrealist productions, begins, at least, to go beyond them. There is little "eloquence" in Fardoulis-Lagrange: the sentences rarely flow here, are not organized into periods, but follow one another—except for sudden, broad illuminations—with a paradoxical dryness. Nor is there anything "fantastic" in him: his characters are creatures of flesh and blood who eat, breathe, and mate like everyone else; the situations—sometimes tragic, but of a tragedy belonging to the police page of the newspaper—are really the simplest of situations. The whole secret resides in the explosion—or the crumbling—of a banal world, one not ruled by any god in any disguise whatsoever and admitting of nothing supernatural, unless it be that very explosion destroying the logical framework, so that in this written world that it affects (for what we have here is, by definition, a world having only a literary existence), things are precipitated, through the powers of language, into a sort of *beyond* or *within* of language. There is a state of fusion or effusion in which common thought collapses, along with its theoretical and practical aims; a state of "powerlessness" [*impuissance*] or abdication, a sort of raw return to a prehuman mode of being, to values exclusively concerned with living: a goal that, in the midst of lives enticed by chaos on all sides, seems to be sought as if by touch—or like dogs sniffing and sometimes scratching the ground with a mysterious determination—by the heroes of *Volonté d'impuissance*, which was written before *Sébastien*, and which forms the content of the present volume from Messages.

In this "fresh and naive" book (as the author sees it)—a book in which ceilings tend to cave in suddenly and there abound puddles of murky humor and quagmires in which we lose our footing—it seems that one can make out the latent qualities that, with *Sébastien, l'enfant et l'orange*, have situated Michel Fardoulis-Lagrange in such a singular position: at the point where what can be most directly produced by a bluntly authentic art intersects with the most inaccessible precincts that poetic expression, denying however modestly that it is in any way reduced to servitude, necessarily preserves.

The Martyr Saint Matorel

*I*n the history of poetry, the death dates of the great poets are by definition mournful, yet some seem more terrible than others and also surrounded by a special aura. More terrible because if death is already in itself something sinister, certain ways of dying are so brutal that they cause an even more appalling disturbance—the ones called "violent deaths," for instance. Surrounded by a certain aura because, instead of being, like more common deaths, the conclusion of a life by an event that is absurdity itself (since death is beyond comparison with life), certain deaths assume the appearance of a full stop, a fermata, giving the life its full meaning by the way it ends.

From this point of view, one can say that Shelley, who drowned in a storm, Nerval and Mayakovski, who committed suicide, Federico García Lorca, shot by supporters of Franco, and Max Jacob, victim of an ignoble racial prejudice, had what one may call "exceptional deaths": Shelley, because the torrential nature of his poetry called for a death in which he would be engulfed by nature unleashed; Nerval and Mayakovski, because suicide is a sign of a certain profound discord with life, a distance that, for more than a century, seemed to correspond to the poet's very condition; Lorca, because the man who sang gitano songs and was a friend of the torero Sánchez Mejías owed it to himself to die in a bloody manner; Max Jacob, because the greatest of all the various contradictory passions seething in him was

Originally a note in *Les Lettres françaises*, no. 15, then a talk given after the Liberation in the Théâtre des Mathurins for a matinee organized by Marcel Herrand in memory of Max Jacob, who died at Drancy on March 5, 1944. The final version appeared in *Cahiers d'art* 15–19 (1940–1944), published in spring 1945.

his ardent desire to be a saint and because by allowing him to end his days a martyr, his murderers, without intending to, gave his life a truly hagiographic ending.

A little of that exuberant life, which might still have remained legendary had it ended in another, less tragic, way, constantly passes through Max Jacob's writings. Whether it was Brittany, where he was born, or Montmartre, where he lived at the heroic period of the beginnings of cubism and which he only left for his refuge at Saint-Benoît-sur-Loire, or whether it was the Orléanais, where one might justifiably have believed he would end his days, everything that in one way or another was part of Max Jacob's life can be found in his poetry. Poetry that is all the more effective because its roots go deep into everyday surroundings, however much pure imagination may contribute to it.

Toward the end of his *Art poétique*, Max Jacob wrote: "I dreamed of recreating earthly life in the atmosphere of heaven." It seems that this sentence holds the key to what is most particular about his poetry, indeed, about the whole of his work. On a level that is sometimes burlesque, sometimes mystical, sometimes both at once, Max Jacob—when he does not abandon himself to a flood of pure lyricism—presents us with the fragments of a sort of *worldly comedy* in which all things, viewed as though from the loftiness of heaven, grow distant, shrink, and at the same time become increasingly delicate and, partaking more of dream than waking life, assume a fantastic appearance and form strange interrelations. Because his style is consistently, inimitably limpid, a certain unity is maintained in this disparate comedy, where all tones are adopted in succession and all registers employed.

If Saint-Pol-Roux (another victim of Nazi Germany) remained the last representative of our symbolist poets and one of the most brilliant, Max Jacob was among those who, shortly before the other war, took poetry in a new direction and created what was called (through a rather perfunctory comparison with the movement that, under Picasso's impetus, was then reinvigorating painting) "literary cubism."

The magnificence of symbolism (which will remain associated, quite particularly, with the name of Saint-Pol-Roux, called the Magnificent) was to be replaced by a less embellished poetry, one less burdened with aesthetic gilding. A poetry that was as simple as water and at the same time as free as air, with a more relaxed appearance than it had ever had before, having thus been freed of the chains that an excessive concern for art had caused to weigh on it almost everywhere, even where overly severe formal constraints had been rejected. A "de-Hamletized" poetry (as Max Jacob called it) whose sometimes bewildering aspect was due not to a taste for the baroque or the peculiar or to a futile attempt at hermeticism in order to seem profound but to the poet's desire to give free rein to his spontaneous invention, to grasp things in all their freshness and enter into as direct a relationship with them as possible.

More than Guillaume Apollinaire (who was too taken with a certain modern picturesqueness and too easily intoxicated by the marvel of his own voice), Max Jacob was the champion of this poetry, and there is some justification for believing that a few years from now his contribution to our literature will prove to be even more important than that of the prestigious companion of his youth, precisely because of the less showy appearance of his writings, which reveal a more distinct break with the aestheticism of the preceding period than do those of the great star of the new poetry, who invented the term "surrealist" to describe it on the occasion of the performance of his play *Les Mamelles de Tirésias*. Although the fame of Apollinaire, hero of the 1914–1918 war, has long eclipsed that of "poor Jacob"—who preferred the relative solitude of Saint-Benoît to the life of a man of letters, then came to a miserable end, interned in the Drancy concentration camp, after having been plagiarized, exploited, betrayed in every way so many times and by so many people—there will inevitably be a settling of accounts that will put in his rightful place Apollinaire's less fortunate friend, whose whole life, before leaning toward the total deprivation by which Christians think to raise themselves to their god, seemed dominated by the need to attain a unique poetry by way of its many possible aspects.

A poetry whose aim, one may believe, is to show—even when it does not go beyond the limits of reality—that our universe, a pure facade to anyone who knows how to see, is a universe whose nether sides are enchanted; and this through the magic of a sensibility that objectifies itself by choosing to employ the simplest speech, a natural and savory French unequaled in the twentieth century, a language of unaffected syntax and vocabulary, though as varied as possible, in which one must recognize what Max Jacob was alluding to when he recommended to those of his correspondents whom he was initiating into the art of writing that they express themselves in the language of a cook or in "the style of the oldest woman in the house." A poetry of feelings and objects rather than a poetry of words, even though puns and other language games often appear in it, whether they be ironic comments on the acrobatics of rhyme or verbal tricks to create associations of things or ideas that would be inaccessible by other means; whether such a deliberate highlighting of the turn of phrase (whose content is indisputable, since the apparent necessity connecting the words convinces us of a similar necessity linking the ideas) might suggest the obviousness of a proverb or dictum; or whether, more simply, the poem or poem fragment thus conceived must present itself in the manner of a children's counting-out rhyme or a popular song, typical specimens of those products of folklore that form the oldest as well as the most universal of poetries. A poetry at once subjective and concrete, in which crude reality (preferably envisaged in its flattest or most vainly anecdotal form), primal truths, comical aphorisms, oratorical effects often exist side by side with the effusiveness of a great interior or cosmic lyricism, in a combination of invented elements and elements received directly from outside (or with the speed of things already made) comparable, to a certain point, to what the cubist painters did with papier collé and their use of fake wood and marble, fragments of the outside world incorporated into the picture. A poetry that was increasingly clarified, like the very life of its author, who constantly sought, through his many lapses and relapses, to free himself of sin. A poetry whose intentions were, finally, classical, though it was always opposed to grandiloquence and ornamentation, anxious to slip into the mold of the least affected forms and dedicated, more and more frequently and continuously as it evolved, to the themes that one may regard as the most generally human: the love of nature (which meant, for Max Jacob, a way of venerating it while also being on intimate terms with it), the dread of death (the subject of many poems as well as meditations included in the voluminous stock of unpublished works still to be brought out), heartaches, life's various miseries. A poetry that, even though it is not truly mystical, abounds in themes directly inspired by Catholicism: devotion to God or the Virgin Mary, the intervention of angels and demons, repentance, aspiration to salvation and fear of divine justice, images from the life of Christ, etc. A poetry in which these pious themes gradually predominate, the theme of hell, among others, which obsessed Max Jacob and which he depicted sometimes in a style reminiscent of Châtelet or certain lavish operettas such as *L'Œil crevé* or *Le Petit Faust*, which provided him with so many catchy tunes to sing for the amusement of his friends, sometimes (and this was most often the case) as an everyday or everynight thing, borrowing details of its appearance from our banal world, as dreams do, taking the events of our current life as raw material and arranging them in unexpected constructions.

As though—was he perhaps being loyal to the two traditions he could have claimed as his own?—he were straining his ingenuity to give proof of his origins as both a native of Quimper and the son of antique dealers who was brought up in the Jewish faith, Max Jacob displays, in handling these themes, sometimes the subtlety of a heresiarch or a cabalist steeped in Illuminism, the Talmud, and astrology and sometimes the candor of a Breton peasant going off on his local processional pilgrimage or a good woman from the church society repeating her prayers and hymns over and over again. Beyond that subtlety (from which it would have been very hard to disengage himself completely) and beyond that feigned candor (but feigned to the extent that he had a sincere taste for it, because it was deep within him despite all his cunning and guile), he frequently achieves the grand tone, "the eternal cosmopolitan style" of which Baudelaire felt he could speak in relation to Chateaubriand, Alphonse Rabbe, and Edgar Allan Poe and which can be found only in writings based on a whole representation of the world or the human condition.

In the domain of the novel and its related forms, world literature owes no less to Max Jacob than it does in the domain of poetry. Portraits whose models are supposed to paint themselves, without apparent interference by the author—like those selectively presented in *Cinématoma* (where one sees them file past like filmed carnival characters)—portraits that offer something as new, technically, as the interior monologue used by James Joyce and recent American novelists; letters from the *Cabinet noir*, followed by commentaries by the imaginary recipients or third parties; forms as original as the pieces in the famous collection *Le Cornet à dés*, whose preface is equivalent to a manifesto and in which Max Jacob brought together a number of prose poems, having developed the genre to its highest point of perfection so that it appeared, among his works as a whole, the prototype of a *written* poetry—different from the quite various forms of *oral* poetry that he practiced elsewhere—a poetry that ignores the various resources of sound that tend to turn a poem into a song.

It would seem that Max Jacob, as a poet, was determined to be a welcoming host for refrains and images and to allow things to be reflected in him, themselves bearing a whole world of feelings; often, this song sung by things blends with the poet's own song, but the *I* that is then expressed seems to be simply the *I* of one of them, not that proud *I* of the romantic poet central to the organization of everything else. As a novelist, Max Jacob also seemed to be able to let the characters he had imagined or observed respond to their own emotions; it is not the author who directs the tale toward a duly premeditated end with a more or less sure hand but rather his creatures who appear to be guiding everything as they please, endowed as they are with sufficient vitality to assert themselves with their various expressions, tics, rhythms, and forms and only do what they like, the author mingling his voice in their concert from time to time not as their master, nor as a spectator with a cool, sagacious eye, but as a witness who pities or enjoys, admires, sometimes praises, and most often lectures.

For as a prose writer, Max Jacob is, essentially, a moralist and author of characters. There isn't a single novel of his that does not pursue, through its thousand passing incidents, an apologetic end whose purpose reverts, in the final analysis, to depicting the misery of man without God; there isn't a single satirical work of his that does not imply, beneath the criticism of bourgeois customs, a veneration for the tranquil, traditional virtues that the town of Saint-Benoît symbolized for him and that he never ceased to admire at any moment of his life, though it was so chaotic, so tormented by contradictory impulses. The characters he puts on stage—each endowed with his own way of speaking and moving (the author disappearing behind them or rather projecting and incarnating himself in them, as Max Jacob did in his imitations, side-splitting improvisations that no one could ever forget)—the marionettes he sets in motion (for what we have here is truly a theater, where everything is observed "through the wrong end of the opera glasses," to use the expression placed at the beginning of the first part of the collection *Le Roi de Béotie*), these puppets soliloquizing or confronting one another in stunning dialogues, are coherent figures, complete "characters" and not mere aggregates of psychological notations. In this, too, one could say that he shows himself to be of a classical orientation and certainly an heir to what is pompously called *le Grand Siècle*, that is, an era when the mania for analysis was not rampant, as it is in our day, and when no one yet was trying to reduce the great human motivations to the dust of mechanical reactions.

Yet we must be deflected from this overly brief classification not only by the spontaneity and multiformity of Max Jacob's genius and all the outbursts to which his irrepressible irony compels him but also by the immense place occupied in all his work, prose and verse alike, by confession. Examinations of conscience in *La Défense de Tartufe*, memories and other elements (real or imagined), such as dreams and visions, used in a number of prose poems, avowals and cries from the heart that emerge here and there in his other poems would inspire one to place him in the line of writers who—like Villon, Rousseau, Nerval, and, closer to us, Verlaine—have given the largest part of their art to an expression of their personal emotions. So much so that it would falsify everything to try to situate Max Jacob too precisely and, even more, to try to enclose his image abstractly in a merely literary frame.

Loving street art and local art (antidotes against aestheticism and objects naturally attractive to a spirit concerned with Christian humility), knowing how to put himself on an equal footing with all things, large and small, and with all people, on an equal footing even with that God in which he firmly believed, Max Jacob seems to have maintained intimate relations with everything that can be encountered in our world, real and unreal, relations similar to those ascribed by the Catholic church to certain of its great saints. "Burlesque" and "mystical"—two epithets taken from the title of one of his first books (the works attributed to the fictitious Brother Matorel, a transposed figure of the author)—are the two poles between which Max Jacob's inspiration has always oscillated, an inspiration whose best element, though far from the only one, will have been a sort of *quotidian fantastic*, sharing the qualities of dream and vaudeville, enchantment and humor.

To the younger writers he taught, discovered, or inspired (that is, a great many men of my generation), Max Jacob has left, beyond his work—inexhaustible in what it can teach—the memory of an unparalleled life as an example on which to meditate. A life tormented as much by long years of poverty as by the sharp conflict between the many urges of passion and the sincere faith that had led him, Jew that he was, to become a Catholic. A life traversed from one end to the other by the most complete devotion to a vocation as poet that changed gradually into a vocation as Christian. A life wide open, without any inclination toward evasion, to whatever fate might introduce, no matter how painful. A heterogeneous life, an ardent life, which the brutes who claimed even yesterday to rule our world ended with a sordid martyrdom, at the close of the winter that preceded our liberation.

Would they have acted otherwise, those executioners who caused him to die because he was a Jew, if, as instruments of some obscure providence, they had wanted to give the career of a poet beyond all others what could be its most authentic consummation, according to the bitter laws that regulate the disposition of lives destined to become legendary?

Elie Lascaux

A History of France, by Henri Martin; *A Popular History of Sciences, Inventions, and Discoveries from the Earliest Centuries to the Present*, by Adolphe Bitard; *Ancient Castles, Feudal Residences, Fortresses, Citadels, and Historic Ruins of Europe, along with the Traditions, Legends, or Chronicles Associated with Them and an Account of the Exploits of the Owners of These Manors*, a work signed "M.B.R." and published by the Librarie populaire des villes et des campagnes; La Fontaine's fables, Corneille's plays, Bossuet's funeral orations; a catalogue from the Musée Grévin; programs from various shows: the Comédie-Française, the Opéra, the Alcazar de Paris, the Cirque Médrano. These are some of the books and odd little publications that can be found either carefully bound and arranged on shelves or lying around haphazardly on a corner of a table in Elie Lascaux's study. I should add to the list a collection of old songs, the veritable vade mecum or bible that he carries with him wherever he goes.

Lascaux strolls through countrysides and towns, loves open-air shows as much as those that take place in confined spaces, walks in search of old churches and castles, is as much a tourist as were the fraternal artisans who used to roam France—he belongs to that race of gawkers that has produced so many poets, Nerval probably remaining the most typical representative.

Making concessions to the anecdote more freely than is proper for a painter of today, infatuated with pretty details (even precious ones), accustomed to painting only what is, for him, surrounded with its own halo of sentiment (emotion aroused directly by a certain

Preface to an exhibition of paintings by Elie Lascaux in the Galerie de la Pléiade (housed at the Editions Gallimard), June 29–July 20, 1945.

fragment of nature or indirectly by an object, a site, a structure linked to a certain memory of a period of history or a certain element of his own private life), giving free reign to his capacity for reverie often enough so that in many pictures the framework of normal reality is disturbed (tormented, in any case, by a cluster of relations that muddy the ordinary classification of things, so that the sky, for instance, is treated as equal to the earth, a winding road as equal to a raveled cloud, a bottle of vintage Bordeaux as equal to a cock's crest and the red of a sunset), sitting before the outside world as he sits in the theater—it is by becoming passionate over everything he sees, by intervening almost in spite of himself in the action (or, rather, mingling the action with what is going on in himself), that this spectator from the gallery, this authentic "child of paradise," converts into duly structured pictures the fruits of his experience as a native of Limousin who went off to Paris one day to seek his fortune.

As close to so-called popular painting as to so-called erudite painting and deriving his originality from the convergence of the two, Lascaux, not entirely a man of his century, as is the case for quite a few poets (who seem anachronistic because anyone who ignores immediate contingencies easily appears to be lagging behind his time), Lascaux, viewed by some as a "naive" painter, nevertheless participates in what is conventionally called "the modern spirit." In fact, in his work one is constantly encountering the mark of that *quotidian marvelous* that seems to be one of the poles around which poetry revolves these days. But in his work this marvelous assumes the air of a backdrop for a comic opera or the stage set for a fairy play, innocent of malice, because Lascaux, who in his art goes straight to the point, likes what he likes without any shadow of irony and, when it comes to thread, uses only the white.*

White thread: a twisted strand that is visible even though so slender, a light rigging for childish stories that have not yet ceased—far from it!—to move and enchant us.

*["White thread" refers to the expression "sewn with white thread," that is, too apparent to fool anyone.]

Henri Laurens, or
Sculpture in Good Hands

Some sculptures seem to want a pedestal, others obscene graffiti; some sculptures are made for palace courtyards or tombstones, others would be more at home in particular houses than in public squares or museums. There is legion-of-honor sculpture and brothel sculpture, ancient sculpture (found in cool churches or extracted from the ground), exotic sculpture (brought back from overseas or discovered in a dusty curiosity shop), popular sculpture and aesthetic sculpture (the latter to be placed in a park surrounded by flowers with names ending in *ium* and *ia* or in a studio with or without green plants). All these various kinds of sculpture, each in its own way, create niches for themselves (small or large) in space. Each has its fans, or at the very least some sort of audience, gazing at it with an eye that is, depending on the work, earnest, lustful, admiring, or distracted.

But another kind of sculpture is content simply to be there. Within the reach of one's hand. It does not seek to embellish, nor to draw the eye or impress. It is even less anxious to imitate. It wants only to populate the void of the atmosphere, create a discreet, friendly, but also undeniably evident presence in it, a little like an open-air equivalent and three-dimensional realization of what Erik Satie referred to as "furniture music." This kind of sculpture is what Laurens has devoted himself to constructing; it is an art that has its

Preface to an exhibition of sculpture by Henri Laurens at the Galerie Louis Carré, October 19–November 19, 1945.

admirers (this is quite clear) but, animated and endowed with the same perceptible radiance as a person, is more likely to have *friends*.

Something so pure, though beyond all austerity, so natural though on the fringes of all naturalism, so gracious without affectation, so dense without being heavy, so large without being pompous, so qualified to furnish proof of all the epithets with which friendship and love, too, are so freely prodigal, so capable of provoking a flood of these epithets without tasteless solicitation or vulgar publicity—we hardly knew anything like this before. On an equal footing with us and also situated in an extraordinarily distilled world, this thing could be given to us only by someone who could think lucidly but was not yet completely freed of his attachments to flora and fauna; only Henri Laurens—with his gentle equine eyes— could have given it to us: the image of what a free life could be in the new golden age whose coming he longs for; the reflection of this fabulous treasure in his eyes, filled with wonder but as serious, also, as the eyes of a child watching a circus.

In the light we need in order to see clearly, in the air we need in order to breathe, it would seem that Laurens (who, at the time of the great outburst of artistic creativity, showed that he was an inventor; witness his "constructions," which are as important in the history of cubism as are papiers collés) today finds a way to offer people of goodwill—with his own hands, which are not those of a centaur or a conjuror—the rarest meal in so simple a form as a little bread and water, symbols of frugality but also tokens of life and commodities whose barter is a touchstone of humanity itself.

Introduction to The Flight

*F*or a number of us, Tristan Tzara—who was the main promoter of the dada movement at the end of the last war—has, for a long time now, been the man *who made stones speak*. A savage poet, upsetting everything, mocking bourgeois conventions and the framework of logic, trampling on the fallacious constructions of a Reason that seemed justified only by the fearful need to keep man enslaved. Attacking language as though it were public enemy number one and changing that tool from a means of communication with others into an explosive that caused a return to chaos, all hierarchy among things and all order destroyed; an eye aligning itself with a door handle, a heap of old scrap iron with the imaginary mechanism regulating the movement of the celestial spheres, rust with blood, the warm gruel of our viscera with the rock crystal of the proudest thoughts, the heart's most secret motions with the slow mutations that take place in the core of metals while birds migrate, while grass grows, covering the bones of moles, and while revolving lighthouse beams preside over the periodicity of menstrual periods as over ships' departures and arrivals. He made everything speak: a tree's leaves were words of a new type of elocution; bark became sentient and close to a cry, like skin. In this enormous festival, man lost his little academic form, ceased to be the center of the world, and, all boundaries having been broken, merged with the limitless jumble of the

This essay was read at the Théâtre du Vieux Colombier on January 21, 1946, to introduce a reading-performance of Tristan Tzara's *La Fuite* (The Flight), directed by Marcel Lupovici, and was subsequently published in *Labyrinthe* 2, no. 17 (1946), from Geneva.

universe. A truly panic festival, a vast massacre in which a communion took place, as in the ceremonies of so-called primitive peoples, where a pact with the forces dominating nature is sealed through spilled blood, orgiastic dances, insane squandering of riches.

This is how I see Tristan Tzara during the nihilistic phase that dada was for him.

Where poetry was concerned, he had summed up what must be called his doctrine (however negative it was) in the famous aphorism THOUGHT FORMS IN THE MOUTH. Meaning that the edifice of reason is only a battle of words, that all our mental activity comes down to a futile faculty for speech. But also meaning that, for the poet, thought truly exists in words, in their savor, their resonance, the way they take shape in our mouths, draw from our mouths a human warmth, mold themselves in the intimacy of our organs, emerge from us quite remote from all geometry, desiccating in its abstractness.

The extreme importance he has always attached to language—man's essential attribute—is the common denominator between *nihilist* poetry, which Tzara's poetry was for many years, and *humanist* poetry, which his poetry is today. When he made stones speak, this was really, for him, a way of humanizing them. By allowing a lyricism to flow into him that was in some way mineral and biological, he abandoned himself to the flow of things, identified with them, impregnated them with humanity. Language as he used it—freed of its discursive chains—became an instrument of rupture and conquest, a sign of man's freedom, even when it seemed to belittle man, reduce him to no more than a small packet of organic sensations, hardly more alive than the uncountable quantity of inanimate beings among which he moved. Thus, Tzara's poetry, so close to things and so like them that it often seems to be simply their bewildered stammering, has consistently tended to become a tool in man's hands, a means of grasping these things, a vehicle for a profound contact, an Ariadne's thread allowing him to rediscover himself through the fantastic labyrinth in which we stray because of our condition and the insanity of the current order of our social relations. At the same time, from an exasperated revolt that made him deny himself, hurl himself recklessly—as though dismembered or volatilized—into the diversity of our material surroundings, Tzara moved to the idea of a proletarian revolution, which is no longer man's simple refusal to accept his condition but a clearly decided desire to transform it as much as possible, to take action so that one can at last speak a human language rather than an idle chatter obeying a species of court etiquette, empty words, nonsense, utterances unrelated either to our fate or to the truth of things, because our bourgeois world is such that all contact is broken and we all live in it like strangers.

Thus, as though through a natural dialectic or in the same way that an ebb tide follows a flood tide, Tzara has come from a poetry that tried to be entirely glued to things, in some sense dehumanized, to a poetry in which external elements appear only in order to allow man to rediscover himself in them, as in signs that he himself has drawn. There is no kind of repudiation in this; simply the inevitable development of a thought that has gone down and touched the bottom and must rise again. And no doubt Tzara had to begin by cutting man into pieces and scattering his limbs to the four corners of the world so that he would then be led to put him back together in a new way.

Immediately after the exodus (which he must have experienced in 1940, as a little later he would experience the adventure of the maquis in the department of the Lot), Tzara wrote the dramatic poem he called *The Flight*. Its governing theme is the rending, the constant divorce, the separation that corresponds to the very rhythm of life itself. The flight of the child who must tear himself from his parents in order to live his own life. The divorce of lovers who cannot remain together without losing their freedom and who must deny their love if they are not to deny themselves. The death of one generation, from which a new generation gradually splits off to rise in its turn. The flight of every living being who separates from others, suffers and causes suffering but cannot do otherwise, because in order to realize himself he needs a certain solitude. The flight of men. The flight of seasons. The flight of time. The implacable course of things, turning like a wheel. And lastly the historical flight: the exodus of 1940, the disorderly retreat, the dispersal of every man and woman along unknown roads, through tumultuous railway stations where civilians and soldiers mingle. Defeat, collapse, confusion, because this total disarray is needed if a society is to be reborn that involves different relations among men, among women, among men and women.

We rediscover in this poem on the theme of flight, for which his actual experience of the exodus of 1940—coming unexpectedly, like a sign of the times—was the main crystallizing agent, the sense of vital pulsations, here operating on a human level, that underlies all of Tzara's poetry. It seems clear that without this flight, this separation from oneself and this kind of return to one's origins, this kind of end of the world or end of man, which he had first experienced when he repudiated everything and admitted to living only the life of things, Tzara would never have acquired the profound knowledge, more organic than rational, through which he has arrived today at a poetry in which thought is authentically the work of the mouth, the utterance of a man who puts into words everything he feels, and perceives the rhythm of his life more clearly because every word he says is the fruit of a voyage through his viscera, of a maturation in their labyrinth, where there is more to learn than in the fixed and disembodied light of any paradise.

Bernarda's House

As opposed to drama, which is nothing more than a news item (because it is based on accident or psychological contingency), we have tragedy, the plaything of destiny, an action that appears to obey a necessary development and result from predestination; there is no situation in it that does not seem decreed from all eternity so that the protagonists may show their true measure, no hero whose conduct does not seem to betoken a kind of vocation. At grips with this necessity, which reigns supreme, the tragic man struggles, suffers more than a thousand deaths, and only arrives at the end of his action ragged or completely broken.

To our modern minds, it seems that the theme which most clearly expresses the nature of tragedy (the passion of a man confronting an opposing fate and the burden of certain acts whose weight he must bear) is the conflict in which the hero, striving toward some accomplishment, comes up against the severity of laws that he cannot break without unleashing catastrophe. Within a world that is well ordered—if not through the will of the gods, at least through the decrees of man—there is this foreign body: the individual rebelling against a geometry that has nothing in common with his fundamental liberty. On one side we have order, the constraint of social rules, hierarchies, and norms; on the other, the light or dark forces that tend to destroy this balance, the fire burning in the man's heart and inducing him, no matter whether for good reasons or bad, to step outside the law. He has met more than his match; it is a scandalous

This review of García Lorca's *House of Bernarda Alba*, performed at the Studio des Champs-Elysées, first appeared in *Les Temps modernes* 1, no. 6 (1946).

crisis, one that must logically lead to the physical destruction or moral defeat of the troublemaker and whose consequences may sully the reputations of those close to him.

It is this sort of conflagration, in which what could not yield except by failing altogether is seen to rise up against an armature of oppression, and an Evil represented by the most naked human desire is seen to rise against a Good that is only an egotistic concern for respectability; it is a similarly radical challenge that is portrayed in *La Casa de Bernarda Alba*, the last play written by Federico García Lorca, a man profoundly marked by tragedy, since he sang—in one of his most beautiful poems—about the bloody end of Ignacio Sánchez Mejías, the famous torero whose friend he had been, and was himself shot down in Grenada by supporters of the inhuman Franco regime.

Like the rumblings (muffled at first, then closer and more precise) that accompany a storm or like the rustling and crackling indicating that things are not working properly in the small, tightly controlled world ruled by the haughty landowner Bernarda Alba, noises from outside are heard very early, as soon as the backdrop of the drama, which is the idea of hierarchy, has been visibly established: a cascade of scorn that overwhelms in turn, in the order of the social rank they occupy, the mistress of the house, the housekeeper, the maid, and last, the beggar woman, whose presence on the doorsill is an insult. As a keystone, there is religion; and as a possible hell, the brothel, where the daughters of the austere Bernarda have a good chance of ending up if their chastity as recluses confined by a mother in mourning should be violated in any other way than by husbands actually less interested in them personally than in the material goods they may possess.

A few noises, occurring in the wings, mark and punctuate the growing tension of the three acts: the song of the harvesters, which causes Bernarda Alba's daughters to feel their confinement more painfully; the uproar of peasants stoning an unwed mother who has gotten rid of her child; the bucking of a rutting stallion; a gunshot fired in the direction of the seducer by the mother, who is most concerned for the family's honor; the toppling of a piece of furniture, which tells everyone the offending girl has hanged herself.

Also in the wings, an almost mythological place: the olive grove, a sort of sacred wood where acts of carnal depravity are consummated and to which it is known that a certain woman or girl was carried off one day more or less with her consent. Likewise a figure from the borderlands is this vagabond in spangled dress, of whom it is told that she once came to dance before the foreign harvesters.

Women effectively ravaged by the absence of coolness and who thirst for an embrace as much as they thirst for water in their absolute dog days, the daughters of Bernarda Alba, prey to the pangs of an unslaked desire and to the annoyance of the dry air, are the solitary and hateful stars of a closed universe that must explode sooner or later because here the needs of the body and the heart are not taken into account, but only the needs of a class pride that causes their mother to oppose the enjoyment of their femininity in her overriding exigency to remain unblemished in the eyes of neighbors she disdains, just as the spotless floor of the house must be kept irreproachably clean. In this closed world, hard as the greedy earth, only one impulse toward escape: the mad grandmother, hugging a ewe to her heart and dreaming of the ewe's fecundity, as though in such a strictly ordered life, the misfortune of being mad represents the easiest way to return to something natural. In a prison where all are so divided and deprived, no positive escape can be plotted; the daughter who, competing with her older and richer sister, would try to satisfy the desire she has to be taken by a man will immediately stumble into scandal, and even her gesture will be as good as buried, since her mother will declare that she died without having been deflowered.

Sensual ardor and the heat of the sun, a dearth of air and suffocation in a privation of the passions, black clothes and a total eclipse of inner radiance—everything merges here, though there are no symbols, nor do the physical elements, with their deceptive boundaries, appear as emblems: the motion that drives one daughter toward the pitcher or the pot of food is the same that drives the other toward the arms of a man; there is no difference of level here between the physical and the moral elements of an atrocious situation. A single perspective, which is that of poetry itself, in which everything that occurs is equally evident and the distinction between center and periphery, container and contained, a human being and her surroundings, internal states and external phenomena, disappears.

A tragedy like this should be performed in a style that is consistently restrained—except for rare outbursts—and not with a violence that heightens the drama to the detriment of the poetic throb and its persistent oscillation of resonances.

June Days

I know very little about my paternal grandfather. There's his tomb at Père-Lachaise, in which my father is buried too: it is a secular tomb, without a cross or any symbol at all, and my grandfather was the first to be buried in it. There is also a portrait of him hanging on a wall that I remember having seen every day for years when I lived with my parents; this portrait was done by his son Jules, my father's younger brother and, it seems, a very skillful engraver, and showed my grandfather when he was already old, full face, seated, his bust taken (I believe) in a frock coat, which was the fashion at the time, a garment apparently made of a grayish material, portrayed by a crowd of tiny lines that restored all its folds, the result of a patience equal to that which had tackled the bold, dry face hidden behind a dense growth of white or whitening hair, moustache, and side-whiskers. And, finally, there is a rather voluminous record book bound in rough black cloth, a book I have leafed through two or three times, perhaps, four at most, in the course of my life. It contains my grandfather's memories of the 1848 revolution and the famous June days that followed the closing of the national workshops, as well as his deportation to Algeria and Belle-Isle-en-Mer, when, like many of his companions, he had to submit to the repression of the riot in which he had taken part.

Written by him in 1887 or 1888 when he was bedridden by pains in the joints that could be relieved only by shots of morphine, a drug for which he acquired a taste, this memoir is illustrated by colored

Introduction to *Jours de juin* (June Days), by Jacques-Eugène Leiris (fragment of a manuscript entitled *Jadis*), published in *Les Temps modernes* 1, no. 7 (1946).

pictures (views of Belle-Isle, of Lambessa) cut out of newspapers of the time and carefully pasted onto some of the manuscript pages. The record book is not available to me now, and I can speak of its illustrations only from memory. Am I going to say that they depict seaports, docks armed with heavy cannons, three-masted ships? If I said that, I would perhaps be the more or less willing dupe of my imagination, which is so eager to transform my father's father into a sort of Jean Valjean standing with his foot chained to an iron ball before a convict-filled Toulon. So I will simply say that a few years ago my mother had a copy made for me of the memoir contained in this record book and that the fragment offered here is an extract from that copy.

As for the author himself—who was presented to me, during my entire childhood, as a model of republican virtues—I have the following information about him from family tradition.

A native of Brie-Comte-Robert, in the Seine-et-Marne department, where his parents lived rather meanly off the yield of their estate, "Les Minimes," he was at the time of the June days no more than a humble employee of a business in Paris, the city being not yet industrialized enough for bohemians and loose-living shop girls to have been transformed into objects of folklore. "Very well educated in a Regional Institute" (if I am to believe my father's sister, who was a teacher by profession before marrying a roofing and plumbing contractor), he belonged to that category of Frenchmen who put freedom foremost among their demands and made their independence from the monied forces an article of religion. A democratic fervor of which he had already had an example in his own grandfather—a member of the Convention and head carpenter who must have lost all his property at the time of the depreciation of the promissory notes—when he outfitted his workers to fight against the Royalists of the Vendée. A fervor perhaps not entirely unlike the anger that inflamed his father during the evil days of the end of the Empire and led him to push a cossack out the window (though it was only a ground-floor window, in fact) when the man was too attentive to my great-grandmother. A fervor that certainly animated my grandfather until his last breath and did not cool during the five years of exile which were the price he paid for his actions as a rioter. Having managed, several years after he was freed, to be appointed stationmaster in the Charenton locality, thanks to the support of Drouyn de Lhuys, then minister of foreign affairs, he decided against taking the job (which, modest though it was, would at least have assured him a living), because in order to occupy the position he would have had to address a petition to Napoleon III, which he regarded as incompatible with his dignity as a republican.

These are the few items I have been able to gather as to the curriculum vitae of this grandfather who had no positive contact with me except by way of a portrait I saw constantly, a record book I rarely opened, and a tombstone on which I read, when I visited it last All Saints' Day, the words "Jacques-Eugène Leiris 1819–1893" inscribed at the top of a list that has gradually come to include half a dozen names. Shall I add that his wife's maiden name was Loetitia Deneix, that she was born April 6, 1834, at Bercy, and that she had received her school certificate? A slight detail, certainly, and the sort to make one smile (just as one can react with some sense of irony to the sight of a piously framed diploma). Yet it was a detail that certainly had its importance for my grandparents. Did they not belong, after all, to a time when education, a very recent conquest for the majority, seemed to be one of the mainsprings of human emancipation and appeared somewhat in the guise of a good angel triumphing over the powers of darkness?

Divine Words

Marcel Herrand, who was the first to stage a play by Federico García Lorca in Paris (his *Blood Wedding*, which opened not long before the war), is now presenting *Divine Words*, a play by Valle-Inclán that also belongs to the great tradition of Spanish theater.

In contrast to tragedy steeped in an extremely fine, though popular, poetry, tragedy characteristic of Lorca, composed entirely of balanced tension, we have here something baroque, always on the point of excess, oscillating between the crudest, picaresque-style realism and the most intense lyricism and imbued with the extravagance of a gothic novel.

A half-paralyzed, idiot dwarf whose right to push his cart from fair to fair to earn some money is being disputed; an old sacristan with incestuous desires; his wife, in love with her body; vagabonds of all sorts (such as an exhibitor of a performing dog, an effeminate young man, and a bogus pilgrim)—these are a few of the characters whose comings and goings and whose sometimes noble and sometimes sordid speeches (limited to "F——!" in the case of the dwarf's vocabulary) animate this succession of scenes in which the spectator sees file past him a series of types of human behavior whose consistently inspired nature the author wished to stress, one might believe, by calling the whole thing *Divine Words*.

Divine words: in many cases, certainly, they are the words of the Holy Scripture; but they are also—taking the form of dictums, proverbs, almanac maxims, and basic truths—the sorts of impul-

This review of Ramón del Valle-Inclán's *Divine Words* at the Théâtre des Mathurins was published in *Les Temps modernes* 1, no. 7 (1946).

sive words, words nourished on common knowledge, that spring, as though inevitably, from the mouths of different characters to express their basest sentiments as well as their highest exaltation. What we see here is not so much a satirical intention as a desire to show certain violently contrasting aspects of life in their naked truth, by choosing as the particular milieu one of those rural regions where the level of material existence has remained very low and the Christian religion, still permeated with archaism, proves to be a strange alloy melding, beyond any preoccupation with morality, an authentically mystical emotion with elements of the most narrow superstition.

In Galicia, where the action of *Divine Words* takes place, estates have been broken up into such small pieces that many men have had to leave their native villages and go find work as dockhands in the towns or live as outlaws in the mountains. Whence, in the case of Valle-Inclán's characters, the absence of any clear distinction between peasants and vagabonds, which one could attribute to the author's imagination, even though there is nothing arbitrary about it, it being instead a positive reference to a real situation. It is a fantasy with a naturalistic basis, comparable to what Erskine Caldwell's *Tobacco Road*, that masterpiece of "black humor," is for the poor regions of the South in the United States; also comparable—and here we return to Spain—to Pablo Picasso's piece of genial buffoonery, *Le Désir attrapé par la queue*, in which poetic invention and the hirsute intrusion of what could represent the shameful parts of the anatomy of our lives coexist in the same way against a background of banality.

The sacristan's beautiful wife, Mari Gaïla, is the sumptuously fleshed she-devil who leads this dance. As well endowed with "divine words" as she is with flaming senses: a pathetic weeper when custom demands that one grieve for the dead, a witty singer of *coplas* when it comes to amusing customers at fairs, skillful in conversations where her interests are at stake, quick with invective and also knowing how to restore to the most childish rigmaroles to conjure—

though in vain—the Evil One that torments her, as though to illustrate William Blake's assertion that the true poet is of the devils' party without knowing it. A great drinker of *aguardiente* (as are all the other characters, for that matter), something of a sorceress (broom roaster and buck rider), the beautiful Mari Gaïla barely escapes total dishonor: surprised with her lover in the reeds, she is knocked about by the peasants, who are also excited by her as by a hot-blooded animal; she will not be lynched, however, nor raped, but only stripped of her clothes, hoisted up on a hay cart, and taken to the porch of the church. And here, the confounding climax takes place: the failed suicide attempt of the sacristan husband, who throws himself off the top of the bell tower without managing even to hurt himself; evidently this is a miracle, and before a crowd that is little by little overcome with respect, he leads his half-naked wife into the church, after recalling the words of the gospel: "Let him who has never sinned throw the first stone!" Ineffectual at first, when the sacristan pronounces them in the vulgar tongue, these words calm the last traces of unrest as soon as he pronounces them in Latin, since, no longer understanding them, the crowd recognizes them as divine.

To attempt to stage in its entirety a work of this sort, so free of prejudice and so disdainful of the conventions of the theater, is almost an act of defiance. Yet Marcel Herrand's production has almost no cuts; its only concern is to serve the text and its only extraneous additions are musical interludes needed to fill the dead time resulting from the many scene changes. Throughout the performance, whose beauty is refreshing, the admirable Germaine Montero, singer, dancer, pythoness, and tart, displays before us the range of seductive artifices of an unfettered woman on intimate terms with the devil, love, and God.

"Should Kafka Be Burned?":
Response to an Inquiry

*U*nless it is pure effusion, the sharing of what one has felt, or else the free play of the imagination creating new combinations, all literature (at the point we have reached in history) seems useless to me if it does not strive to enrich man's potential self-knowledge. In this sense the authentic writer is one who knows himself best as he writes, and, when he appears in print, teaches others to know themselves better, through what he communicates to them of the particular experience that the work has allowed him—for his own use, first—to intensify or elucidate.

Therefore a writer of this sort, like a pure lyric poet or inventor, cannot possibly yield to social or political imperatives, however reasonable they may be. Since the act of writing is for him a means of sudden awareness, he must reject all species of apriority (on a moral as well as an aesthetic level), so as to work on a clean slate, so to speak. It is quite obvious that the imperatives he obeys in a practical sense can be found, in one way or another, in his writings. But if he does not want to falsify anything, he must endeavor to disregard them as much as possible or else to treat them as given facts, like features of his own person, to be brought into play in the same way as any of the other elements given him by his inner experience.

In forming such an idea of a writer's task, I naturally feel as alien to feigned optimism as to deliberate gloominess. My experience is

Published in *Action: Hebdomadaire de l'indépendance française*, no. 93 (1946).

what it is; heartening or depressing, I owe it to myself above all to make it clearer, more perceptible to myself and also to someone else.

As for burning Kafka, I can't see that anyone up to now would dream of it but Hitler's followers. No authentic writing, in the sense I mean, could lead to anything else but an emancipation of man, since what paralyzes us at every instant is our incapacity—either through lack of intelligence or through cowardice—to confront our condition.

The Arts and Sciences
of Marcel Duchamp

One may ask whether, given our modern ways of thinking and feeling, a good part of what is conventionally called aesthetic pleasure does not depend on a play of substitutions: the role of metaphor in poetry (establishing between two different phenomena a relation such that one can be taken for the other), of re-creation in plastic art (replacing a thing or a part of a thing by a new symbol, this substitution of an unprecedented sign for one or another of the more customary figurations doubling the pleasure one could already have taken in the classic trompe l'oeil, a procedure by which is created an object capable of being substituted for the thing that served as its model, except that it lacks one dimension). Whereas trompe l'oeil involves repetition by *identity* (that is, the creation of a copy playing the role of a phantom or double in an environment without depth), the modes of representation invented by cubism, for example, involve repetition through *equivalence*. For the spectators, then, the game would be to perform an act of recognition, as in the case of repetition through identity, but to recognize only after a hesitation, a bewilderment, or at least a departure; so that in the end, it would be as though one were speculating on the principle of identity, causing it to undergo a number of distortions or dissonances, and one's pleasure would lie in the state of suspense associated with these replacements, displacements, deviations, which are close to rebuses or puns.

Published in *Fontaine* 7, no. 54 (1946).

One can try to make the plastic arts, which are normally a *language* (having visual signs—whether traditional or not—just as spoken language uses auditory signs, signs that in both cases create the illusion of adhering to things), into a *writing* (finding purely gratuitous signs endowed with a value just as conventional as the value of the signs of the alphabet in relation to the words they transcribe, and in this way admitting only the most elastic and tenuous link between the sign and the signified). Marcel Duchamp seems to have attempted such a distancing in his famous picture *The Bride Stripped Bare by Her Bachelors, Even*, in which he has applied the most peculiar, sometimes elementary and sometimes specious means to pass from the reality of a group of events or objects to the abstraction of a collection of signs that will be inscribed on a plane that is in this case transparent, a sheet of glass replacing the opacity of the canvas. Thus, the advent of the *Nine Malic Molds* or the *Cemetery of Uniforms and Liveries*, figures already reduced to the anonymity of uniformed things and then further depersonalized like chessmen; thus, the process of printmaking, the actual projection of various points of a solid body onto a surface, instead of the usual geometric *projection*.

Pushing further, and ceasing even to speculate on the margin of uncertainty separating the sign and the signified, one can go so far as to deny any importance whatsoever to symbolization as such and direct all one's interest toward the act of choosing a sign. At this point, what is in question is no longer a sign, properly speaking: the word, form, or object chosen no longer counts except to the extent that it results from a choice, and, its capacity for signification remaining absolutely vacant, it can serve as support for any imaginable intellectual or emotional value whatever. Going to an extreme, eliminating even choice (Duchamp has not failed to do this, with his *Standard Stoppages*, figures obtained by stretching equal lengths of thread horizontally at one meter's distance from the ground and letting them fall, each thus being allowed to change shape "as it pleases"), one can rely on chance alone, personal intervention becoming, in this case, simple acquiescence to what has materialized almost spontaneously in the event.

Whereas the papiers collés—definitely one of the most dizzying heights of cubism—incorporated a fragment of reality into the artificial world of the picture and the surrealist collages foregrounded completed elements to which a more or less allegorical meaning was assigned, either individually or in their disparate assemblage— techniques that, based on contrast or surprise, are both tinged, though to different degrees, with romanticism—there is nothing similar in the very simple and disconcerting invention that Duchamp has called the "readymades," commodity goods or things already made (such as advertising chromos) signed by him, and sometimes supplemented by a few words forming a caption or slightly retouched. Here, the chosen object is simply isolated, qualified, extracted from its environment, projected into a new world; the fragment of reality is not taken in order to be confronted with the handmade parts of the work or to become a symbol, it is taken *in order to be taken* and assumes its power, its singular effectiveness, only from the fact of having been cut off from the rest.

The use that Marcel Duchamp, disdainful of everything anachronistically ascribable to handiwork, has made of elements in series (fixed, stereotyped) does not amount only to substituting for the subjectively calligraphed particular a universal endowed with the same ineluctable character that a printed page has in comparison to a manuscript page (by reason of the absoluteness that enters its final appearance). No mystique here of the *beautiful object* or astonishment of the naive Westerner before the marvelous products of industry. Rather, such a procedure belongs, as one logical link, to the patient enterprise of desacralization or dissection of painting to which Duchamp has devoted himself for so long, intent on using only in a negative way his gifts as a painter, which, as we know, were most brilliant.

If we envisage the American advertising chromo (supplemented by Apollinaire's altered name, a few words without any logical connection at the bottom, and a head of hair toward the left side of the mirror represented in the picture), the design for a bottle of perfume (whose label shows, above a name that is a play on words, a portrait of Rrose Sélavy, the author's pseudonymic personality), the bond issued for a few subscribers to exploit a martingale at the Monte Carlo roulette (printed in three colors—black, red, green—against a white background, with a photograph of its inventor and the inscription "moustiques domestiques demi-stock" [demi-stock domestic mosquitoes] repeated indefinitely), or the check entirely fabricated by the payer's hand and remitted to an art-loving dentist in remuneration for his services (a syllogistic snare, since the check in question is a bad one, but a good one in the sense that it derives its value from the hand that penned it; a way, too, of ironically demonstrating that in our day the commercial value of a work of art has become, in large part, a question of the signature); if we envisage also the idioms taken literally: a geometry book suspended by four threads so as to create a true *geometry in space*; the object called "Paris Air" exhibited in the United States, consisting of a glass vial filled with air before being brought from Paris (the game in this case being not to present anything that is not strictly authentic, a fraud based on the very absence of fraud); if we envisage, finally, more recent creations such as *Rotoreliefs* (records to look at and not to listen to, disembodied paintings no longer resulting from an artist's *making* but from the industriousness of a technician in optics), or the wood and leather valise that contains selected works and thereby becomes a new work, or the card from the United States that, by means of a system of superimposed cutouts, becomes at once a portrait of George Washington, a starred flag, and a sanitary napkin—all these readymades, either absolute or more or less "helped," either immediately given to the author or conceived and realized by him as though they were objects given from outside, indicate a very strong desire to remove from our inventions all signification foreign to them, as though to strip them radically of the possibility of being language and actually see the end of that famous neck of eloquence, so tough and resistant to the efforts of those who have followed—or pretended to follow—Verlaine's still quite innocent advice.* After a series of distancings, decantations, or precautions (proliferating periphrases, as though to be polite or not to deliver any message that is not wrapped in a cushion of silence), the sign remains, stripped of all reference and carefully purged of all discoverable content. Duchamp reaches the extreme point in this respect with the following readymade (planned but, as far as I know, not realized): to enclose an object that can't be recognized by its sound in an opaque box which will then be soldered shut.

A sort of hopscotch—on a patch of ground that appears benign but is pitted all over with metaphysical potholes—a problematic series of domains that reason can travel over only by hopping, such is the sort of image to which it would seem, in sum, that one could refer to understand the type of procedures Duchamp has adopted in a number of what we must call, for lack of a more convenient word, his "works." In this attempt at vacuum cleaning, which his cheerfully detached style situates as far as possible from an asceticism, the inestimable benefit is to have been able to rediscover the activity of play behind an art felt to be too clouded by filters of social convention and religious halos. His pleasure is that of a man who—aware of the limitless system of mirrors among which his condition causes him to be enclosed—refuses once and for all to let himself benevolently be caught in the trap of thinking the moon is made of green cheese and puts himself in a position of full knowledge in order to create his own chamber of illusions; the pleasure not of an artist or artisan but of an ingenious creator replacing the commonly accepted reflections with a multiplicity of other reflections not pragmatically sanctioned but

*[Verlaine's advice was, "Prends l'éloquence et tords-lui son cou," or "Take eloquence by the throat and strangle it."]

just as defensible and producing, in complete freedom, his luxurious stamps and visiting cards, his practical-joke contraptions from the Concours Lépine,* sileni whose bellies glisten with balms and philosophical ingredients.

Once great art has been eliminated, once man has been exorcised of his frank confidence in speech, there would be room for the construction of a new *physics* (or *logic*) *for fun*, open to the elegant solutions of some ARTS AND SCIENCES.

*[An annual exhibit of the work of French craftspeople and inventors at which prizes are awarded.]

Sartre and Baudelaire

To determine what Charles Baudelaire's vocation was (the destiny he chose, summoned, or at least consented to—and not the fate he submitted to passively) and, if poetry conveys a message, to say exactly what, in this case, the mostly broadly human content of the message is. Here the philosopher's contribution proves to be as different from the critic's as it is from the psychologist's (whether a doctor or not) or the sociologist's. Because for him it will be a matter not of weighing Baudelaire's poetry in a precision balance (judging its value or endeavoring to present us with a key to it) nor of personally analyzing the poet who wrote *Les Fleurs du mal* as though he were a phenomenon of the physical world. Quite the contrary, to attempt to relive the experience of Baudelaire, quasi-legendary prototype of the *poète maudit*, from the inside instead of only considering its outer aspects (that is, oneself examining it from outside) and to accept, as an essential basis for doing this, the information he has confided to us about himself in the margins of his real work, such as the facts we can glean from his correspondence with people close to him—this is the task that devolves upon the author of the present work, as philosopher, within limits sufficiently indicated by the fact that the text being republished today was not presented, when it first appeared, as anything more than an "introduction" to a collection of *Ecrits intimes*. A text dedicated—it is of some use to point out—to someone about whom one may observe (whatever opinion one might have of him and his writings) that up to the present it has been his fate, in fact, to pride himself on being a delinquent at the same time as a poet

Preface to *Baudelaire*, by Jean-Paul Sartre (Paris: Gallimard, 1947).

and that society has, indeed, kept him locked away for a number of years.

No claim here—in a study whose parts are arranged in the synthetic manner of a casual overview—to account for what is unique in Baudelaire's prose works as well as his poems; no attempt, which would have been doomed from the start to failure, to reduce to a common measure that which derives its value precisely from its irreducibility; the author of this introduction deliberately stops on the threshold when, in his very last pages, by way of proving the correctness of his approach, he risks an examination not, certainly, of the poetry but of what he calls—thus explicitly defining his limits—the Baudelairean "poetic fact."

No presumptuous endeavor, either, to disassemble any mental or even physiological cogwheels by relegating the person subjected to such an operation to the rank of a thing, a "poor thing" that one looks upon with feigned commiseration, when appropriate, if anxious to show that one is not entirely insensitive. Just as the phenomenologist of *L'Etre et le néant* could never write, in a learned or lyrical style, the "Baudelaire" chapter of some ideal literary textbook, he could also never sanctimoniously poke his paws into an exemplary life of the poet, adding his own explanation to other, sometimes more degrading, explanations. For Sartre, who chose as the tangible goal of his work to construct a philosophy of freedom, the essential task was to derive some meaning from what was known of the person Baudelaire: the choice of self that he made (to be this, not to be that), as does everyone, in the beginning and from moment to moment, up against the historically defined wall of one's "situation." One person will not allow himself to be limited even in the most difficult conditions, another will act defeated in the easiest; and as for Baudelaire, if the image he left us is that of an outcast unfairly overwhelmed by bad luck, some complicity nevertheless existed between him and this misfortune. What we have here, consequently, is not Baudelaire as victim, fit subject for pious or condescending biographers, nor are we presented with either the life of a saint or a clinical case history; rather, the enterprise of one freedom, recounted in a necessarily conjectural way that allows it to be understood by another freedom. An enterprise that seems like the impossible attempt to square the circle (a fusion of being and existence strived for by every poet, each in whatever way is suited to him). An enterprise that has no bloody episodes but can nevertheless be regarded as belonging to tragedy, inasmuch as its motivation was the insurmountable duality of two poles, for us a source—without any possible remission—of disturbance and anguish. An enterprise in which—to quote the conclusion—"the free choice that man makes of himself is identified absolutely with what is called his destiny," and in which chance seems to have no role at all.

Apart from what might be criticized by some about the thesis itself (whose principal postulate concerns the author's ideas about what he calls "original choice"), isn't it rather a mistake to attempt a rational reconstruction of a poet as difficult as Baudelaire was to insert into any sort of scheme? What is more, isn't this manner of breaking and entering (if indeed such a thing is conceivable) such a consciousness excessively casual, if not simply sacrilegious?

One could just as well declare that all great poets dwell in a heaven apart, beyond humanity, escaping the human condition as though by miracle, instead of being the chosen mirrors in which this condition is reflected better than in anyone else. If there is great poetry, it will always be fair to examine those who wanted to be its spokesmen and attempt to enter their most secret places in order to form a clearer idea of what they were dreaming of, as men. And what other way is there, in such an attempt, than to approach them without the fear or stammering of religious awe (armed with as much logical rigor as possible) and at the same time to act toward them (however jealous they may be of their singularity) as though they were *close* to oneself, on an equal footing?

Yet Sartre's undertaking—definitely a very bold one—does not display any irreverence toward Baudelaire's genius nor any lack of recognition (whatever may have been said about it) of the supreme power that poetry represents in him. Set apart as a forbidden domain (the very domain of poetry as such, where rationalism has no role), this poetry nonetheless comes to us as the product of a pen guided by a hand, this hand itself being moved, through writing, by the fact that a man was aiming at a certain goal. Such endeavors—which tend, finally, to enlighten one about one's own undertaking through a more exact knowledge of what certain exceptional beings undertook—are not insulting encroachments. Except in the eyes of a person who would tackle only weak mysteries incapable of resisting a brighter intellect, no corrosive blemish can be reflected on true poetry, whose resonance is made only more profound by every new view of the human being who was its medium, however approximate that view must inevitably be.

To Sartre's credit—he who is so alien to poetry (as he himself admits) and sometimes singularly rigid, to say the least, toward its passionate champions (as demonstrated, for instance, by the summary execution of surrealism that appears in his essay *Qu'est-ce que la littérature?*)—it must be observed that not only has he been able to discover some overtones that had not yet been pointed out in Baudelaire's work but also he has shown that it would be wrong to see only "bad luck"* in a life that, finally, turned out to partake of myth in the highest sense of the word, if indeed the mythic hero is a creature in whom fatality combines with his own will and who seems to compel fate to carve his statue.

*[In French, "guignon," the title of poem no. XI in *Les Fleurs du mal*.]

The Ethnographer
Faced with Colonialism

This text reproduces—in a fairly well reworked version, though still marked by the circumstances in which it was composed—a talk followed by a discussion given March 7, 1950, at the Association des Travailleurs Scientifiques (human sciences section) before an audience composed mainly of students, researchers, and members of the teaching profession.

*E*thnography can be briefly defined as the study of societies seen from the point of view of their cultures, which one will observe in order to try to identify their differential characteristics. Historically, it developed at the same time as colonial expansion by the European nations, when an ever-vaster portion of inhabited lands was being encompassed by a system that essentially consisted of the subjugation of one nation by another, better equipped, nation, a vaguely humanitarian veil being thrown over the final goal of the operation—namely, to ensure the profit of a minority of the privileged. The diffusion of Western culture, conceived as the most perfect despite inventions such as mustard gas (which Mussolini used against the Abyssinians) and now the atomic bomb (with which the Old World is threatened by the American government), the cultivation of regions that would have remained unproductive without this, the advancement of Christianity and of hygiene—these are the reasons most often cited, of all the good or bad reasons that modern

Published in *Les Temps modernes* 6, no. 58 (1950).

colonialism can come up with, for dominating countries and exploiting their inhabitants by alienating them from themselves. As we must not forget, Hitler's Germany also claimed to be embarking on a humanitarian mission when it masked its brigandage behind the idea of a regeneration of Europe and justified its extermination campaigns by a certain eugenics.

Although in principle any society can be studied from this point of view, ethnography has taken for its preferred field of study the "nonmechanized" societies, in other words those that have not developed any large-scale industry and are unfamiliar with capitalism or, as it were, know it only from outside, in the form of the imperialism to which they are subjected. In this sense, then, ethnography seems closely connected to the phenomenon of colonialism, whether ethnographers like it or not. Most of them work in colonial or semicolonial regions dependent on their native countries, and even if they do not receive any direct support from local representatives of their government, they are tolerated by them and ranked together, more or less, with agents of the administration by the people they are studying. In such conditions it would immediately appear difficult for even the ethnographer most enamored of pure science to close his eyes to the problem of colonialism, since he is, willy-nilly, a part of that game, and the problem is crucial for the societies thus subjugated with which he is concerned.

Though it is beyond question that ethnography—if it is not to cease being a science—must be as impartial as it can, it is no less indisputable that, being a human science, it cannot claim to be as detached as a physical or natural science. Despite differences in color and culture, those we observe when we engage in an ethnographic study are always our fellow human beings, and we cannot adopt toward them the indifference, for example, of an entomologist curiously watching insects fighting or devouring each other. What is more, the impossibility of completely removing an observation from the influence of the observer is, in ethnography, even less negligible than in the other sciences, for this influence is much more pervasive. Even if we believe—in the name of pure science—that we must confine ourselves to conducting our investigations and not intrude, we can do nothing about the fact that the mere presence of the investigator within the society on which he is working is already an intrusion: his questions, his conversation, even his simple contact raises problems that the person he is interviewing had never posed to himself before; it makes him see his customs in another light, reveals new perspectives. In the case at least of art objects or religious objects transported to a museum in the motherland, no matter how one compensates those who possessed them, it is a part of the cultural patrimony of a whole social group that is being thus taken away from its rightful owners, and it is clear that the part of his work that consists in assembling collections—if one is allowed to see this as anything other than a pure and simple act of despoilment (given the scientific interest it presents and the fact that in museums the objects have a chance of being better preserved than by remaining where they were)—must at least be considered one of the acts of the ethnographer that by rights create obligations for him vis-à-vis the societies he is studying: the acquisition of an object not normally meant to be sold is, in effect, an infringement of common practices and therefore represents an intrusion such that he who is responsible for it cannot consider himself entirely a stranger to the society whose customs have thus been disrupted.

If, for ethnography even more than for other disciplines, it is already obvious that pure science is a myth, one must also admit that the desire to be purely scholars counts for nothing, in actual fact, in the face of this truth: working in colonized countries, we ethnographers, who are not only from the mother country but agents of the mother country, since it is the state that has commissioned us, are less entitled than anyone else to dissociate ourselves from the policy pursued by the state and its representatives in regard to the societies we have chosen as our field of study and to which—if only through professional astuteness—we have not failed to show, in approaching them, the sympathy and openmindedness that experience proves to be indispensable to making good progress in research.

Scientifically, it is already certain that if our views on them are not to be distorted, we cannot neglect the fact that the societies in question are societies subjected to a colonial regime and that as a consequence they have suffered—even the least affected, the least "acculturated"—a number of upheavals. If we wish to be objective, we must consider these societies in their *real* state—that is, in their current state as societies subjected to some degree of economic, political, and cultural ascendancy by Europe—and not in reference to the idea of some sort of integrity, for it is quite obvious that the societies we are examining never knew such an integrity, even before they were colonized, seeing that there probably is not a single society that has always lived in complete isolation, without any kind of relation with other societies and consequently without receiving some minimal influence from outside.

Humanly, for the reason stated above (the fact that we belong to a colonizing nation and act as civil servants or envoys of the government of that nation), it is not possible for us to avoid taking an interest in the acts of the colonial administration, acts for which we necessarily have our share of responsibility (as citizens and as envoys) and from which it would not be enough, if we disapprove of them, to dissociate ourselves in a purely platonic way. It is up to us, whose profession is to *understand* the colonized societies to which we are attached for reasons often having nothing to do with strictly scientific curiosity, to be in some sense their natural lawyers in relation to the colonizing nation to which we belong: to the degree that there is some chance of our being heard, we must be constantly in the position of defending these societies and their aspirations, even if such aspirations conflict with the so-called national interests and are the object of scandal.

As a specialist in the study of these societies, so unknown to most people in the mother country, and as a traveler to regions of which these same people in the mother country have only the most confused, if not erroneous, idea, it is also up to the ethnographer to make known what they really are, and it is therefore to be hoped that despite the usual repugnance of scholars toward vulgarization, he will not scorn those occasions that may be offered him to express himself elsewhere than in scientific publications, so that the truths he has to express will be broadcast as widely as possible. To dissipate certain myths (starting with the myth of how easy life is in the tropics); to denounce, for example, instances of segregation or other customs that bear witness to a racism persisting even among nations such as those usually regarded as "Latin," who appear less inclined than others to see the White race as the race of lords; to condemn official or private acts he believes harmful for the present or future of the people he is concerned with: these are the elementary tasks that an ethnographer cannot—if he is endowed with any professional conscience—refuse at least to consider performing.

Yet more is involved here than merely arriving at the simple, general affirmation of this duty to inform the public and act as critics. It is understood that every honest intellectual worker able to express himself publicly must not be afraid to take a stand against errors or injustices about which he is one of those qualified to testify; it is understood that he must not hesitate to compromise himself thus, once he realizes that such a denunciation is the most effective means he has of helping to correct the situation and that by doing this, he does not prevent himself from being able to accomplish an even more useful work in an analogous direction. But if we consider above all the fact that ethnographers, specialists in the study of cultures as mass phenomena, are focused by the operation of scientific specialization on the culture of a certain colonized people or group of peoples, it would seem that—beyond those primary duties for which each person must take responsibility and in which, what is more, each case is a special case—there is a more precise task one can expect from these experts. The exact nature of this task and the methods by which it may be accomplished (methods that one can foresee will have to be chosen carefully, given the ethnographer's dependence on the official powers) are, finally, the points on which one would like to see some discussion among those ethnographers who feel a sincere attachment to the groups of people they are studying. The task is a positive one and not simply a protest; it is an active task, concerning the protection of cultures whose vehicles are these groups of people. A protection that one must not confuse with their preservation, as do many ethnographers, whose wish is to see the cultures they have been working on change as little as possible and who, one would quite often be inclined to suspect, want more than anything to be able to continue studying them or delighting in them as spectacles.

A culture—being defined as the sum of the modes of acting and thinking, all to some degree traditional, peculiar to a more or less complex and more or less extended human group—is inseparable from history. This culture, which is transmitted from generation to generation, changing according to a pace that may be rapid (as is the case, in particular, for the people of the Western world in modern times, although to some extent an optical illusion enters in here that makes us overestimate the importance of changes all the more considerable in appearance because they offend our habits) or may, on the contrary, be slow enough for these changes to be imperceptible (as is the case, for example, with certain African tribes whose superficial description as recorded by Herodotus remains more or less viable today)—this culture is not a fixed thing but a moving thing. Everything traditional about it ties it to the past; but it also has its future, being constantly in a position to augment itself with an unprecedented contribution or, inversely, to lose an element that falls into disuse—and this from the very fact that, as the generations succeed one another, it is continually taken up again by newcomers, to each of whom it provides a basis for departure toward the individual or collective goals he assigns himself.

But the moment any culture appears to be in a state of perpetual evolution and is constantly overtaken as the human group that is its support is renewed, the desire to preserve the cultural particularisms of a colonized society no longer has any sort of meaning. Or rather, such a desire signifies, practically speaking, that one seeks to oppose the very life of a culture.

If it arose within the society itself and among the crowd of people that composes it, such a desire could have the significance of a vocation: it would be the society itself that had made a choice concerning its own development, and in that case one could only criticize (approving or disapproving) this desire to preserve. But whatever the case, one would be justified, within the limits of this criticism, in saying that a society that would make such a decision was in some sense crossing out its own history and denying itself as repository of certain forms of culture. One must admit, in fact, that a civilization, of whatever kind it may be, has not attained its true flowering until it has acquired a certain dissemination and demonstrated that it is capable of exerting an influence on other civilizations by providing them with some of the elements of their value systems; but as we know, a colonized society possesses neither the means nor the prestige necessary to exert a true influence: one can speak of the influence exerted, for example, by Negro art on the development of contemporary Western art, but it is still true that one could not maintain that our ways of being or even our representation of the world have been seriously changed by this precious, but minimal, contribution from Africa. Rather than remaining closed in upon themselves (a utopian idea, anyway, given the conditions of the modern world), the more correct line for colonized or semicolonized societies—in the case of great aggregates or of groups of societies with few cultural differences—would be that, while they awaken to an awareness of what they represent that is original, irreplaceable from a cultural point of view (so that a certain faithfulness to their past would be protected), their most active elements direct them toward an attempt to assimilate our technology and educate their people, an effort indispensable to each of these societies, considering its members as a whole, if it is to overcome its handicap as far as local possibilities permit and achieve conditions that might allow the voice of its masses, liberated—and for this reason able to take part in an effective way in the cultural evolution—to deliver a message to the outside world and have it heard. In this sense, the work being done in China now at the instigation of Mao Tse-tung must appear, to everyone who thinks Western peoples are not capable by themselves of creating a truly human civilization, as the beginning of a prospect full of hope. As far as one can judge, such a transformation differs radically from what occurred in Japan during the last few decades, because it is a *people's* emancipation movement and not a simple alignment with the capitalist countries, as is the case with Japan, which has gone from being an old feudal state to being an imperialist power.

In the case of a society that has become too small or has been placed in a situation such that its culture has practically no chance of ever being disseminated, one would hope to see it left to itself, so that it might at least persist as it is. But a society thus abandoned to total isolation—if such a thing were possible—would be destined only to vegetate over a longer or shorter period of time; one would be allowing it, in sum, "to die a natural death." And if, instead of cutting all its contacts, one were to submit it to the system of "reservations" (which does not exclude medical assistance), besides the fact that there is something shocking about putting a society under a bell jar (treating men like animals one coops up in a zoo or locks away in isolation for a laboratory experiment), it still remains that the endeavor is falsified by the few contacts that take place and that there is a great chance that the culture artificially preserved in this way will change rather quickly into a tourist attraction. True, one can allege that the members of the society thus separated have a chance of living more happily than they would if mixed in with our world and all its vicissitudes, but nothing is less certain: we are all too inclined to regard as happy a people that makes us happy because of the poetic or aesthetic emotion the sight of them arouses in us. What is more, we know that such conservation measures, already parsimonious when it comes to the amount of land conceded (as is the case notably in Kenya), are also precarious and subject to revision for economic or military reasons.

In a certain sense, to describe culture as something whose essence is to evolve may seem to provide colonialism with a justification: the need to educate those peoples who are regarded as backward, and to do this for their own good as well as for the good of everyone else, is, in fact, one of the arguments used most readily by colonialists (even though they actually fear and even tend to find various pretexts for retarding an evolution that will inevitably result in eliminating them from the picture). If only to the extent that colonization—however destructive it may be of human values, and however heavy a consumer of work to the profit of a few—not only leads to progress in the areas of technology and hygiene but necessarily implies the founding of a minimum of educational establishments, the colonizers may, without too much presumption, take credit for their role as educators. Yet one must not forget that if there is a definite interest in seeing education spread among these peoples, it is not so that their systems of ideas might be replaced by ours, which nothing—except pragmatic considerations—allows us to consider a priori more valid, but so that these peoples might, as soon as possible, be as well-equipped intellectually as we are, capable of achieving the same practical goals, and consequently in a position to take their fate in their own hands. Such an education, if it is felt to be humanly useful, must logically be carried out on the largest scale and within as short a time as possible; and we must add that it will be accomplished all the more quickly and all the more effectively if the peoples in question realize the imperious need they have for this weapon in the struggle they must engage in to overcome an oppression that is tied to the very nature of capitalism (the concentration of the means of production in the hands of a privileged class) and that continues to be a form of oppression even when it assumes the guise of the most benign paternalism. One must also consider that this struggle is in itself a kind of education: it is not by resigning oneself to living under a guardianship but by becoming accustomed to assuming one's own responsibilities that one becomes fit to govern oneself.

Obliged as he is, whatever his feelings about the colonial regime may be, at least to admit its de facto existence for the time being, the ethnographer is certainly justified in offering opinions (in being, really, a "collaborator" of that regime) to the degree, limited enough in any case, that he is consulted as an expert. As regards education (to restrict myself to the cultural domain in the strict sense of the word), it seems, for example, that an ethnographer—accustomed as he is to taking a relativistic view of civilizations and regarding ideas as indissolubly connected to concrete circumstances —can support only those who believe that teaching in a colonized or semicolonized territory should, at least in the beginning, refer as much as possible to the natural setting and local history, if one wants to avoid uprooting the child and turning him into a person with a purely superficial culture; even though the official authorities have understood the need for this sort of effort, hampered as it is by the demands of an education that tends by definition to excite loyalty, this effort remains insufficient: can one, for example, consider as truly "local" a history of French West Africa of which fully half is devoted to the Europeans' exploration and conquest of this part of Africa? For the same reason, many ethnographers will join those who deplore the fact that when instruction is given in the language of the colonizers (as is the practice in French territories), the child is alienated from his native language in favor of a different language connected to a different system of notions that lose a good part of their content when they are more or less superimposed on—rather than integrated into—different ways of living; from this point of view, it seems that a solution ought to be looked for—as M. Léopold Sédar Senghor has already advocated—in the direction of bilingual instruction (in French and in one of the most common vernacular languages), a method of teaching that would not cause the same uprooting as instruction given exclusively in French and would not expose the child to the risk of later being cut off from the outside world and deprived of the means of defending himself because of his ignorance—or his insufficient knowledge—of one of the great languages "of civilization," as they say.

Within the limits of a general discussion like this (whose aim is not to resolve but to point out certain problems faced by the ethnographer of today in the exercise of his profession) it is, of course, impossible to address all the areas in which the ethnographer may be called upon to do useful work, at least concerning a temporary arrangement of living conditions for peoples who have not yet been emancipated. The organization of labor, the various forms of industrialization, the question of living quarters, the protection of manual trades are a few of these areas, though it is only with the greatest prudence that measures may be taken so as not to risk in the end interfering with the free development of the culture of these peoples, since the measures envisaged may possibly result either in a pure and simple prolongation of the guardianship period or in the accelerated degeneration of what one intended to protect (as is the case with so many moves to promote "indigenous arts").

If it is clear, apart from these reservations, that when ethnography is applied to colonial problems it can perform a number of services and sometimes soften the effect of brutal shocks (as Lucien Lévy-Bruhl pointed out in 1926, at the creation of the Institut d'Ethnologie de l'Université de Paris), it is just as clear that beyond its application within the administrative framework, it can be of some use to colonized peoples in the process of emancipation, who are beginning to think about the meaning of particular characteristics of their traditional cultures.

As for safeguarding cultures, I have already said that I believe it would be useless to preserve them as they are, for, even allowing that one could do it, it would amount to petrifying them and would also mean maintaining the status quo where colonialism is concerned. Without arrogating for ourselves the role of guides—for it is up to the colonized peoples themselves to discover their vocation and not to us, the ethnographers, to reveal it to them from outside—and also without seeking to present ourselves as advisers (which would imply a conceit very close to paternalism), we must nevertheless consider that in studying their cultures, we provide these colonized peoples with materials that can in any case help them define their vocation and that we are only fulfilling our functions as scientists in the strictest sense by allowing them to profit from this work, which, for the simple reason that they are its subject matter, primarily concerns them. To create archives for these peoples—including the very ones whose history, because they know how to write, may be composed of more than just oral traditions but who do not have available to them methods by which they could engage in a positive study of their own social life—to create archives that they will be able to use as a resource is an undertaking whose interest is obvious, from the point of view not only of knowledge in general but of the self-awareness these peoples may acquire. This is technical work that in the current conditions really we alone can do, given the necessarily tiny number of natives of the countries in question who have had the inclination and the possibility to devote themselves to ethnography; work whose results we must, however—in order to give it its true scope— disseminate as widely as possible, so that from now on they may be known to the greatest possible number of intellectuals—if not to a wider public—in the colonized countries. Such studies, showing that these cultures, reputed to be less advanced or cruder than ours, are worthy to be taken seriously and are often, indeed, marked by true greatness, can in fact only help those who are their more or less direct representatives to get rid of the inferiority complex that has been fostered among many by the colonial regime, a complex that induces too many of them to regard as the only "culture" deserving of the name that which they have learned from the Europeans, who constitute a privileged caste in their country. In this sense, even though the study of those societies that are less affected than others by colonization and thus seem "archaic" (or, perhaps more correctly, "anachronistic"), even though the study of such societies distances us from the study of more current questions and can become a sort of alibi, it has the undeniable interest of informing future members of these societies (if they do not reach the point of disintegrating completely) of approximately what they once were like. If we succeeded in disseminating these works as they should be instead of publishing them almost exclusively for ourselves and our colleagues in foreign countries, the benefit would be that henceforth all colonized peoples able to read us would have an account of what various members of the group of peoples they belong to have been able to accomplish through their own means.

Of course such studies are urgent, since societies that have essentially been preserved until now are being constantly threatened by a more or less rapid and more or less profound transformation by European penetration, if not simply by internal decadence. However distant the prospects that the groups that motivated them will put them to use, it is indispensable that certain researchers devote themselves to these studies. But one must react against—and alert students to—a tendency too common among ethnographers, at least where France is concerned: the tendency to attach oneself by preference to peoples one can qualify as relatively intact, either out of a love of a certain "primitivism" or because, in comparison to others, such peoples offer the attraction of a greater exoticism. In doing this, one risks—and this has to be emphasized—turning one's back on crucial problems, in somewhat the same way as those colonial administrators (such as one hears of in sub-Saharan Africa) who praise the "fine bushman," contrasting him to the more "evolved" townsman, and judge the latter with all the greater severity because, compared with the modern representative of the eighteenth-century authors' "noble savage," he is harder to administer. On the other hand, to allege that such peoples, whose culture seems to us purer, are, say, more authentically African than the others, who are regarded as adulterated, is a value judgment clearly equivalent to one that would have Breton peasants, for instance, be more authentically French than the inhabitants of large cities, because the latter live at the crossroads where many different populations mix. It is in no way paradoxical—and no less legitimate, in any case—to declare that on the contrary, of all the Africans (since I have chosen this example), the most interesting, humanly, are those who are more "evolved," whose eyes are opening to things in a new way, and it is among these people (too often regarded, as a consequence of a mistaken generalization, as mere imitators greedy for consideration or position) that one encounters the most authentic Africans, by definition; that is to say, those who, being fully aware of their condition as colonized people of color and tolerating less and less comfortably the capitalist oppression introduced by the Europeans, have become promoters of emancipation for themselves and for those who are their brothers even less by race than by condition. This is to say that, whatever one's opinion, from a political point of view, of a movement such as the Rassemblement Démocratique Africain, one cannot claim that it is not authentically African simply because it has found a weapon in Western culture and an ally in the French Communist Party; what is more, for the historian of customs if not for the ethnographer, there is some piquancy in the observation that people have maliciously chosen to point to the role of "foreign" propaganda in the fact that large numbers of people in French sub-Saharan Africa (and especially in the Ivory Coast, which is controlled by numerous White colonials) are now discovering their situation as victims of exploitation and organizing to fight this exploitation, whereas the offensive against this movement and its social demands developed precisely when it was a question of opening these same territories to investments by American capital.

Strictly from the point of view of scientific research, it seems there is a good deal to learn from contact with those known by the very displeasing term of "evolved" peoples. Among these people, in whom, by the very progress of acculturation, we find only a small number of the traits we have become accustomed to observing among other Africans, we have some chance of perceiving certain characteristics and asking ourselves if their continuing presence might indicate that they correspond to what was most profound, most personally inherent in the cultures that can be seen in them, as though these had undergone something one might then compare to a decantation: traits—or rather an appearance—that would represent that aspect of a people's culture that is less directly subject to the vicissitudes of history and would constitute precisely the *particular way one has there of being a man*, this way embodying, for a long period at least, what one could justifiably regard as the very originality of this people.

Thus, either way one looks at it, it seems it would be a mistake to reduce the field of ethnography to that of folklore—as happens all too often—and, by giving preeminence to the societies reputed to be the least contaminated (which means those that have remained, so to speak, cut off from our modern life and seem somewhat like survivors), ignore the people on whom the ascendancy of Western civilization has made itself felt most strongly: those of the towns, for example, who are described, according to the social class they belong to, either by that annoying term "evolved" or by the hardly less unpleasant "detribalized."

With this really very simple goal in mind—to orient French ethnography in a direction I will not hesitate to describe as more *realis-*

tic, fully aware of how vague and uncertain such a term is—it would be suitable to habituate students (who are too easily seduced, when it comes to the direction of their future research, by the attraction of myths and rituals, an attraction certainly justified by the immense interest this part of the research presents, if only because in a given society myths and rituals represent the "tradition" in the strictest sense of the word, but an attraction that should not allow one to forget that myths and rituals lose at least a good part of their meaning if, as one studies them, one neglects their social context even a little), it would be suitable to habituate students to regard as just as deserving of the interest of the best of them an undertaking that to many seems so much less rewarding: the study of societies on the completely down-to-earth level of daily behavior or, for example, food (so often insufficient or ill balanced) and standards of living.

From this "realistic" perspective, it would also be desirable to study colonial societies *in their entirety*, with research bearing not only on natives but on Europeans and other Whites who live in them (or paying particular attention, at least, to examining relations between the natives and these noncolonized peoples). Such a study could not fail to bring out how much, from a human point of view, relations between colonials and colonized peoples can be detrimental to both parties; the situation is an unequal one that can only demoralize both parties, encouraging excess in one, servility in the other.

Another point to which peoples' attention must be drawn is the following: If one regards ethnography as one of the sciences that should contribute to the development of a true humanism, it is clearly regrettable that it remains, in some sense, unilateral. I mean by this that although we have ethnography engaged in by Westerners studying the cultures of other peoples, the inverse does not exist; the fact is that none of these other peoples has so far produced any researchers able—or in a practical position—to make an ethnographic study of our own societies. From the point of view of scholarship, then, there is a sort of imbalance, when one thinks about it, that falsifies perspectives and contributes to anchoring us in our pride, since our civilization lies out of range of examination by societies that are themselves quite within range of our own examination.

It goes without saying that I have no intention of advocating what would be a hopelessly idealistic dream, given the current state of relative strengths: to train ethnographers in colonized countries from scratch so that they could come to us on a mission to study our ways of life. I am not unaware of the fact that even if such a project were not utopian, it would not resolve the problem, since these researchers would do their work using methods we had taught them and what would be thus created would be an ethnography still strongly marked by our stamp. The completely theoretical question I am raising here thus remains unanswered, but there is something in an analogous sense that is quite possible to achieve and also has its own precedents: to train native ethnographers to devote themselves to research either in their own societies or in neighboring societies. By systematically developing, alongside ours, an ethnography suitable to the natives, one would obtain studies of the societies in question conducted from two points of view: that of the researcher from the mother country who, whatever his efforts to put himself on an equal footing with the society he is observing, can do nothing about the fact that he is from the mother country; and that of the colonized researcher, who is working in his own milieu or a milieu close to his own and whose way of seeing things, one can hope, will differ to a greater or lesser degree from ours. The training of a sufficient number of colonized ethnographers—whether or not it results in truly new perceptions about the regions studied—would be useful at least in the sense that the colonized peoples, while becoming alienated from their customs (as is inevitable), would retain a more vivid memory of them, one would think, because they would be able to appreciate their meaning and value through studies done by their

own people and because those same people who would devote themselves to studying their own ways of life would ipso facto adopt toward them the attitude—the position of an observer encompassing
the scene with his glance in order to situate things in their correct
places—of someone who had left them behind rather than having
purely and simply repudiated them.

Finally, it is important to point out that the orientation of ethnographic research, whether it corresponds to an organized program
or is abandoned to individual whim, is always governed by the idea
we have, in this Western world we belong to, of the inherent interest
in examining certain problems felt by us to be the most urgent or the
most important, for various reasons that may be excellent but, even
in the best cases, are never more than *our* reasons. In this connection,
it would be suitable to develop and systematize contacts between
ethnographers based in Paris, for example, and intellectuals from
colonized or semicolonized countries living in Paris: politicians,
writers, artists, students, etc. One would take one's inspiration,
when orienting one's research, from the desires expressed by these
different categories of intellectuals, who would be anxious, for the
sake of what they feel to be the *real* needs of their country, to see certain problems analyzed. Theoretically, such participation on the
part of representatives of colonized peoples in the direction of research concerning them would be only normal in a country like
France, which admits into its own assemblies elected representatives
(though very few, it is true) from these same populations. Practically, if one observes to what extent the policy of this country, whose
empire is now graced with the title "French Union," remains in its
forms as well as in its goals a colonialist policy (as is evidenced by
events such as the bloody repression and the low-level police tactics
used to silence Madagascan claims, not to mention the Vietnam
War, a murderous operation, ruinous for both sides, that was waged
in disdain for the great principle by which every people has a right to
self-government), it is undeniable that one can hardly see more than

a pious wish in the wish expressed above. At the rate things are going, one can, in fact, believe to be only minimal, if not completely nil—barring a complete reversal of circumstances—the chances of seeing any official development of the sort of ethnography I would like, which would primarily aim to serve the interests (as they themselves may see them) and the aspirations of the peoples currently being colonized. For the present, one is compelled to state that, on the contrary, if an ethnographer openly displays total solidarity with the object of his study, he in many cases actually risks seeing himself deprived of the very possibility of accomplishing his missions.

From the most narrowly national point of view, however, it is certain that, the colonial regime being a state of things that everyone (even those who hope to see it prolonged) recognizes to be essentially temporary, since the economic, social, intellectual, and other development associated with colonization tends to give the people in countries subject to this regime the opportunity to emancipate themselves, the only sane policy would consist in preparing for this emancipation in such a way that it can come about with the least damage possible and therefore in seeking to encourage it rather than hold it back, since a policy inclined to prevent people from emancipating themselves almost certainly, in the end, turns against the nation that attempted this repression. In this sense a form of ethnography dissociated from any spirit of colonialism, direct or indirect, would probably contribute to ensuring for the future a minimum of good understanding between the mother country and its former colonies, at least on the level of cultural relations.

From a broader point of view, one should recall that, as we too live under the domination of economic forces we cannot control, we are subject to our own oppression, and it is hard to see how the construction of a world freed of this oppression could take place unless all those who must submit to its consequences, whether they are colonized peoples or not, unite against the common enemy represented by a bourgeoisie too attached to its position as dominant class not to seek—consciously or unconsciously—to maintain at all costs such a state of oppression. So that when one regards them no longer from the point of view of the privileged minorities but from that of the great masses, the interests of the nations who have become the promoters of ethnography and those of the peoples they are studying appear, finally, to converge.

It remains true that if the ethnographer perhaps sinks his own ship, as far as the colonizers are concerned, by attempting to speak too frankly, by attempting to give his enlightened assistance to peoples currently fighting for their freedom, still he may, as far as the colonized are concerned, be no more than an interfering busybody; for material liberation—the preliminary condition for any pursuit of a vocation—can come about only through means more violent and more immediate than those available, as such, to the scholar.

So long as he has not resolved to strive for his own liberation by taking part in the battle being fought in his own country, the ethnographer torn by the anxiety just described will not cease to grapple with his contradictions.

Stones for a Possible
Alberto Giacometti

To speak of Alberto Giacometti as he himself spoke of Henri Laurens—by way of allusion, analogy, evoking an image with no analyzable relation to the trait to be revealed, rather than by way of argument or description.

In 1933, while I was spending the summer in Brittany—the land of menhirs, dolmens, and cromlechs—shortly after returning from my first trip into sub-Saharan Africa (a trip that Giacometti later told me he had held against me because I went there in an official capacity), I had a series of dreams from which I take the following fragments without changing their chronology at all:

—On the ground floor or in the basement of a kind of museum containing a gymnasium in which children are playing, there is a trick rather like the classic funfair or amusement park attraction known as the "Phantom Train"; it is called "Marriage" and perhaps it is a sort of Aunt Sally? Opening a door that resembles a theater flat, I go in. Here there are a number of chairs with folding seats like the seats in a concert hall; obliquely, at the far end, I see a small theater, hardly larger than a toy, that looks very much like the sort of organ that is covered with moldings and embellished with figures and that

Published in *Derrière le miroir*, nos. 39–40 (1951), the catalogue of a Giacometti exhibition at the Galerie Maeght in June of that year. An earlier version of these notes, translated into English by Douglas Cooper, appeared in the London magazine *Horizon*, no. 114 (1949).

usually forms the central part of a merry-go-round. At the idea that, obeying the rule of this attraction, I am going to have to be conveyed among all these chairs, and that I will have to avoid touching them for fear of electric shocks or other even more disagreeable surprises, and that I will have no control over which path I take or how fast I go, I am seized with fear and I run off, abandoning the friend who is with me.

—In the half-sleep of morning, a dream I have just had and after which I have awoken—immediately or not?—takes the form of a rectangle the color of red ink that stands out, in a distinctly defined shape, against a piece of paper. This rectangle, perhaps actually *cut out* of the paper—and I don't really know whether this is somewhat stiff cardboard rather than just paper—is at once a proscenium (similar to those in Elizabethan theaters) and a human beard. Outside this rectangle an "old friend" happens to make a remark, an "old friend" who appears to me wearing the features of a bearded man whom I afterward will recognize as the Italian consul at Gondar, a city I lived in when I was in Abyssinia. I will abruptly forget this remark, the utterance of which figured as a sort of commentary on or moral to the whole reverie; I will forget it at the very instant when, having emerged from my half-sleep, I am about to write it down in a notebook. Despite some efforts, all I will succeed in unearthing amounts to this: a brief proposition indicating two alternatives and probably ending with "we have to ——ate or ——pose," a sentence of which I know only that the second of these two infinitives is something like "oppose," "dispose," or "impose."

—Coming out of a reception where I have stood leaning on a cane that doesn't belong to me, whose handle—not curved into a crook but straight—is made of wood that is very gnarled, though polished by use, and where, so positioned, I have seen, among the other guests, a woman who is the wife of an Italian diplomat, I go to a sort of garage whose floor is damp with rain, in order to answer the call of nature. Facing a rather small garden, which serves as a sculptor's studio, I do it. On an open-air workbench there are some fragments (particular pieces or just debris?) of medieval or Renaissance works of art. The garden, which I can only glimpse, separates the garage from a house with open windows, which is the sculptor's house.

—In half-sleep I try to remember a couplet that seems to be a phrase containing a condensed revelation. Believing that I have grasped it clearly enough so that it can't escape me, I sit up in my bed and pick up a pad of paper on which I want to make a note of it. Even though all I have to do now, in order to write it down, is to let the point of the pen or pencil run freely over the white paper, I stop short and see that it is impossible for me to remember it. Perhaps, in the second verse, there were the words "roses" and "fire"?

Giacometti's Italian-Swiss background. His professional familiarity with minerals may explain why he seems to be carved out of rock. Yet there is no heaviness, nothing bearlike, about him; does a certain soberness in his gestures disguise his affinity with the lean animals (ibex and sub-Saharan African goats) that prefer to live on the steepest slopes?

In his not very mobile face, under his crown of woolly hair, a cannibal laugh often widely reveals his teeth. A character from a commedia dell'arte of the time of the Etruscans, perhaps, in which Harlequin the medicine man confronts Punchinello the child-eater; or perhaps a werewolf, if he must be compared to an animal (one that is prone, of course, to peculiar transformations). Note also that cannibals, who are more refined than is usually believed, have been credited by one sociologist with the invention of the fork.

Giacometti's art as a questioning of the viewer himself by means of the work: a girl with her knees half-bent as though for an offering to the man looking at her (a position inspired by a little girl the sculptor once saw in his native country); a figure pointing out to a third figure something that can belong only to the viewer's world; objects presented in the manner of experimental apparatuses or reduced models of funfairs; etc. Above all, a woman upright, her arms hanging, as motionless as a question mark.

Rectangular panels arranged vertically in a circle: a construction imagined by Giacometti and then worked out on paper, to recount several events that happened to him for the most part over the past few years and whose conducting wire was a dream that he wanted to note down; each panel corresponds to one of the events described, and the whole system expresses their interconnections in time and space. This apparatus inevitably reminds us of one of the objects Giacometti made when he belonged to the surrealist group: sculpted in plaster, it was a sort of scale model of a funfair, and if the person looking at it should happen to fall into it, his adventure would unfold through the different parts of it.

To set up votive stones, to materialize experiences, to give lasting substance to the elusive or fleeting quality of an event, to fix realities using methods that, when necessary, borrow from naturalism whatever is indispensable if he is to convince us, but nothing more: this is, roughly, what Giacometti appears to be doing; he seems to have chosen a three-dimensional art as his most consistent way of expressing himself, because this is the most difficult art to extricate oneself from without cheating.

One of Giacometti's major preoccupations: the scale on which the human being is represented in a work of art. What he finds striking in Jacques Callot's etchings, for example, is the smallness of the figures, who are lost in vast spaces and appear to be seen from a certain height.

Giacometti's statues—larger in the courtyard of his house or in the street than in his studio (littered with pieces of plaster that for a long time threatened to invade the little room in which he slept in spite of the cold and the rain). This difference, because a creature always unfolds when it is no longer confined; more reasonably: because it is in the open air that one can judge human scale.

Until now, almost no one but astronomers concerned himself with the *apparent diameter* and the *real diameter* of what he was looking at. Giacometti shows that he can make this sort of distinction when he fashions figures whose "natural height" doesn't depend on their height in meters and centimeters.

People standing, people walking, people crossing paths in a place that may be public or private, an arm by itself, a nose springing out like the enormously indiscreet interference in a face: a few ways sculpture has of *putting in an appearance*, following one of the various systems conceived by Giacometti. And this is in the large atmospheric box in which we live, a very different space from that of a museum.

In good weather or bad, individuals with no other relation to one another than the fact that they are all walkers going each in his own direction. No common denominator for them, except—possibly—for the woman who is also there but isn't moving and at whom these nameless men gaze—without complicity, each for himself alone.

To enumerate, to count, to survey desirable creatures, to recapitulate, to gauge, and to leave in suspense. Figures not so much grouped as juxtaposed and each of whom—without its solitude being in the least broken—is all the more emphatic for being situated or framed by the others. Here, what is singular increases by becoming a fragment of a plural, what is relative surpasses what is absolute, and the comparative says more than the superlative.

What you see when you walk down the sidewalk and everything strikes you at the level of your two eyes. What you only glimpse from your window.

Whereas usually a piece of sculpture is an object with space around it (exactly the opposite of a cannon, which is a hole encircled by bronze), Giacometti is now engaged in creating space that contains one or several objects.

What might make us believe that Giacometti is capable of Byzantine subtleties: the faultless attention he pays to questions that are very simple (though for this very reason more difficult to grasp than many others, even if one limits oneself to pondering their terms), questions posed by the way people and things present themselves to us.

Confining himself to what is characteristic of man: to stand upright, to walk by moving his two legs one after the other. Recently, sculpting domestic animals too.

For several years, after an accident from which he escaped with one of his feet seriously injured, Giacometti was never seen walking without the help of a cane; then, one fine day, he decided to give up that implement, and as soon as he made that decision he moved about without any support. In the same way, his sculptures always stand upright without either cane or crutch.

A glittering trolley with small bottles and surgical dressings belonging to the Bichat Hospital that appeared in 1938 before the admiring eyes of the man with the broken foot and that reappeared twelve years later when the sculptor needed two wheels to isolate an effigy from the ground and fictively endow it with a capacity to move in spite of its absence of movement. Perched above the axle of this component of the vehicle (which is itself mounted on blocks), the woman no longer touches the ground, and it is she herself who incarnates the sculptor's admiration for the trolley circulating among the beds.

The sudden memory of a forest or of a clearing, depending on whether a random grouping of figures turns out to be denser or more diffuse. Instead of being destroyed like so many others, the figures had accumulated as though they had been made just for this grouping—in which they will have come into their final transformation.

Feminine bodies arranged in a row, the same way girls in a brothel present themselves to be chosen. At the Sphinx a vast expanse of gleaming floor relegated the nude bodies to an almost sacred distance; at the rue de l'Echaudé, on the other hand, their proximity (not very appetizing, finally) was almost aggressive within the four walls of a cramped room. The different heights of the supports and the scale itself of the figures made them farther away or closer, just as did the greater or lesser expanse of floor.

To integrate the support into the action, to make it a part of the sculpture, and so an object or piece of furniture with which the viewer is on an equal footing. Sometimes the opposite happens and the support separates, either suggesting the space of a stage or platform open to everyone (though in fact limited), or extending in lines defining the three dimensions of a cube of air in which the things are situated, or indeed becoming a container for the protagonist.

After the highly polished solids of the beginning (steles or shingles soaked for a long time, which are all that remain of the perception of a living body), after the openwork constructions and the games that refuse to close off space, what we have now are pin-sized figures and larger figures that are still thin, images of the vertical position, small proliferations of human structure around a plumb line.

The period in which these tall effigies were painted, dabbed with little mostly rust-colored touches, as though this clayey color had been drawn to the surface by the need to give them blood.

Are they statues that have returned to their natural state following some accident or some treatment that remains to be defined? Or are they natural bodies promoted to the rank of statues after slight alterations or a ripening period?

How these latest sculptures of Giacometti have taken on the look of *objets trouvés*. All things considered, one would be inclined to believe they were idols or mummies that had come out of hopelessly dry sand or volcanic soil. Compare with them the desert concretion known as the "gypsum flower"; certain results in the earth of the process of erosion; utensils warped by burning lava or directly corroded by a wave of heat?

Extreme reduction of matter, following a law of economy that seems to determine both the quality and the quantity of the attack on it. No more than a little, the smallest bit of matter needed, and by its own action stripped of all luster, as though to show plainly that richness lies elsewhere.

To scratch down to the bone, to what is indestructible. Or else—the opposite—to add space when one seems to want to eliminate a few ounces of material.

Between geological matter and air, there is the shared surface.

Something of the ruins of Pompeii and the wall paintings that have remained fresh in spite of wind, storm, ashes. In happy discoveries of the sort that archaeologists make, millennial antiquity converges with the flashing rupture of time: the sudden unveiling of a face forever contains all of the long past. As for his own discoveries, it seems that Giacometti—directing his hands as one would direct workers proceeding with excavations—would like to dig them up, fully outfitted, from his own brain.

Intense concern for speed, without which there could be no creation. In contrast to the patiently elaborated work of art, here we have the thing that suddenly appears, all the more manifest because it seems to have sprung up without any history and without any roots: instantaneous and outside of time. From this point of view, to destroy something completely is more worthwhile than to correct it. Seeing the sorts of slaughters that Giacometti has been indulging in, I have sometimes wondered if for him sculpting means making something that he can then demolish.

Make, perfect, destroy, then make again, perfect again, destroy again . . . out of a desire to be rigorous, up to the moment when circumstances require that the thing be finished, and it is halted just as it is, the desire for rigorousness having simply been supplanted by submission to circumstances, just as one law succeeds another.

The problem of *real presence*—posed and solved by Giacometti, whereas it seems to have escaped almost all of our sculptors, who are either pure architects or the makers of mannequins whose stuffing doesn't prevent them from being absent. In the same way, Negro sculptors are trying not so much to represent their models as to allow them to be there (and they are prepared to let their figures later crumble into dust).

A stone in the shape of a head is at once a stone and a head; but could one say the same thing of a head made of stone?

When it is painted, a bronze escapes its condition of being a sculpture more easily than when it has kept its metallic look. If *Man Fall-*

ing was left out of the series of works that Giacometti subjected to
this treatment in 1950, was that because a fall cast in bronze is never
in danger of solidifying into a statue?

"Rose mallow," "saint of the abyss," "white phantoms" falling "from
our burning sky": a sequence of themes from one of the most famous
Chimeras by the man whom posterity will perhaps simply call "Gérard," as his friends did,* a sequence of themes I would also be
tempted to apply to the series of feminine figures sculpted during all
these past few years by "Alberto," who says he absolutely does not
come from Ile-de-France but from a country with severe cold
weather and plenty of mountains and snow.

*[Leiris is referring to Nerval's sonnet "Artémis," in *Les Chimères*.]

Note on the Use of Catholic Chromolithographs by Haitian Voodooists

*A*s shown not only by its name—which comes from the word *vodoun*, in the Fon language of Dahomey, designating what one can briefly call "spirits"—but also by many similarities observable in the rituals, dances, and songs, as well as in the names of divinities and various elements of the special terminology, the religion commonly called "voodoo," for which Haiti is one of the main centers, was created from a nucleus of originally Dahoman beliefs and practices. Though categorically condemned by the official church and at best tolerated by the government, this religion—which is based on the idea of possession and may be regarded, in spite of its disrepute among so many people, as a sort of national creed for the Haitians—is practiced almost openly by a majority of the people, though Roman Catholicism is their faith, and proves to be strongly steeped in Christian elements in its ritual as well as in its liturgy. The use of Catholic prayers and hymns in the ceremonies (along with truly voodooistic prayers and songs), the presence of the crucifix in the *houn-fors*, or sanctuaries, and the use of Catholic devotional images (chromolithographs, most often from Cuba) to represent the *loas*, or "mysteries," which are also called "saints" because they are syncretically identified with saints of the Catholic church, give striking evi-

Published in *Les Afro-Américains*, ed. Pierre Verger, Mémoires de l'Institut d'Afrique noire, no. 27 (Dakar: Institut français d'Afrique noire, 1953), pp. 201–207.

dence of this mingling, whose origins one can trace back—without prejudice to its later developments—to the fact that during the colonial era baptism was legally imposed on slaves almost as soon as they arrived on the island of Santo Domingo.

During the brief visit I made to Haiti (from September 24 to October 26, 1948, under the auspices of the Institut Français de Port-au-Prince, whose director was M. Simon B. Lando), I was able to make some observations about the way in which a correspondence was established between a certain *loa* and a certain Catholic saint depicted on a chromo, on the basis of a series of fifteen images, all close to the same size and shape (25.5 to 26 centimeters high; 18.5 to 20 centimeters wide), that I had acquired during various visits to the covered market of Port-au-Prince, paying a half-gourde for those on thin paper and a gourde (or one-fifth of a dollar) for those on heavy paper, nine of these images coming from Cuba (seven marked "L.N.V.," one marked "Misiones Parroquiales Cuba" and "La Nueva Venecia," and then one without any particular mark), whereas six (marked "C.G." with a tiny ornament) were printed in Italy.

In the case of each of these chromos, which are now part of the collection of the Département de l'Iconographie at the Musée de l'Homme and of which I saw numerous equivalents during my visit on the walls of those rooms in the *hounfors* called *cay' mystère*, or "house of mysteries" (species of "holy of holies," each referring to a particular group of divinities), I made inquiries to find out exactly which *loa* each of them corresponded to, addressing either the women who were selling them in the market or, as a double check, other informants. The identifications thus created and the reasons spontaneously invoked to justify these equivalences seem to permit us to infer that the likening of a saint to one of the divinities in the voodoo pantheon is based at least as much on the sharing of attributes or elements of the setting that create a visual likeness as on a system of general correlations that is independent of such formal conjunctures.

For example, my informants set up a correspondence between *Papa Legba*, who is the god of crossroads and of routes that allow men to enter into relations with the other gods and is pictured as an old man who leans on a forked stick (as does, invariably, the initiate possessed by him during ceremonies), and the following images of saints: Saint Lazarus ("San Lazaro") represented as an old man covered with sores (which two dogs are licking), his forehead bandaged, walking with the support of crutches and holding in his left hand a wooden clapper; Saint Anthony the Hermit ("San Antonio Abate") dressed in sackcloth and bearing a tall staff with a small bell on it, blessing a group of domestic animals against a background of wooded countryside with a burning house; Saint Anthony of Padua ("San Antonio") in a monk's robe holding the Infant Jesus paternally in his arms before a book of prayers and some flowers, in an outdoor setting including a vast cloud with cherubs on top of it. The same image of Saint Anthony the Hermit, in which the pig who escorts the saint is depicted along with other animals (horse, donkey, ox, sheep, dog, rooster, ducks dabbling in a pond), is also believed to represent *Simbi Pétro*, a spirit whose "services" require the sacrifice of a pig (as is the rule for the *loas* of the *pétro* series) and always take place near a body of water.[1]

---

[1]According to Milo Marcelin, *Mythologie vodou (rite arada)*, vol. 1 (Port-au-Prince: Les Editions Haïtiennes, 1949), p. 16, "Legba is generally identified with Saint Anthony the Hermit (because, they say, of his sexual frigidity) or with Saint Anthony of Padua (surrounded, in his chromos, by all sorts of domestic animals). But according to a *houngan* (voodoo priest), who told me this himself, if one wishes to represent Legba, one uses the image of Saint Anthony the Hermit in the *Rada* ritual and that of Saint Anthony of Padua in the *Pétro* ritual." For his part, Jacques Roumain notes, "Whereas in Dahomey, Legba is a phallic god, he has lost this characteristic in Haiti, and in Cuba he is even identified with Saint Anthony because of his sexual frigidity." (*Le Sacrifice du tambour-Assoto(r)*, Publication du Bureau d'Ethnologie de la République d'Haïti, no. 2 [Port-au-Prince: Imprimerie de l'Etat, 1943], p. 19).

The *pétro* ritual, which inclines toward magic, is apparently more recent than the *rada* ritual, which, according to Major Louis Maximilien, "in its most basic aspect perpetuates the true religious traditions of Dahomey" (*Le Vaudou haïtien: Rite*

The saint who corresponds to *Damballa Wedo*, divinity of springs and streams whose symbol is the snake, is Saint Patrick ("San Patricio"), whom one sees represented in full bishops' clothing driving the serpents that had infested Ireland into the sea.[2] It seems that what matters here is simply that the saint is represented with snakes, regardless of the fact that his relation with them is one of enmity, not of sympathy.

Ayda Wedo, Damballa's wife, was mentioned by my informants in connection with an image of Saint Elizabeth of Hungary ("Santa Elisabeta—Regina d'Ungheria"), who is shown with her forehead encircled by a crown and her head surrounded by a halo of rather large diameter consisting of a very delicate double line standing out against the sky—an attribute reminiscent of the rainbow with which Ayda and Damballa Wedo are associated.[3]

An image of "Nuestra Señora de la Caridad del Cobre"—in which the main figures are the Virgin standing on a crescent moon, invoked by a young Black kneeling in a boat where two rowers are fighting against a foaming sea—offers more complex interpretive possibilities, and one can obviously expect that it will be put to various uses, given its many themes and characters (besides those already named, there are three cherubs, as well as two girls in blue tunics carrying a banner with the inscription MATER CARITATIS IN

Radas-Canzo [Port-au-Prince: Imprimerie de l'Etat, n.d.], p. 150). The same author points out that "numerous pétro loas are replicas of radas loas" (p. 151).

Among the chromos I collected, an image of Saint Anthony the Hermit (and not of Saint Anthony of Padua) shows the saint surrounded by animals; in any case, for Marcelin's informants as for mine, the image in which a pig appears refers to a *loa pétro* (either Simbi, or Legba invoked in the *pétro* ritual).

[2] According to Marcelin (*Mythologie*, p. 57), for certain believers, Damballa Wedo, who is imagined to be White, "is not Saint Patrick, who, according to them, is his son, Odan Damballah Wedo. They identify him with (Saint) Moses, saved from the waters, for, they say, Damballah stutters like him. A *houngan* . . . told me that Damballah Wedo, a *loa Rada*, was Saint Moses and Damballah La-flambeau, called also Saint-White, a *loa Pétro*, was Saint Patrick."

[3] Marcelin (*Mythologie*, p. 69) identifies this divinity with "Our Lady of the Immaculate Conception, represented in Catholic chromos as crowned with stars, dressed in blue and white, standing on the earth's globe before a crescent moon, with a snake beneath her feet."

FLUCTIBUS MARIS AMBULAVIT). The attention of certain of my informants was primarily drawn to the boat, actually, and they associated the image symbolically with the god of the sea, *Agwé Taroyo* (whose most important attributes are a boat and an oar); but the attention of certain others was particularly drawn to the principal celestial figure, in whom they recognized *Clermézine* or *Clémerzine*, daughter of the water god *Clermeil* and regarded as being related to the moon. These two interpretations are not at all contradictory (since *Général Clermeil* is considered the commander of Agwé's guard and consequently part of the same series); but a third interpretation introduces a god situated rather differently: a Haitian researcher already cited, Milo Marcelin, reports that "certain practitioners of voodoo in Port-au-Prince identify Agaou [god of wind and storm, who is part of the retinue of the peasant god *Zaka Médé*, brother of *Cousin Zaka*] with Saint Roch, others with Saint Michael, and still others with the little Black who appears in the chromos of the Caridad Virgin, kneeling in a boat with his hands joined."[4]

Corresponding to *Erzilie Fréda* or *Grande Erzilie* (as to her namesake or double, *Maîtresse Erzilie*), the goddess of love whose symbol is a heart in the white flour drawings, or *vévés*, that are her sacred emblems—as they are for the other *loas*—and who is entitled to all sorts of luxury items and adornments, is an image of the Mater Dolorosa ("Dolorosa con joyas") shown covered with expensive jewels and surrounded by many hearts, among other numerous ex-votos.[5]

The secondary figure in an image of Saint James the Greater ("San

---

[4]"Les Grands Dieux du vodou haïtien," *Journal de la Société des Américanistes*, n.s., 36 (1947):51–135. According to the same author (*Mythologie*, pp. 89–90), "the Caridad Virgin, goddess of the sea, is probably a double of Erzili. She *walks* with Agoué"; in Cuba, she is apparently identified with the Afro-Cuban deity *Chun*, who is pictured as a "lithe, glowing, long-haired mulatto." Since *Erzilie*, guardian of the gentle waters, is reputed to have had numerous love affairs and most notably to have become the wife of Agwé, we thus return to the essential idea of a relationship between the chromo of the "Caridad Virgin" and the gods of the sea.

[5]According to Marcelin (*Mythologie*, p. 77), "Maîtresse Erzili" is also identified with two Black virgins: that of Altagracia (also called the "Virgin of Higüey," the name of a town in the Dominican Republic) and Our Lady of Mount Carmel.

Santiago," literally "Saint Saint-James": the place name Santiago, designating a Cuban town under the patronage of the Spanish Saint James of Compostela, has become, as it happens, the name of the saint himself), an image depicting Saint James on horseback, with sword and shield, fighting the infidels and escorted by a knight in armor carrying a red flag with a white cross on it, produces two interpretations: for all my informants, the main figure is the blacksmith and warrior god *Ogoun Ferraille* or *Ogoun Fer* (whose most important attribute is a saber and whose color is red, as in the case of the other Ogouns), but for some the figure in the background is *Ogoun Badagri*, brother of Ogoun Ferraille, whereas for others he is a *guédé*, a spirit of cemeteries; the reason for this is that the helmet with lowered visor worn by the figure in question recalls the chin bandage and other attributes of the dead (such as cotton in the nostrils) often assumed by initiates incarnating the *guédés*, which would also explain why the latter are reputed always to speak through their noses.[6]

Some of the people I questioned recognize as an Ogoun a red-coated "San Miguel, Arcángel" holding a scale in his left hand and in his right a sword with which he is preparing to pierce the devil, and they assume he is Badagri himself. One "San Giorgio Martire," an equestrian figure also clothed in a red coat, armed with a sword and slaying a dragon, is also considered an Ogoun, and perhaps the one called *Balinjo*.[7]

[6] According to Marcelin ("Les Grands Dieux," pp. 85ff.), "The chromos representing Saint James the Greater wearing armor are interpreted as portraits of Ogoun Ferraille. For some the visor of his helmet is a bandage that prevents him from seeing and thereby restrains his fury; for others it is a veil with which he has been adorned by Badagri, his father [and not his brother], who is jealous of the assiduous court he has been paying to Maîtresse Erzili and the favors he has obtained from her. This ironclad knight is also called Saint Philip, and he is made out to be the twin brother of Saint James the Greater." It is this ironclad knight identified as the brother of Saint James that certain of my informants have recognized as Ogoun Badagri and others as a *guédé*.

[7] Harold Courlander (*Haiti Singing* [Chapel Hill: University of North Carolina Press, 1939], p. 40) mentions Ogoun Balinjo as the brother of Ogoun Badagri. Both are warriors and blacksmiths, and it is quite probable that the presence of

Identified with *Cousin Zaka*, a rural god one of whose main attributes is an *alfor*, or wickerwork satchel, is Saint Isidore ("San Isidro"), represented as a peasant carrying a leather satchel slung across his shoulder and praying with one knee on the ground and his hands joined, while in the background an angel guides a plow pulled by two oxen.

Baron Samedi, father of the *guédés*, whose emblem is the tombstone cross and who is also called "Roi Degonde" (from Saint Radegunda, founder of the abbey of Sainte-Croix), will be seen in Saint Expedit ("San Espedito"), represented as a Roman military leader holding his martyr's palm in his left hand and in his right a cross bearing the word HODIE, while his right foot tramples a crow holding in its beak a banderole with the word CRAS on it and on his left, flat on the ground, sits a helmet with its visor raised. The identification is essentially based on the presence of the cross and of the helmet, likened to a skull (according to some, because of its form, which is liable to cause confusion in people who have never seen a helmet before, as is the case with the inhabitants of the Haitian hills; according to others, because a skull is what was actually represented in old specimens of the same chromo). According to Milo Marcelin,[8] however, the similarity between the saint's name and the word "expedition," designating the sorcery rituals in which Baron Samedi plays an important role, has something to do with this identification.

Similarly, the *loa Brave Guédé*, all of whose attributes are black, is recognized in a picture showing Saint Gerard ("S. Gerardo Majella") dressed in a bluish black soutane with a long wooden crucifix in his

---

flames in the picture of Saint Michael (the fires of hell) as in that of Saint George (tongues of flame coming out of the dragon's mouth) has something to do with the identification; according to custom, in fact, people possessed by Ogouns show they are not afraid of fire by walking on hot coals and handling red-hot iron bars. We must note, however, that in the interpretations given of the picture of Saint Anthony the Hermit, identified with Papa Legba, the fire in the background is omitted.

[8]"Les Grands Dieux," pp. 120–121.

left hand, leaning his right elbow on a table on which we see an instrument of mortification along with some lilies or other white flowers, which replace the death's-head that appeared (it seems) in old examples of the same chromo.

Quite naturally, too, one recognizes the *marassa*, or twins (who are worshiped in Haiti as they are in Dahomey and numerous other regions of Africa), in a picture showing Saints Cosmas and Damian ("SS. Cosma e Damiano") standing side by side, both in sumptuous gold-embroidered garments (one in a sort of green caftan and red pall, the other in a red caftan and green pall), one holding a ciborium and the other a book, as well as each his martyr's palm.

It also happens that one picture may give rise to completely contradictory interpretations, depending on which details are stressed. This is the case, for instance, with one of my chromos showing, in the shadow of a tall tree, a young Saint John the Baptist ("S. Giovanni Battista") dressed in a sheepskin, a lamb on his knees and in his left hand a cross made of two branches tied together with the words ECCE AGNUS DEI: according to one interpretation, the picture represents the *loa Jean Pétro*, and one can assume that the reason is not only the similarity of the names, since *Ti Jean Pétro* is a tree spirit envisaged as a small man without feet or with only one foot,[9] two characteristics that may correspond as well to the tree as to the apparent absence of legs in the young Saint John the Baptist shown sitting down; according to the other, what we have here is not a *loa* of the *pétro* series (spirits to whom it is customary to sacrifice pigs, as we saw earlier) but a *loa* from the *rada* series, given the presence of the sheep.

I must note, furthermore, that among other Catholic holy images

[9]This trait may justifiably be seen as originating in Africa, since a belief in spirits that haunt tall trees and are sometimes conceived as having only one leg, or one leg longer than the other, can be found in West Africa in the form of the belief in *dyinous*.

I saw in the home of a *mambo*, a famous priestess from the Croix des Missions, on the outskirts of Port-au-Prince—Mme Ildevert, or Soustinie Minfort, to give her her *nom vaillant* (that is, her assumed name)—I noticed a picture of "Nuestra Señora de Montserrate" surrounded by four singers and six musicians, all adolescent, dressed in black robes and white surplices, a picture that represented, as it happened, the goddess Erzilie. Now, about a month earlier I had seen a version of this same picture being used, through a similar process of syncretism, in the Changy chapel near Carangaise de la Guadeloupe, one of the main places of worship where descendants of the "coolies" gather, people generally of Dravidian race who came from the Indies to the French Antilles as salaried workers after the abolition of slavery; whereas for the Haitian practitioners of voodoo she is Erzilie, these Hindus from Guadeloupe use her to represent *Maryemen* (or *Madyemin* or *Mayêmé*, which may come from "Marie aimée" [beloved Mary]), a female goddess whom they liken to the Virgin Mary—as is the case, in voodoo, with Erzilie—and to whom a black stone statue is dedicated on the main altar of the chapel: a figure entirely covered with a great white veil exposing only the face: when this veil is drawn aside the statue is revealed to have four arms, holding in its outer right hand (the one farthest from the body) a representation of a sword, in the inner right hand a bulging object that would seem to represent a gold disk, in the outer left hand a branch of "Indies lilac," or *vêpêlé*, and in the inner left hand a trident (none of these attributes being reminiscent of the mirrors and various implements for adornment that, in Haitian sanctuaries, one so often sees arranged on a dressing table dedicated to Erzilie). In this deity—whose chapel is occasionally visited by Guadeloupeans of African ancestry who mingle with the faithful of Hindu ancestry—one can apparently recognize a goddess of smallpox: *Mâriyammei*, or "Mother Death," in other words one of the *grâmadevatâs*, "village deities," who, associated with the worship of vegetation and especially common in Dravidian regions, have been absorbed in part into Sivaite theology;[10] the very name of this goddess with her ambivalent maternal character can only have facilitated her identification with the Virgin Mary.

Finally, if almost all the chromos one sees in voodoo sanctuaries are pious images, particularly representations of saints, there are some that are completely profane from the point of view of the Catholic religion. Thus, visiting the *hounfor* of the *houngan*, or priest, Jo Pierre-Gilles (at Croix des Missions, not far from Mme Ildevert), I was able to see, in a *cay'* devoted to *loas* of the *pétro* series and—as far as I can remember—to the *Simbis*, deities of rain and fresh water,[11] two copies of the following chromo, among other chromos representing pious subjects: two nude bathers (or nymphs?) standing by the side of a stream in a green landscape.

This hasty investigation of the fifteen chromos bought in Port-au-Prince would tend to show, then, that it is often on the basis of a purely circumstantial detail, what one could almost call a pun using things rather than words (such as, for instance, the lowered visor of the helmet likened to the chin bandage of a dead person), that the correspondence between *loa* and saint is established; for such a connection to be made, there need not be any similarity in the content

[10]Louis Renou and Jean Filliozat, *L'Inde classique*, vol. 1 (Paris: Payot, 1947), p. 487. Because she was moved by the beauty of *gandharvas*, whose images she saw reflected in water, this goddess lost her ability to gather liquids, since they turned solid at the touch of her hands; condemned by her husband to be burned alive, she was saved by her son, her body remaining covered with scars, and she became the goddess of smallpox. The association between the element of water and the female principle is certainly a very general one; it is nonetheless interesting to point out this myth, which makes the Dravidian Mâriyammei (rediscovered in Guadeloupe) into a deity related to water like the Haitian Erzilie (endowed with the same ambivalent character and, furthermore, also transplanted, since the voodoo songs describe her as "Dahoman" or "Dahomey").

[11]The aquatic nature of these deities is most notably marked by the fact that their leader, *Papa Simbi*, is generally identified with Saint Christopher crossing a stream of water with the Infant Jesus on his shoulders. Of the same god it is said that he captures children who go to certain springs or streams to draw water or bathe (Marcelin, "Les Grands Dieux," pp. 131–135).

Art and Poetry in the Thought of Paul Eluard

Let language become concrete!
ELUARD, *The Physics of Poetry*

*E*luard the dadaist, Eluard the surrealist, Eluard the Resistance fighter, Eluard the Communist party member, and, if they don't want to leave anything out, Eluard the unanimist from the beginning: so many different figures that literary historians will perhaps take pleasure in discovering in Paul Eluard, sifting through his life and separating it into different periods, as though one could coldly carve up the unity of his destiny without running the risk, in breaking it up, of missing precisely what created that unity and must therefore correspond to the permanent and essential part of his life.

From a strictly formal point of view, of course, there is no denying that such divisions can be made in the work of Paul Eluard, as they can in the work of many artists and poets, but when, pursuing this at first purely superficial examination, one begins to concern oneself with deeper motivations instead of a mere surface blossoming, a certain continuity appears, so that one soon sees the image of a single Paul Eluard forming, a Paul Eluard who found his way—not without detours, conflicts, setbacks, and tribulations—"from one man's outlook to every man's outlook," a Paul Eluard who, on a strictly poetic level, gave sight priority over vision and situated above the eva-

Published in *Europe* 31, nos. 91–92 (1953) (special issue, "Paul Eluard").

siveness of lyricism the use of the word in all its force as a human instrument of exchange and connection.

Like Hugo, like Baudelaire, like other great pioneers of modern literature, Eluard left us, in the margins of his immediately creative work, a number of accounts that clarify the significance of that work and allow us to understand the goal he assigned poetry as well as art in general.

In July 1919, when he had just barely emerged from the war, Paul Eluard published the preface to his collection *Les Animaux et leurs hommes* in the fifth issue of *Littérature* (which was to become one of the principal dada magazines). In a few lines, he formulated the premises of a program that his later thinking, as well as the course of his life and the progress of events, would of course lead him to put into practice in accordance with an outlook that he would continuously broaden and reanimate, though nothing basic to the program was ever touched:

> The vanity that drives men to declare this or that beautiful or ugly and to take sides lies at the origin of the highly civilized error of several literary epochs, of their sentimental exaltation and the disorder that results from it.
>
> Let us try, though it is difficult, to remain absolutely pure. We will then see all that connects us.
>
> And let us transform the unpleasant language that is good enough for gossipers, a language as dead as the wreaths on our identical brows, let us reduce it, transform it into a language that is charming, true, one of common exchange among us.

Like all the promoters of the dada movement, Eluard first attacked aestheticism and its arbitrary judgments, a source of confusion and false sentimentality: beyond beauty and ugliness, there is room for some purity, and it is here that men may rediscover themselves; the language without virtue, the language of gossip, must be replaced by an authentic language, whose charm will foster a communion among speakers. The poems in the book thus prefaced are only examples of this distilled language, language reduced to the simplicity of counting-out rhymes or proverbs and brought to a maximum of transparency.

All questions of literary technique aside, language will remain one of the dominant themes in Eluard's thinking and—one could say—the very texture of his thinking. Speaking is an attribute of man, and the language he speaks gives the exact measure of his humanity. But, as Eluard was to write in a dada manifesto published by *Littérature* in 1920, "man respects language and worships thought; if he opens his mouth, one sees that his tongue is under glass and the naphthalene of his brain stinks up the air." To restore life to language and at the same time to attain a state less revolting than that of a mummified humanity, it is therefore indispensable to eliminate this religious attitude and go on, in some way, to emancipate the word; this was apparently the first goal Eluard assigned himself and the goal his poems strived for during the whole period in which he was to speak for the pure joy of speaking, "speak without having anything to say," speak in order to use that marvelous plaything, the specifically human faculty of speaking.

It remains true, nevertheless, that language for the sake of language, no matter how it may sparkle with poetry, and even if it is as unsophisticated in its syntax as in its vocabulary, proves to be as vain as art for art's sake. The word is a means of communication, its primary function is to express and to communicate, so that it necessarily refers to something other than itself. Certainly Lautréamont could legitimately declare that "nothing is incomprehensible," that is, there exists nothing in the world to which man is not capable of giving some signification, including his own prophecies and even the most apparently gratuitous of his verbal constructions; but the same Isidore Ducasse decrees in another connection: "Poetry must be made by everyone. Not by one person." A poetry that would be the achievement of everyone could not, by definition, be the speech of a single person discoursing only for himself, and true poetry—a poetry that, at the extreme, would be universally shared and become a collective activity—must therefore first bring into play what is common to all human beings. "To express everything is our moral law, to express everything is the very condition of life, of the hope we have in it," one will read in *Les Sentiers et les routes de la poésie*, a work that appeared in 1952—the very year of Paul Eluard's death—and that today stands out as a literary summation or testament, which the poet also intended for the largest possible audience, since it is a collection of radio broadcasts. "Yet I have never found what I write in what I love" was already the conclusion of a poem of 1921: the recognition (at least circumstantial) of a gap, a hiatus that kept love—or lived poetry—in the margin of the closed world of writing. And two years later, in the tenth issue of *Littérature* (which was soon to be succeeded by *La Révolution surréaliste*), one finds this footnote to the poem *Au Cœur de mon amour* expressing, in a provocatively humorous way, another aspect of this desire for a poetry without limits: "Every poem that does not bear my name is an imitation," as though the author wanted to say that the identity of the poet does not count, since poetry is unique in its diversity and the poet is never more than its spokesman. At the same time that all distance between love and poetry must be abolished, then, poetry must be made universal, and it is to the extent that it is integrated into life that it will become a place for exchange, meeting, where not only the lover and his love but all men and all women will be able to join together and recognize one another. At this time, like his companions—the future surrealists—Eluard still seems remote from any reflection on the practical problems posed by the fact that man exists in society; at least he already knows that art and poetry have no meaning except as ways to break the barriers standing between the self and the world and also between the self and others.

We know how much importance surrealism attached to dreams, inventions, and, more generally, all the products of the imagination that touched man's depths most closely. But we are less aware that for most of the writers and artists clustered about André Breton who participated in this movement, what was originally involved was much less a matter of escaping into a convenient nonreality than of conquering the imaginary and annexing it to life. Paul Eluard—whom Aragon, in *Une Vague de rêves*, dubbed "that outburst of the stars" and of whom Breton, in his introduction to *Capitale de la douleur*, declared that he had to give measureless praise to his "agonizing *motions of the heart*"—would be one of the most rigorous surrealists and one of those who most strongly stressed the concreteness of a goal from which his gaze would never be allowed to turn away. "The surrealist painters," he was to write in *L'Evidence poétique*, which appeared in 1936, "all joined in the same effort to free vision, to bring together imagination and nature, to consider everything possible as real, to show us that there is no dualism between the imagination and reality, that all that man's mind can conceive and create comes from the same vein, is of the same substance as his flesh, his blood, and the world around him." "Surrealism," he would declare in another passage of the same text, "works to show that thought is common to everyone; it works to reduce the differences that exist among men and, in doing this, refuses to serve an absurd order based on inequality, deceit, cowardice." Here the desire to arrive at the total man seems expressly joined to the desire for revolution: the total man is he for whom real and imaginary are one, he who has recognized that he belongs to nature and no longer perceives the products of nature and his own creations on different planes; he is also the man who recognizes other men as his fellows at the same time that he is recognized by them and, on an equal footing with each, is bound to them by a truly human relationship, something inconceivable as long as humanity remains divided into unequal classes.

If, in order to lead men to take total responsibility for themselves, it is important to teach them that thinking is a privilege they share and that this thinking is not, for all that, separate from the world but, on the contrary, an integral part of it and can act on it to make things real that originally existed only in spirit, art and poetry represent major elements in this revolution.

Where art was concerned, Eluard, like most of those involved in the surrealist movement, stressed the plastic arts, which he essentially saw as a language having the same goals as the language of poetry and constituting an instrument by means of which men could come to an understanding with the world (since, for an artist like Picasso, "there is only communication between what sees and what is seen, an effort at comprehension, at relation—sometimes at determination, at creation") and to an understanding among themselves based on this very understanding with the world. "Language is a social phenomenon," he wrote in the same text on Picasso, which was reprinted in *Donner à voir*, "but can we not hope that one day drawing, like language, like writing, will also become a social phenomenon and that along with them it will move from the social to the universal. All men will communicate through their vision of things, and this vision of things will serve them to express the point they have in common with one another, with things, with one another as things, with things as one another. When that day comes, true clairvoyance will have integrated the universe with man— which is to say, man with the universe." In this future, which it is our responsibility to build, everything will, consequently, depend on the view men take of the world, a view through which their humanity will assert itself to the extent that it expresses their association among themselves and which ("true clairvoyance" and not hallucination, since all agree about it) is not only the absorption of the universe by man—to whom the plastic arts henceforth propose, in the realm of the imaginary, a humanized world at the same time that they transform in a positive way the vision he has of the ordinary world—but also the fusion of man with the universe in which his reconciled gaze loses itself, he who is both a gaze unifying the universe and a fragment of that universe, if one accepts that (to quote Eluard's early observation in *Au-delà de la peinture*, a study of Max

Ernst) "a truly materialist interpretation of the world cannot exclude from this world the person formulating it."

As for poetry—that poetry which is not "poeticized language" but, as truthful poetry, "allows man to see in another way, other things," and is not unaware (as Eluard was to say in 1949 in the first of his radio broadcasts) "that there are deserts of sand and deserts of mud, waxed parquet floors, untidy heads of hair, rough hands, stinking victims, miserable heroes, superb idiots, all sorts of dogs, brooms, flowers in the grass, flowers on tombs"—its three functions are to form the "armature of language," to be "an object lesson," and to fight "to bring men together again."

Whether it is the achievement of someone quite ordinary—even a child or a mad person—or of experts ("impersonal" or "personal," "involuntary" or "intentional," to use Eluard's terms), poetry opposes "language as dead as the wreaths on our identical brows" with an effective language, one that is always renewed because it is essentially creation, and one can say that in this sense poetry gives life to language, preventing it from solidifying and restoring to everyday words, which it combines in ways that are always startling, the emotive power that has eroded from them under constant use.

From the point of view of knowledge, it is also an "object lesson," since it is what teaches others—with its collection of axioms and images condensing truths or establishing relations between different realities—what has been *seen* by the poet, who can be compared to a lookout man "keeping watch," Eluard says, "like anyone else, for the obscure news of the world and the unlikely problem of the grass, stones, filth, and splendors that lie beneath his feet." Because he is not a visionary seeing only for himself but one who discovers and reveals to others, one must say of the poet—to quote one of the key phrases in Eluard's entire poetics—that he is "one who inspires rather than one who is inspired." Seeing, showing, and showing himself—because for him everything is "an object of sensations and, consequently, of feelings," and because with him (endowed with sight by that very same poetic faculty that dedicates him to showing himself) "hope, hopelessness become concrete, along with sensations and feelings"—he needs partners who see what he has "given them to see" and who are his equals, themselves capable of showing what he has seen and equally capable of showing themselves in their turn by showing what they themselves have seen, without which poetry would remain the activity of a few visionaries instead of being a ground where truths are exchanged in total reciprocity, truths that would be mere illusions if they were not shared by everyone, each making his own contribution to this common good. Doubtless this is how one must understand these aphorisms—at first glance cryptic—from *Premières Vues anciennes*: "The poet *sees* to the same extent that he *shows himself*. And reciprocally. Some day every man will show what the poet has seen. End of the imaginary." And farther on: "Poetry will not become flesh and blood until the moment when it is reciprocal. This reciprocity is entirely a function of the equality of happiness among men. And equality in happiness would raise that happiness to heights of which we can as yet have only the feeblest of notions."

The moment there is no concrete, true poetry experienced and practiced by everyone, the poet will take it upon himself to work at the creation of this total poetry and engage in "a fight to bring men together," a fight to which he will commit himself fully (with his hope built on a foundation of the "somber truths that appear in the work of the true poets") and which will tend to become the armature of his poetry. This is why that same movement toward others that had gradually led Eluard to give more time to what was expressly love poetry than to the sort of poetry in which free invention was the chief characteristic (at least to all appearances) also led him to make his poetry a militant poetry in the most complete and highest sense of the word: a poetry not only of a militant politics, whose fighting arm it was, but of man fighting for man and for poetry itself, as sign and means of attaining an integral humanity. Here it is impossible to separate what was logically deduced from premises posited once and for all and what was experienced day by day, through the menacing convulsions of history and personal ordeals, those hard "object lessons" or crucial experiences which demonstrated to the poet that no one can break through his solitude by associating with a single being but that he must connect with everyone (or with one, in the fight for everyone). "I will love the person close to me, I will make myself loved, I will prolong my life. Thus do men and women know, in the same way, their strength and their weakness, they receive their light from these three mirrors: the mirror of procreation, the mirror of society, and the mirror of intellect. Production and reproduction, sympathy and fraternity, reflection and conjugation." In these few sentences from the radio broadcast of *Prestiges de l'amour*, Paul Eluard situated decisively what art and poetry represented for him: among the three ways of dominating their fate that present themselves at the same time to men and women, the first two ways implying going beyond the individual (whether he produces usefully and reproduces, or whether he unites with others in social action), "reflection and conjugation," which are characteristic of art as of poetry in that they reflect the world and bind men together, also appear as ways of abolishing the temporal boundaries that reduce to nothing each human being taken in his isolate state.

Having, like so many others, started off with poetry as a mirror for the whims of the heart and spirit, no doubt Eluard will have achieved his ultimate greatness by arriving—without the cunning of religion—at a prophetic poetry, in which is reflected a future that it not only points out to one and all but tends, at the same time, to transform into act, a poetry in which language, whether it articulates these future truths or formulates truths of experience, "is not mere stenosteno or something dogs don't have" but is always charged with efficiency and life.

A Marionette of Ubu

*B*ecause of a meeting on a Normandy beach some forty years ago between a professional in the Guignol puppet theater and a fan of that too-often disdained form of theater, the Musée des Arts et Traditions Populaires has recently acquired a historical item:[1] after passing into the possession of M. Gauthard, puppeteer of the Buttes-Chaumont, the hand puppet representing the central character of the scaled-down version of *Ubu roi* produced at the Quat'Z'Arts on November 10, 1901, by the "Théâtre Guignol des Gueules de Bois" (with the assistance of the Anatole marionette theater, which Emile Labelle directed on the Champs-Elysées), then published as *Ubu sur la Butte*, under the rubric *Théâtre mirlitonesque* (Paris: Sansot, 1906), was given by its owner—along with other plays and sets—to someone he had known at Houlgate, and today the widow of that person, Mme Méry-Picard, feels—quite correctly—that she should hand over to a national museum this material form of the figure about which Stéphane Mallarmé wrote, in a letter addressed to the author of *Ubu roi*, when most people were scandalized by the stage creation of it done by the Théâtre de l'Œuvre on December 10, 1896: "You have set on its feet, with a rare and durable clay in your fingers, an amazing character along with his people, and you have done it as a sober and sure dramatic sculptor. It enters the repertory of high taste and haunts me."

This review, requested by Georges-Henri Rivière, head curator of the Musée des Arts et Traditions Populaires, Paris, was first published in *Arts et traditions populaires* 1, no. 4 (October–December 1953): 337–338.
[1]Coll. ATP 53.21.1.

Presented recently at the Librairie Jean Loize, where it was one of the most important pieces in the very moving and erudite Alfred Jarry exhibition opened under the auspices of the Collège de 'Pataphysique, the marionette of Père Ubu given by Mme Méry-Picard to the Musée des Arts et Traditions Populaires must be distinguished from another three-dimensional effigy of the legendary character, older and known to have been reproduced (most notably) by M. Paul Chauveau in his *Alfred Jarry ou la naissance, la vie et la mort du Père Ubu* (Paris: Mercure de France, 1932) as an inset plate at page 100: a marionette that Jarry, helped by his sister Charlotte, made for the performances at the Théâtre des Pantins (January 1898, less than two years after the flesh-and-blood *Ubu roi*) and that is today owned by M. Sacha Guitry after having belonged for many years to the late Mme Rachilde.

Fifty-five centimeters high and with a breadth of forty centimeters when his arms are open in a cross, Père Ubu—as he was presented at the Guignol des Quat'Z'Arts—is topped with the pear-shaped head that is a consistent feature in the iconography of the character, whether in Jarry's wood engravings (such as the "Véritable portrait de M. Ubu" and the "Autre portrait de M. Ubu" published in 1896 in the *Livre d'Art*, then in the original edition of *Ubu roi*, or the "Grande Image de M. Ubu et des Quatre Hérauts Porte-Torche," which refers to the Heraldic Act of *César-Antéchrist*) or in the drawings done by Pierre Bonnard for the little *Almanach du Père Ubu* that appeared in 1899, all images reflecting aspects of a creature whose inventor expressly indicated that it was the public's "ignoble double, who had not yet been introduced to it" ("Questions de Théâtre," *La Revue blanche*, January 1, 1897), having one month earlier described it in the negative way appropriate for stressing its universality: "This is not exactly M. Thiers, nor the bourgeois, nor the boor: rather, it is the perfect anarchist, along with the quality that prevents us from becoming the perfect anarchist, which is that it is a man, whence cowardice, dirtiness, ugliness, etc. Of the three souls

Plato distinguishes—of the head, the heart, and the stomach—only the last, in him, is not embryonic" ("Paralipomènes d' Ubu," *La Revue blanche*, December 1, 1896).

Above a chin so diminished it almost merges with the cheeks rises a head with a pointed apex whose tiny, bright-pink bald patch is haloed by a yellow circle, hair of the same color as the eyebrows in little mounds overhanging the oblique ascending slits of the eyes (the two of them together describing a circumflex) and also the same color as the drooping moustache framing gluttonous lips of a pink similar to that which illuminates the long, pointed nose with its vast, magnificently proportioned wings. As such, the physiognomy of the character does not deviate—or scarcely—from the description provided in the "Paralipomènes": "If he resembles an animal, his face is most of all piglike, his nose similar to the upper jaw of a crocodile, and his whole caparison makes him in every way the brother of that most aesthetically horrible sea creature, the sea louse." As it happens, the body is not wrapped in a large coat stamped with a whorl on the stomach but clothed in a strict uniform: a black tunic closed at the neck, with broad gold braid edging the collar, which is doubled on the inside by a white collar that protrudes as a border, the edges of the sleeves, pocket flaps, and closing edge of the tunic also being lined with braid, while a simple blue unornamented sheath forms the pants.

Thus treated, militarily outfitted and (apparently) on the point of shouting "Pschitt!," Père Ubu appears to resemble quite closely—except for his clothes—the civilian who was his model, the teacher at the lycée in Rennes whose portrait Alfred Jarry painted when he was an adolescent ("Monsieur Hébert, Prophaiseur de Pfuisic," a painting appended to a copy of *Ubu roi* that once belonged to Laurent Tailhade and was exhibited by Jean Loize as number 217 in the catalogue). Like the one made for the Théâtre des Pantins, this marionette is purely for the puppet theater and for this reason turns out to be a little different from the emblematic Père Ubus, certain features of which were apparently inspired in Jarry by an image from the *Songes drolatiques de Pantagruel* (a series of 120 anonymous engravings published by Richard Breton, Paris, 1565) and whose visible form seems to us already fixed for eternity the moment the caricature originally drawn by a group of schoolboys is promoted to the rank of *Ubu roi* and the mocked teacher to that of a mythological figure.

Thanks to the Guignol, Père Ubu, the product of a piece of tomfoolery on the part of some schoolboys, will retain all the freshness of a popular puppet at the same time that the genius of Alfred Jarry has nailed it—not so much a star as a starfish—to the firmament of symbolist literature.

Picasso and the Human Comedy,
or the Avatars of Big Foot

I Pagliacci—literally "the buffoons" or more commonly in French, *Paillasse* [Buffoon]—opens with a prologue that I will summarize here from a program from the Rome Opera, which I kept from an evening in 1949 when I saw a performance of Ruggiero Leoncavallo's famous work at the Baths of Caracalla, a vast open-air place where the Roman opera performs during the summer season: "In keeping with the custom of Italian pantomime, before the curtain goes up, one of the characters from the drama appears before the public. His task is to call the audience's attention to the events that are going to unfold on stage; he is most anxious to make them aware that under the actors' makeup and costumes, hearts are beating, hatred causes rage, love sings powerfully. He asks the spectators that they not be fooled by the costumes the actors are wearing onstage, but that they see, beneath the fiction, the reality of life such as it is taught us by the drama that is going to be played." The artist whose function it is to induce the spectator to make the leap over the footlights that show him the actors under a false light while the latter, dazzled, have before them no more than an indistinct void, the artist who appears before the public after having for a moment parted the slit in the middle of the proscenium arch to make his way through, is none other than the baritone playing the role of Tonio, the cripple, the one who in the play will reveal to the buffoon Canio that his wife

First published in *Verve* 8, nos. 29–30 (1954), on a series of 180 drawings by Picasso, November 28, 1953, to February 3, 1954.

is betraying him and who because of this will determine the course of the drama; in any case, he appears with no apparent makeup and, like someone torn unexpectedly from the mystery of the wings, wrapped from head to toe in an ample hooded cloak.

Reality or fiction? This is the crucial question posed by theater, and this is the problem of art in general: To what extent is what we are shown pure artifice, entertainment that is more or less refined but in any case classifiable as an after-dinner pastime? To what extent does it implicate something that assumes a vital importance for us, comparable to the importance of the tragedy Hamlet brings about when he finds it necessary to evoke what lies heaviest on both his own heart and the heart of King Claudius, the crime in which the latter was the all-too-willing protagonist and of which the former received, like a terrible inheritance, the task of making himself the avenger? Reality or fiction: there is no true art—and such is the art of our great Pablo Picasso—in which fiction is not at every moment covering over a reality as authentically felt as it is for Hamlet, as he causes a plot to be played out that is at once appalling for the murderer who recognizes himself in it and stimulating for Hamlet because it temporarily frees him from his obsession, or for Canio, when, surreptitiously, he transforms the pantomime into the setting for an interrogation and then a punishment of the guilty party, with actual blood in the end oozing through the floorboards and his own heart torn beneath the tawdry clown suit. It is on the level—reached by far too few—where the extreme of *verism* merges with the extreme of fantasy that one must situate the series of drawings and lithographs, most in black but some in colored pencil, that, toward the end of 1953 and the beginning of 1954, constituted for Picasso the journal, not verbal but visual, of a very bad "season in hell," a crisis in his private life leading him to the most general sort of questioning. On the occasion of a personal event involving the feelings, *everything* will be called into question again for anyone who has any awareness whatsoever; if—as is the case for the man of the blue period, of the mountebanks, of cubism, and now of the dove, after so many other periods—the person involved belongs to the species known as "geniuses," the low-level intrigue (melodrama- and vaudeville-style) is transcended, and the anecdote becomes myth.

A buffoon who no longer believes innocently in his own high spirits and no longer makes people laugh, an old lover who no longer seduces: this is how Chaplin appeared recently in his confessional film *Limelight*, and it could seem that with this theme of the twofold decadence of the comedian and the Don Juan—a coupling of two clichés worn threadbare but renewed by what irresistible and bewildering subterfuge—the bottom of the bog was reached: isn't it literally the end of everything when art as well as love slips away, prey as they are to the malignity of time, which deprives us little by little of our various capacities to seduce and soon nullifies what might have been special about us? Yet there is a fact even less acceptable, which is that the creator—however invulnerable he may be in the domain of art and capable of meeting the attack of the years in the manner of a torero, for whom each charge of his adversary is another opportunity to shine—the creator with his inexhaustible resources is no more than a man, despite everything, and just like the poorest of second-rate comics he is, despite his magic, which has been more invigorated than eroded by his heavy accumulation of experiences, a creature subject to aging and death. A stroke of genius will never abolish lost time, one could say, parodying Marcel Proust as well as Stéphane Mallarmé and disputing the validity of their faith in art as a means of finding oneself again and neutralizing death, despite time, whose torrential flight so stuns and disorients. Toward the end of *A la recherche du temps perdu*, Proust invites the reader to a sort of Last Judgment in the form of a fashionable evening party at which the narrator rediscovers the people he knows, who have been lost from sight for a number of years: each one, having aged, looks as though he had "put on a face," and for a moment the memorialist thinks he is attending a masked ball. In many of the drawings and lithographs composing the ball to which Picasso invites us, old themes and characters—taken up again ironically—are exhibited in their frivolous or miserable truth, having succumbed to age; but for Picasso, who is not an idealist, there is no formula that allows one access to the illusion of eternity that is "time regained": far from helping him by stopping him short in his fall as age inexorably drags him down, his grasping these old themes or characters carried along by a current that they are not allowed to fight seems to tell us that all one can do is testify to the violence of this current.

In the fifth act of *Le Désir attrapé par la queue*, which Picasso wrote in 1943, the main character says, "Already the Demoiselles d'Avignon have an income of thirty-three long years," this character being the grotesque Big Foot who, in scene 2 of act 3, cries out as he welcomes his lover the Tart: "This is the sort of luck I had this morning, at biscuit time with figs, half fig, half grape, and so fresh. One more day and its black glory."* The fact that the *Demoiselles d'Avignon* (a picture Picasso originally thought of calling *Bordel en Avignon* because that was actually its subject) still dazzle us with their youth and freshness, the fact that the renown of their portraitist, today as much showered with praise as he was once disparaged, now reaches even the working-class milieus of the most distant countries, changes nothing, and—for this man, so much alive, whom no force in the world would be able to put to sleep and whose keen humor allows him to walk with a brisk step under the weight of his startling celebrity—the triumph experienced by him and immediately acknowledged by almost all the others will never be more than a black sun. "My chilblains! My chilblains! My chilblains!" moan the feet of the protagonists of *Désir* just after their owners have de-

*[The translation quoted here and below is that of Sir Roland Penrose, *Desire Caught by the Tail* (London: Calder & Boyars, 1970). Leiris misdates the play; it was written in 1941 (and was first performed in Leiris's home, in 1944, with Camus directing, Leiris reading the part of Big Foot, and Sartre that of Round Piece. The line from act 3, scene 2, is addressed to Round Piece, not to the Tart.]

posited them for the night at the doors of their respective rooms in the hallway of "Sordid's Hotel."

With its range of elements in tiers from the most wretched (guts tumbling down, blood spreading, urine, dung, sweating men spitting water after rinsing their mouths) to the most delicately nuanced (the brushing or wrapping of the fragile biped by the weighty mass of his four-footed enemy, the sparkling of a rapier turning to fire or ice, the floral unfolding of capes with soft folds or of cloth the color of blood, cloth supported, as by a rod, by the muleta's stick), through the ambiguous stage of sordid luxury (the paper twists of the banderilla, the rich stamped leather cases in which the rapiers sleep, the tired, fat baggage hollowed with long gashes sewn back up by the zip fastener, the ancient Hispano-Suiza into which the maestro and his whole cuadrilla pile themselves), isn't the very image of Picasso's work given us by the bullfight, in itself and along with its trappings? An image that is a particularly good likeness in the case of the collection of graphics of the winter 1953–1954, since in it is manifested in the clearest fashion (it seems) the constant osmosis of opposites—so striking in Spain—that marks Picasso's art as it does the spectacle of the bullfight, both of them oscillating between the rawest realism and terrifying escapes that go beyond the limit.

A faena based on natural passes—and true "naturals," those that are executed with the muleta held in the left hand (the simplest and at the same time most dangerous pass, because during it the whole of the man is fully exposed)—thus this group of scenes drawn by Picasso appears as described in the language of tauromachy, scenes in which art envisaged as a whole, with its many aspects (painting, literature, circus, dance, etc.), and love in all its forms constitute the almost exclusive subjects and which, having come into being "from the tip of the pen," so to speak, seem to represent moments of total abandon: no plastic problem to resolve, only put down on paper what is in one's heart or what comes to mind, without any aesthetic censorship or repugnance for the cliché; "When you are very old, in the evening, by candlelight . . ." and the snows of yesteryear will alternate with "Laugh, clown, laugh!"

Whatever themes Picasso has handled in the course of his various periods, they have almost always been closely associated with his life: elements of his daily setting, human beings he had been attached to sensually or sentimentally, pitiful or picturesque characters from his early years, epic compositions ushered in by Guernica, figures from classical myths or strictly personal legends, all of these subjects—either drawn from life as he lived it concretely or derived from a more or less imaginary existence—have a specific relationship to the body or heart of the artist and can be exactly situated in his life story, his intimacy with the things he painted being so great that it is as though there were a correlation between their lives as they moved ahead and his, and as though, far from remaining fixed, as pieces of groundwork no longer to be touched, they continued to accompany him, jostling one another, mingling, and tolerating numerous avatars.

The Pegasus carrying a winged female dancer on the curtain of *Parade* will one day merge with its sinister companion, the picador's horse; in act 4, last scene, of the play *Les Quatre petites filles*, it will be seen spilling its guts and carrying on its head the owl whose prototype was a household pet and who was so often represented in painting, in sculpture, and especially in ceramics: "An enormous white winged horse enters dragging its bowels, surrounded by wings—an owl is perched on its head—stops for a moment in front of the little girl and disappears off the other side of the stage"; later, in *La Guerre et la Paix*, this same Pegasus who was first a circus horse will plow a field, led by a child. Resting or flying, solitary or combined with a woman's face, the dove of Peace also has its history: it was originally inspired by the fully living pigeons Picasso had for a long time in his studio on the rue des Grands-Augustins and whose precursors were perhaps the pigeons that the painter Ruiz Blasco, the artist's father, had adopted for his favorite theme, leaving it to his son Pablo to paint in the feet when he was old enough to take part in the work that was the family's means of subsistence; in one of the recent drawings, the dove has alighted upon the hand of a seated naked woman who is holding it out to a clown standing with an olive branch or some other leafy stem in his hand. Not very different from their homologues, the bearded athletes (close to the world of animals and plants because of the mossy hair on their faces and entering these nonhuman realms along with the minotaurs, centaurs, or pans), the bestialized men or humanized animals that are the minotaurs run here and there, banquet, abandon themselves to debauchery, and are sometimes put to death in an arena or, now blind, walk with their heads raised to the stars, leaning on a stick, accompanied by Antigone as a little girl; the one in the *Minotauromachie* plunges forward, his arm stretched out before him as though to ward off everything that could oppose him or as though to unveil a terrible mystery, the other protagonists of the half-dark, half-light tragedy being a little girl with a lighted candle and a bunch of flowers, in a short dress and a broad beret, facing the monster, a woman with a rapier, in a torero's costume that reveals her bare chest, a fallen horse on which this woman has collapsed, her eyes closed and her head bowed, an almost completely nude man climbing a ladder and turning to look behind him, then two women watching from the bay of a window on whose sill two pigeons sit; in *La Fin d'un monstre* (a drawing from 1937) a nude woman holding a lance offers a mirror to a minotaur pierced by an arrow; finally, in the series from a few months ago, the minotaur will no longer be more than the bearded athlete holding up as high as his face or chest a bull's head of the sort Spanish children use in their imitations of the corrida: in the full light of midday or in the shadowless light of a brothel scene, he has lowered the mask.

Of the characters from classical mythology, it seems that Picasso has concentrated especially on those that seem to incarnate, permanently, a metamorphosis: the Minotaur, the centaurs, the fauns.

Just he himself undergoes constant metamorphosis (since he never petrifies in one style), he likes to metamorphose what falls within his reach or into his field of vision, unless he becomes, expressly, the painter of a metamorphosis. Does a hag whose skull, face, and jaws are made of two little toy automobiles glued wheel to wheel differ essentially from a minotaur, the body of a man whose head is explicitly the head of a bull? Is making something else out of a picture by Manet, El Greco, Cranach, Courbet, or Poussin really a different procedure from the constant invention of new signs for the figuration of the same objects, and isn't it the case that to use the work of an earlier painter for one's own purposes is to treat it as something integrated into life, something one can't allow simply to lie there, that one must in some sense help to accomplish its natural evolution? Nothing (one is forced to believe) could remain inert once it came under Picasso's eye or into his hands. Whether he transforms them for the moment or becomes the witness of the adventures and changes experienced by his characters, he shows the same inability to accept the idea that any creature or object whatsoever should simply be there, as it is, forever, the same inability to leave anything *in repose*.

In the drawings and lithographs in which Picasso seems to have become the historiographer of his own themes—which are the expression of his life and for which time flows as it flows for him—one is struck by the abundance of masked characters in whom the governing idea of metamorphosis reappears, but in a ridiculous form: Can a disguise that allows itself to be recognized as such be anything but the caricature of a miracle, an abortive attempt to make oneself other than what one really is? When one catches someone in the act, isn't he anything but a tragic character, isn't he—by definition—an imposter or a buffoon who belongs to comedy? Already in the ballet *Parade*, Pegasus on the curtain was followed, on the stage—as though to provide a clownish replica of the mythical quadruped—by a grotesque horse whose four legs were the four joined legs of two dancers, and in the series of plates from the past few years representing scenes of knighthood, several of the lords are mounted only on simulacra of caparisoned horses, actually pages in disguise.

It would seem that Picasso has always been aware that a myth is destined to turn into an old wives' tale sooner or later, that there is hardly a ceremony that is not also a carnival and that the marvelous necessarily goes hand in hand with charlatanism. The white and black sides of metamorphosis, expressed by the mountebank who, with his costume and his tricks, touches on the supernatural but at the same time represents only a masquerade.

During the nineteenth century—a period that begins, with all due respect to the chronologists, with the French Revolution in 1789 and ends with the Russian October Revolution—alongside the myth of the artist as demiurge (built upon religion's rubble and first assailed by Rimbaud, who fell silent after pointing out all its vanity) there was the myth of the artist scorned: Baudelaire's old tumbler (*Le Vieux Saltimbanque*), Nerval's "famous Brisacier," the actor hissed off the stage, then the chastised clown from Mallarmé's sonnet (*Le Pitre châtié*) and later, in Raymond Roussel, the under-study, hero of the novel *La Doublure* (written at a time when the author, a visionary, thought himself a demiurge), and finally, in the last film of Chaplin, our contemporary, the-man-who-no-longer-makes-people-laugh and before whom the hall empties. From the point of view of romanticism and its modern extensions, the artist is always out of the ordinary, because of either his excessiveness or his deficiency: conquering or tortured god, prophet who reveals or madman whom one ridicules, "his giant's wings prevent him from walking"; alone in the world and opposing the world, this exceptional being has, like a courtesan, his splendors and his miseries. In his early years, Picasso painted beggars, invalids, ill people, prostitutes, or certain of his companions (such as Jaime Sabartés) captured in their solitude, characters whose common trait was to be outcast, members of the marginal society that included the artist and whose most perfect image was that of the mountebanks, shady creatures who are at once organizers of fairy shows and starving vagabonds. It was in reference to conversations the two of them had toward the beginning of the blue period (whose color is the color of melancholy) that Sabartés wrote, in *Picasso: portraits et souvenirs*: "He believes that Art is the son of Sadness and Pain (and we agree). He believes that sadness favors meditation and that pain is the very basis of life."

A bitter argument against life as society has shaped it for us, a challenging of reality as a whole, romanticism oscillates between lyricism and irony: when the poet stops transfiguring, it is in order to demystify by embarking upon a sharp criticism. He who uses irony as a mask and as a weapon is in a good position to know that under the laughter there are often tears and that if the truth is only theater, beneath the theater there is a truth: sons or nephews of the disquieting punchinellos one already finds in the younger Tiepolo, in *L'Homme qui rit*, and in the tragic clown (Triboulet, whom Shakespeare prefigures with Yorick's skull and out of whom Verdi will create *Rigoletto*) join the unfortunate tart (Fantine, *La Dame aux camélias*, who in Italy will be the "fallen woman," or *La Traviata*) to illustrate the fact that we cannot rely on appearances; with *Pagliacci*, in which the two themes culminate—to cry under the mask of laughter, to be true under the false pretense—we have perhaps reached the archetype of melodrama.

To look at the undersides of the cards and find out what is happening off stage. Behind an appearance of play there is something serious, behind the seriousness there is something comical: the clowning of the creature who is assuming grave airs, the misery of the one whose job is to amuse. However this may be, there is a source of entertainment to be found in dismantling the mechanism of it all. In his recent drawings Picasso shows us, on the one hand, the great artist as a ridiculous man and, on the other, the clown as a touching figure, as if they were counterparts and he was fully aware of being a little of one and a little of the other, despite the transcendence of his genius. Everything, romantically, is based on the exchanges that take place between appearance and truth, so that many people have given in to the temptation to find a justification for appearance in this game. But Picasso conducts his spiritual pursuit with too much wisdom to become a more or less willing dupe; he does not flee into a dream nor reject what is too human: beyond appearances, which are constantly challenged, worn down, and transformed, reality never ceases to be there ("I am here, I am always here," Rimbaud said).

Picasso, who has gone all the way around it, knows very well the limits of art, he who was a child prodigy and who, possessing the technique of a great master at the age of fifteen, did not stop inventing new processes, perhaps because for a virtuoso like him it was the only way to continue along his road without becoming bored. Yet what Picasso has done is to go beyond art rather than to negate it: there is no greater enemy of "art for art's sake" than he, but at the same time no life has been more completely devoted to art than his, for what he stresses in art—the product of the imagination—is that it is a specifically human activity. The exact part that is most suitably assigned to art—that of a passion to which one dedicates oneself without acquiring delusions of grandeur—and the absence of any illusions about the vocation of the artist are perhaps expressed in Picasso by the frequency with which he has dealt and still deals with the theme of the painter and his model.

In the illustrations for Balzac's *Unknown Masterpiece*, the painter and model theme refers to the properly pictorial activity: the confrontation between the craftsman and the model that is the motif of the work and sums up the living world. Painter and model, man and woman: on the level of art as on that of love, it is always a matter of the duel between subject and object, eternally standing one before the other and separated by a gap that no one, whatever his genius, will ever be able to bridge. One of the illustrations shows, as an equivalent of the studio colloquies, the bull rushing at the horse, the very image of a merciless fight.

Timeless and almost mythological in *The Unknown Masterpiece*, painter and model are duly particularized in the drawings of these last few months, which sometimes verge on caricatures or portraits: models not necessarily very beautiful, sometimes destroyed by age or wearing objects of everyday usefulness such as wristwatches, ankle socks, or shoes; painters of all stamps (young and old, nearsighted and sharp-eyed, driven and easygoing); most often an old or ugly man confronting a wonderfully beautiful young woman, such as the Tart in "Big Foot's artistic studio." Explicitly, the painter and his model are only one particular instance of the confrontation between man and woman, a confrontation that is itself contained within the confrontation between the conscious being and the *Other* facing him. In a number of drawings, therefore, the painter is replaced by the most diverse sorts of characters: the freak paying court, the masked cupid, the sad clown (escapee from the period of the mountebanks), the monkey (that also comes from the earlier period), the old man who has something of the buffoon about him as well as of the Chinese wrestler and whose sardonic laugh announces that he knows a great deal, the carnival king on horseback or on foot, etc. . . . a variable number of acolytes joining each of the two parties (a group of watchers facing a group of people watched, who either present themselves as a spectacle or offer themselves to be chosen for an act of venal love), even a third party, who ultimately is none other than the painter himself represented in the picture as though, at the end of this game of masks and substitutions in which that other species of disguised creatures, animals on their hind legs, sometimes intrudes, the artist had gotten caught in his own trap and lived on, he whose role was to represent the others, only as a representation, a witness unconnected to the action, a voyeur, a shadow, a silhouette, a Don Juan whose punishment, after the conquest of the thousand and three, would be to metamorphose into a motionless statue of the Commandant.

On one of the pages of the amazing series, a bearded painter standing and striking an attitude considers with satisfaction (like a matador after the decisive thrust) the picture he has painted of a nude woman in the pose of a bacchante who has fallen down. A burlesque sort of triumph, as burlesque as the studio scenes with figures admiring the picture: mystification by way of the work of art, which all (fans, critics, and colleagues of both sexes) examine with interest without paying any attention to the fleshly charms of the sleeping model and also without understanding much about what they are looking at, so that in the whole business there is no one who is not mystified, unless it be the one who is sleeping.

In this immense masquerade, reminiscent of the English Christmas pantomime as well as of the commedia dell'arte and the Dance of Death, the stupefying skill of the artist seems itself to be an irony: never has so much artistic genius been more gaily deployed to make fun of art, and never has anyone demonstrated in so peremptory a way that, finally, nothing essential has changed—put into check by physical decline, before the checkmate of absolute separation—for this man who does everything he wants to with his brain and his ten fingers. Behind all the spectacles, each one more dazzling, that this artist who so lives up to the name dispenses like a "producer," and despite the renown that can result from it, nothing has changed for him and he remains just as defenseless as most mortals: a clown who puts on his eyebrows looking into a little mirror, in front of his nursing wife or a dangerous beauty drawing on her stockings. No man—however clever he may be—escapes the human condition, and neither art nor love can eliminate the passing of time, which, as we leave our chaotic youth, leads us through a game of blindman's bluff in which the winners (the "jackpotters," as they are known in Big Foot's house) are also losers.

The Minotaur, Dionysiac even as he is put to death, and the bacchic faun are replaced along the way by a mask of pure comedy or banal nightmare; the masked man—artificial or spectral man— supplants the animal man, from genesis one passes on to the harlequinade, the hybrid of legendary times gives way to the transvestite; the golden age, which could be represented by love when sensuality was still a fairy play, is succeeded by the age of tin, when, for the man who has become more and more perceptive, the colloquy of lovers hesitates between a dialogue of deaf people and the sort of sophisticated game perverts might enjoy ("To love intelligent women is a pederast's pleasure," as already Baudelaire wrote, in his *Fusées*, Baudelaire who elsewhere saw art as proof of man's taste, which he believed contemptible, for prostitution).

"Who am I? A man without a name," Don Juan says to Doña Isabella at the beginning of *El Burlador de Sevilla* by Tirso de Molina.[1] "By the window at the end of the room, bursting it open suddenly," we read at the conclusion of *Le Désir attrapé par la queue*, "enters a golden ball the size of a man which lights up the whole room and blinds the characters, who take handkerchiefs from their pockets and blindfold themselves and, stretching up their right arms, point to each other, shouting all together and many times, You! You! You! On the golden ball appear the letters of the word: 'Nobody.' "

We illuminate, we point to ourselves and we point to another person because in finding him we would like to find ourselves, but we blind the other and we are blinded ourselves. Between the anonymity of indiscriminate desire and the whole comedy of watchers watched, blind people who are (or who are not) seen and who cause others (or do not cause others) to see, there is only time, which inexorably polishes us down, and if one seeks to grasp SOMEBODY, one will only encounter NOBODY.

---

[1] It was at a lecture on Don Juan given by José Bergamin on February 5, 1951, at the Sorbonne, that my attention was drawn to the reply of the trickster of Seville in which the hero presents himself in the negative guise of the "nameless man."

Nobody, not even oneself: the emptiness is so complete that there can no longer be a question even of solitude; nothing survives except, as long as we remain alive, the human tension we share with everyone and that joins us to everyone. Could it be that this "nobody" and this "everybody" represent the two poles, complementary rather than opposed, between which, against a rhythm of *dramma giocoso* that excludes all idea of hope or hopelessness, the life of Picasso is played out, Picasso who shares with the great public puppet Charlie Chaplin, as we cannot forget, the privilege of being the most glorious artist of our time, as we also cannot forget that both of them—almost simultaneously presenting themselves onstage with barely any makeup on, with almost brutal awkwardness—are contemporaries of a worldwide social revolution?

of the symbol: a superficial, fragmentary, and, in short, fortuitous analogy seems to be enough in many cases. Apparently the use of a certain chromo to depict a certain *loa* is, at least in large part, a matter of convenience, and the flexibility of certain identifications is illustrated rather clearly by a fact reported by Milo Marcelin:[12] the sea god Agwé, symbolized by a boat or a fish and because of this identified with Saint Ulrich (shown in chromos with a fish in his hand), was identified during the last war with Saint Ambrose, because pictures of Saint Ulrich had become very difficult to find; thus dealers in chromos sold, as representations of Agwé, pictures of Saint Ambrose that had been corrected by adding a fish to them, held in the saint's hand.

The plurality of attributes and names for a single deity or a single saint (giving rise to a very extensive and complex interplay of elements among which identifications can be made), the extreme elasticity of the possibilities for comparison (which can be made, as in the case just cited, even beyond any commonality of attributes), the variability of the representations associated with a single deity, and the variability of the interpretation of forms make one think that one must expect virtually anything when historical conjunctions and social conditions favor a syncretic process. A systematic study of the way in which images of the Catholic saints are used in the various social groups to represent non-Catholic deities would certainly provide interesting insights into the often deflected mechanisms whereby systems of correspondence are established between one religion and another.

[12] *Mythologie*, p. 103.

This Void: Jean Aubier

*B*AGATELLES: as soon as they are excused from serving the learned speechifiers, this is what constructions and words become. Thus unbound, how they knot up again! And how they mingle as they like, as forms and colors may, too, tangles of vines under our lowered eyelids.

In Venice, where the *Fenice** flowers anew every year, was it a bagatelle—the conversation of the three, writer, painter, publisher, who decided to join forces for the bouquet of this book? Yes, if friendship is only an aroma that uplifts us. No, if without such an aroma living is only vegetating.

Bagatelle or not, this life has come to an end for one of the three. In 1952, before the dead waters of Venice, neither the writer nor the painter (any more than the third) had a sharp enough eye to see that in 1956 their games with words and colors would unfold before this void, Jean Aubier, like useless VEGETAL offerings.

Untitled insert for *Bagatelles végétales*, illustrated by Joan Miró (Paris: Jean Aubier, 1956).
*["Phoenix" in Italian, and the name of a theater.]

Through Tristes Tropiques

Tristes Tropiques. This title, which may at first seem like a
wink at lovers of exoticism, in fact corresponds without a shadow of
deception to the object it designates: a book that not only disputes
the validity of the fairy tale of the easy life in the tropics but harbors
numerous literary genres coexisting like different species of trees in
the luxuriance of a warm forest, for in this essay, which is also a memoir and a travel account, we find, next to bits of autobiography and
pages of ethnology or speculations enriched by picturesque notations, formal portraits or descriptions, several short poems in epi-
grammatic style (presented, it is true, as though in quotes), and even
some element of tragedy; it is a book, too, whose dominant tone,
within the proliferation of ideas, is melancholy, even though a sharp
humor (like a thorny bush) and a bucolic freshness constantly enter
in. There is nothing paradoxical in the fact that one of the most important passages in this work, which is essentially based on the experience of an observer taking care to be rigorously objective, is a
hymn to Jean-Jacques Rousseau: like the man whom Emile Durk-
heim already treated as a precursor of sociology, the author of *Tristes
Tropiques* is not content with a humanism of pure reason but seeks to
arrive at a complete view of man encompassing his twofold existence
as a product of culture and a fragment of nature; from the beginning, his perspective is an all-embracing one, and his account, far
from being simply the secretion of a mind that is expert in the historical and social sciences, will prove to be one of the most signifi-

This review of *Tristes Tropiques*, by Claude Lévi-Strauss (Paris: Librairie Plon, 1955)
was first published in *Les Cahiers de la République* 1, no. 2 (1956).

cant of the new romanticism that our twentieth century has seen develop under the aegis of specialists with vast ambitions—such as Marx and Freud—and that one can describe as *superrationalist*, in the sense that it attempts to integrate the tangible and the rational. In this free and passionate piece of research, it is quite natural that the tale, either epic or lyric, and the anecdote, even the pun, should take their places next to the piece of documentary investigation recorded on the spot as well as the logically argued inference, for in order to understand man one must make use of everything one has, as the free and passionate Rousseau was one of the first to show.

A piece of writing apparently done by fits and starts and without regard for spatial or temporal unities (since the author transports us as though on a flying carpet from sea to savannah, from savannah to forest, from forest to city, and vice versa, moving from one type of tropical misery, illustrated by the almost unpopulated Amazonia, to a second, represented by the overpopulated southern Asia, juxtaposing several trips he made and going back from the very recent period in which the New World was a refuge for those forced to emigrate by the spread of Nazism to the period when this continent, then almost mythical, seemed an Eden in the eyes of the Europeans who discovered it and who were to plunder its marvelous civilizations to such an extent), the book is, in truth, carefully structured. When Claude Lévi-Strauss declares that in ethnography, a science whose object is to know human cultures in their diversity in all places if not in all times, he has found a kind of "history which joins that of the world and my own at its two ends," he is indicating, in these few words, the entire framework of his book. Almost at its very outset, we in fact encounter that "intense curiosity" that the young Lévi-Strauss had concerning geology, the science of the earth as such and a discipline that sometimes yields the profound joy of witnessing a sort of fusion of time and space, when, for instance, one can see with a single glance fossils from two different ages separated by countless years showing on either side of the seam of two layers of earth and attesting to the enormous chronological gap between them. At the end of the more mature philosopher's meditation, as though it were necessary that something beyond humanism counterbalance what in some sense came before humanism, we detach ourselves from the human plane to touch on astrophysics and biology, when the author—in a vertiginous leap—envisages the evolution of cultures toward uniformity as a simple moment and a particular instance of the movement of the universe in the direction of a final inertia and then considers his own person not as an *I* but as a temporary aggregate of living cells that is itself only an element of the almost-as-precarious *we* formed by the humanity with which this pseudo-I is integrated. In the meantime, as though at the pivotal point of the infinite spaces in which man loses himself, there is Claude Lévi-Strauss with a philosophy degree in his past, his vocation as an ethnologist, the groups he studies as he travels the area that for the geographer is defined by the tropics, the singular characters he has contact with in Paris or elsewhere, and the human problems he tries, with all his intelligence and all the force of his character, to elucidate.

From the opening (where the great theme of geology bursts upon us suddenly like a warning), an almost continuous movement to broaden the field and elevate the debate leads us from what the author tells about his personal training, a chapter from a story that is properly his own while illuminating that of his generation, to a point where, after examining the value of Buddhism (the most ancient attempt at a total understanding but also the highest, since here knowledge reaches the limit where it is identified with lack of knowledge) and after contrasting it with the other great systems of Christianity, Islam, and Marxism (whose legitimacy at a certain level is not criticized, despite the pessimism of the general tone of this overview), he leaves the territory of history as such to emerge into the history of the world. Having reached the end of a tour of humanity that certainly will not have made him come out of himself but will have led him from a purely accidental "himself," if one may call it that, to a "himself" that is able to embrace the universal, he concludes by positing as a supreme quality in man, whatever society he belongs to, his capacity to "detach himself" temporarily from the harsh constraints of history through the contemplative grasp of the bond uniting our species, engaged as it is in almost constant "beehive labor," with other elements of nature. In the midst of this long and complicated journey, one experience seems to have been crucial for the traveler-philosopher: the relations he formed professionally with several Indian tribes in Brazil, societies in which material conditions are most rudimentary but in which one is wholly a man, for there one is not smothered in numbers nor alienated by the exigencies of a mechanical civilization, and there each person's milieu is proportionate to him.

Of the four societies described in the main part of the book, which is the properly ethnographic part of it, the first two offer Claude Lévi-Strauss the opportunity for two brilliant demonstrations, carried out as though at a blackboard. An examination of the face and body painting among the Caduveo that the women traditionally perform and a comparison of the structure of this tribe with that of neighboring tribes show how a social problem can be resolved on the (almost oneiric) level of art by those involved, for one must finally "interpret the graphic art of the Caduveo women, explain its mysterious charm and its complication, at first sight gratuitous, as the phantasm of a society that is seeking, with unquenched passion, the means to express symbolically the institutions it might have, if its interests and superstitions did not stand in the way." An analysis in keeping with the general education which, the author tells us near the beginning of the book, he derived from geology, Marxism, and psychoanalysis, namely that "understanding consists in reducing one type of reality to another; that true reality is never the most obvious and that the nature of what is true is already visible in the care it takes to hide itself." In the same way, a study of the distribution of huts in the Bororo villages (a sort of topographical projection of the social structure) and another of the funerary cult lead to this other truth, which is essentially one involving the dissipation of a phantasm or the lifting of a mask: "The representation a society forms for itself of relations between the living and the dead amounts to an effort to hide, embellish, or justify, on the level of religious thought, the actual relations that prevail among the living." It would not seem a violation of Claude Lévi-Strauss's thought to propose that if there exists, at some extreme, a naked truth, it is only the truth of the void; for if disguise is inherent in all truth, knowledge, dedicated as it is to passing through an infinite series of demystifications, cannot logically come out at any other truth than that of the lack of knowledge. "Every effort to understand," he writes in the very last pages of the book, "destroys the object we had attached ourselves to; it calls for a new effort, which abolishes it for the sake of a third, and so on until we reach the only enduring presence, which is that in which the distinction between meaning and absence of meaning disappears: that from which we started out. It has been twenty-five hundred years since men discovered and formulated these truths."

Even though the chapters devoted to the Nambikwara may be regarded as the *happy* part of the book (its idyllic part, since evidently contact with this population, in whom he thought to encounter "something like the most truthful and the most moving expression of human tenderness," provided him with a sort of equivalent of that "green paradise of childish loves" of which Baudelaire dreamed nostalgically), Claude Lévi-Strauss believes that his research into elementary forms of social life fails here because he in some sense exceeded the goal he had proposed for himself (beyond the directly scientific interest of the undertaking) by going among the Nambikwara. For in the case of this tribe, which confronts him with "one of the poorest conceivable forms of social and political organization" and in whose simplicity he believes he has found that state Rousseau speaks of "which no longer exists, which may never have existed, which will probably never exist, and of which we must nevertheless form correct notions in order to make a sound judgment of our present state," the sociological experience itself eludes him: "I had sought a society reduced to its simplest expression. That of the Nambikwara was reduced to such an extent that in it I found only men." Finally, another disappointment awaits the researcher among the Tupi-Kawahib, whom he had been able to approach only at the cost of many hardships: "I had wanted to go to the extreme point of primitiveness; wasn't I satisfied, here among these gracious natives whom no one had seen before me, whom no one, perhaps, would see after me? At the end of an exciting journey, I had my wild men. Alas, they were all too wild. Since I had found out about their existence only at the last moment, I had not been able to set aside enough time to get to know them. The limited resources at my disposal, the physically debilitated state in which my companions and I found ourselves—and which the fevers following the rains were to aggravate even further—allowed me only a brief period of schooling in the bush instead of months of study. There they were, quite prepared to teach me their customs and beliefs, and I did not know their language. They were as close to me as an image in a mirror; I could touch them but not understand them."

However irritating the frustrations lying in wait for anyone who dedicates himself body and soul to the profession of ethnographer in order to form a concrete view of man's deeper nature—or, to put it differently, a view of the social minimum that defines the human condition across the possible incongruities of different cultures— and even though he can aspire only to reveal relative truths (the attainment of an ultimate truth being an illusory hope), this is not the worst of the difficulties he faces. If he is not to taint his investigation by a lack of objectivity, he is in effect obliged to adopt the position of impartial observer, detached from the system of values he inherits from his own culture and likewise detached from the cultures he studies. This attitude must, it would seem, truly "disable" him, since it tends to deny him any opinion or any action within the society he belongs to and within those he is studying and forces him to refrain from playing any part in any society, which amounts to preventing him from assuming his condition as man. Yet it is the ethnographic study itself that will rescue him from this positively unlivable situation. It will, in fact, teach him that all societies "offer certain advantages to their members, taking into account a residue of iniquity whose magnitude seems approximately consistent" and that, since none of them is favored from that point of view, his ultimate task is to try to determine, using all these cultures, whose originality deserves to be respected, and without making a moral choice between one or another of them and his own, what is "the unshakable basis of human society." On these conditions, he is not condemned to remain suspended in the void because he has not found a practical application for his activity: certainly he cannot set out to act on other cultures to change them (given that such interference from outside would be more or less destructive by definition); nor can he offer his own society some other society as a model (since no society, including his own, is fundamentally good or bad); but he will help put us in a position to use our knowledge of societies *in general* "to extract those principles of social life that we can apply to reforming our own customs," that is, the customs of the one society we can "transform without running the risk of destroying it; for the changes we introduce into it also come from it."

Thus, however restrictive may be the limits assigned by Claude Lévi-Strauss to the possibility of a commitment on the part of the ethnographer and however strong the reservations (which is the least one can call them) he expresses here, as in many parts of the book, about progress, he nevertheless leaves one possible route open for action. With all types of civilizations suffering and the increase in our control of the physical world denounced as resulting in a harsher subjugation, since our spirit itself is now a prisoner of determinism and therefore dominated by what it has conquered, all prospect of a future to whose preparation it was worth dedicating oneself seemed closed; but in a dialectical twist quite characteristic of his style, Claude Lévi-Strauss finds a way out at the very moment the reader might have believed that he was deliberately using his sharpest and subtlest thinking to negative ends: "The zealots of progress run the risk of misunderstanding, because they set little store by it, the immense wealth accumulated by humanity on either side of the narrow furrow on which they keep their eyes fixed; by overestimating the importance of past efforts, they disparage those that remain for us to make. If men have always toiled at one thing, which is to make a livable society, the forces that moved our distant ancestors are still present in us. Nothing has been staked; we can take back everything."

Claude Lévi-Strauss may not have found what he was looking for as a sociologist among the Nambikwara and the Tupi-Kawahib, but there he lived in brotherhood with men. In societies like those of India, however, which has proved capable of awe-inspiring creations but suffers, as though from a disease, from its overly dense population (whence the caste system, a means of feeling less crowded by denying part of the species status as human beings), "the gap between the excess of luxury and the excess of misery explodes the human dimension." Whereas Indian America, despite its decrepitude, offers delightful examples of balanced groups such as must have existed during the Stone Age (when mankind lived in a state midway between primitivism and our mechanical age), this part of the Asiatic world presents us with a spectacle of excess, the image of what awaits us if it is true that a society that has become demographically overcrowded "perpetuates itself only by giving rise to servitude" (as seems confirmed by the evolution of Europe over the past twenty years) and if we know of nothing with which to oppose this spreading scourge, "the systematic depreciation of man by man." Whereas in Indian America Claude Lévi-Strauss finds the glimmer of a more harmonious past, southern Asia presents him with a disquieting anticipation of our future, and it is consequently as though, for the traveler of *Tristes Tropiques*, the two great types of displacement he achieved physically in space correlated with imaginary displacements in time, one backward and the other forward. "A journey is inscribed simultaneously in space, time, and the social hierarchy," he writes in one of his early chapters, pointing out that a distant place is not simply exotic but that it evokes a certain period different from that in which we live and that our status also is changed there, since we become almost always richer or poorer according to whether the cost of living is lower or higher there in relation to our resources. Far from being a simple occasion of geographical uprooting, the journey thus conceived represents an experience with many aspects and certainly one of the most complete experiences a conscious individual can undergo. Wherever they occur, and without there even being any need to displace oneself, it is experiences of this kind that—like Marcel Proust's *time regained*—seem to make up for Claude Lévi-Strauss (detractor of journeys or at least of what is most properly "journey" about them) the special moments that allow life still to have some meaning, even though it is undermined on all sides by nonmeaning, and that are at once the justifications for and catalysts of our activity.

To trace, as a geologist, the line of contact between two layers of earth of different ages; to approach an Indian tribe (prepared finally to declare that the modern traveler is only an "archaeologist of space, vainly seeking to recreate exoticism from fragments and debris") and relive the adventure of the men of the sixteenth century discovering the New World; to witness anachronistic dances in the Brazilian forest where the concubines of the rubber harvesters (themselves miserably poor and horribly exploited) turn up in smart outfits, although the rest of the year they are dressed in rags; to find on the same altar at the foot of the Kashmir mountains three bas-reliefs sculpted in styles that reveal a succession of different traditions (Hinduism, Hellenism, Buddhism); to be able, by meditating on

our species, "to understand the essence of what it was and continues
to be, within thought and beyond society": these experiences are certainly distinct and correspond to different stages in Claude Lévi-
Strauss's development, but they have in common the fact that, like
the Proustian illumination, they are all to some degree experiences
of grasping the flow of time. When, after arriving at the discouraging conclusion that "as for the creations of the human spirit, they
have meaning only in relation to it and will fall into disorder as soon
as it disappears," Claude Lévi-Strauss—in an abrupt reversal similar
to Hamlet's when he is recalled to his specific duty by the sight of
Fortinbras's army marching toward the slaughter—declares, "And
yet, I exist . . . ," and opts for that *we* which no one can challenge
without reducing himself to nothing, then it is to times like these
that he appeals almost immediately, seeing them as humanity's only
chance. What possibility does he grant man, in the end, of "detach-
ing himself" as he contemplates a mineral, inhales a fragrance, or exchanges a look of understanding with a pet, if not through rejecting, now and again, the chronometric time in which history and
work are inscribed, through plunging into nature, which surrounds
us spatially and also bathes us in a time that merges with the time of
myth and poetry?

Whether or not one acquiesces to such propositions as are out-
lined in this complex book, which is (it must be stressed) the record
of a piece of research and not an ex cathedra account, whether or not
one feels that despite the author's affirmation that he cares as much
for men as for knowledge, the book privileges a certain disenchanted
reverie, as opposed to immediate action aiming at the material im-
provement of conditions for all people, the fact remains that such a
piece of testimony—quite apart from its literary quality—is enormously valuable, even if only to the extent that it poses essential
problems in a manner as vivid as it is lucid and that, by its very richness, it gives rise to ardent and (as is only right) interminable con-
troversies. For there exists no idea worthy of the name that does not
provoke discussion.

Their Morals and Ours

The fact that a Bolshevik like Leon Trotsky should set out to define the broader features of a system of morals seems sufficient cause to provoke indignation or mockery. Some people believe that one cannot decently broach the question of morality if one is a Communist whose actions conform to the famous Jesuit adage, "the end justifies the means." For others, it is precisely because Trotsky was a romantic and not a realist like Stalin that he was able to explore such a question, one unrelated to the problems of strategy and tactics, which alone are worthy of the attention of a true revolutionary. In both cases, these rejections can have only one meaning: namely, that once it is a question of proletarian revolution, it is understood that politics and ethics are incompatible, whence the impossibility of any alternative besides either carrying out an action with a concern only for the desired victory or embracing values next to which practical exigencies have very little weight.

These days, in widely different social circles, simplistic views of this kind lead people sometimes to justify Russia's invasion of Hungary by pointing to the need to maintain a solid bloc of Communist countries around the Soviet Union, sometimes to condemn it unconditionally in the name of an abstract ideal of liberty (too easily forgetting that the democratic nations ceaselessly flout the idea of liberty in their relations with colonized or semicolonized peoples). Which makes the little book that Trotsky wrote shortly before the

Written in January 1957 as the preface to Leon Trotsky's *Leur morale et la nôtre* (new edition, followed by "Bolchevisme et stalinisme"), to be published by Editions Juillard in their series "Lettres nouvelles," ed. Maurice Nadeau.

last world war, *Their Morals and Ours*, in which the author shows how strategy and morality are linked for any consistent Bolshevik, seem very current despite the lapse of twenty years. For those who are induced by the present havoc to lose hope, purely and simply, in communism as a militant humanism and who impute to the very tenor of the system a degeneration whose main reason should rather be sought in the concrete situation in which the Russian socialist state finds itself, this little book—paired with the essay "Bolshevism and Stalinism," which appeared a bit earlier—indicates at least on what theoretical bases a rectification can be brought about.

Of course, Leon Trotsky does not for a moment dream of playing the saint who takes great immutable principles as his axes of reference, whereas human reality, morality's only point of application, is an essentially changing thing. His thought remains that of a historicist and, in particular, of a Marxist for whom the class struggle constitutes the "highest law" and who mercilessly assails classical democrats. But if, taking the bull by the horns and assuming full responsibility for his position, he declares that violence and cunning are legitimate in the fight against the exploiters, admits that in a period of civil war one makes use of the hostage system (as he himself did in 1919) and that in such a period one stops holding public trials, if, in other words, he in some sense evinces that Bolshevik amorality so offensive to bourgeois ideas, in another sense he rebels against the pseudorealism of those who feel that any means is permissible as long as it results in a point gained for the side that in principle is that of the proletarians.

Given that there is a "dialectical interdependence between the end and the means," that an end is always the means to a further end, and that an achievement is always dependent on the paths taken to achieve it, it is clear that certain means cannot be tolerated by anyone whose ultimate objective is to abolish the exploitation of man by man; not that such means are impure in themselves (for no act, whatever it may be, can be judged out of its context) but because, all things considered, it turns out that these means deflect from the goal to which the long chain of subordinate means—to ends that become in their turn means—should lead. This discrimination among means according to a criterion that goes beyond the notion of immediate efficacy allows us to begin to understand a morality based on grounds that are simply those of a well-understood strategy.

"The proletariat can and must liberate itself on its own." From this sentence in *La Sainte Famille* that bluntly indicates the revolutionary goal capable of justifying any means sufficient to it, Trotsky derives his golden rule and the reasons for condemning that betrayal of the authentic cause of the proletariat, the bureaucratic deviation recently labeled "the cult of personality." This, not because he subscribes to the idea (which he finds corrupt) of a total "freedom for the masses" but because he demands of a Communist party that it actually be the centralized organization of the proletarian avant-garde and act in the interest of the greater number instead of being the tool of a privileged minority.

From this point of view, the crime committed by the Soviet leaders toward the Hungarian people appears in its true and sinister perspective: that of a counterrevolutionary act, for the least one can say—to consider only the political results—is that the Hungarian proletariat, having risen against an apparatus that was the agent of its oppressors and not the instrument of its emancipation, has just been rendered incapable, for a long time to come, of ensuring the management of its work by its own organizations. The fact that Russia's proletarian army should have been employed at such a task is a crime toward the whole of the proletariat, which must be united, not divided.[1]

From this same point of view, it is easy to see that Tito, for instance, acted as a Marxist when he wrested Yugoslavia from Stalin's

[1] It seems to me now, eight years later, that I should have written: "The fact that the proletarian state of Russia should have allowed a situation to develop in a partner country such that it had to engage in an armed intervention is a crime. . . ."

despotism, and one can understand why the guardianship of the French Communist Party had to be rejected by Aimé Césaire, who believed the emancipation of the workers of Martinique had to be their own doing and not that of their "big brothers."

Marxist strategy is in itself an ethic, since it teaches man how he must maneuver to establish conditions favorable to a common pursuit of this ultimate goal: the greatest extension of each person's power over nature and his own destiny. Thus if Trotsky moralizes and moralizes as a strategist, he does so as a Marxist aware of the fact that the doctrine is at once scientific and normative.

From an ethical point of view, it would seem that if the only means to be recommended are, as Trotsky writes, those that "increase the cohesiveness of the proletariat, inspire its soul with an ineradicable hatred of oppression, teach it to scorn the official morality and its democratic followers, fill it with the awareness of its own historic mission, augment its courage and its self-abnegation," in short, those that develop in it solidarity in a single revolt, a critical spirit as well as a devotion to a broadly humanitarian cause, the obligation thus to consider the means one by one and especially to reject everything that tends by fraud, police terror, or demagogy to tame and dupe the masses is an imperative at least as strict as those of the eternal morality dear to the bourgeois democrats for whom it is in truth, in a transitory way, only a class morality.

From a political point of view, and on the level of revolutionary theory, inseparable from revolutionary practice, wouldn't the best first step to a guarantee against the ravages of so-called Marxist-Leninist authoritarianism in the domain of action and in that of culture (here and there debased to the level of a catechism) be this reminder of the exact nature of the enterprise that must be carried out: a liberation that cannot be achieved either from outside or under the more or less interested aegis of a clique of leaders but must be the work of the oppressed themselves, thinking and acting through a party whose only purpose would be this liberation?

Michel Butor's
Mythological Realism

You are holding in your hands a brand-new copy of *La Modification*, a novel by Michel Butor. You are cutting open the pages of the book, and as you perform this light task, you read a few paragraphs at random. What strikes you right away?

In every country, novels are written—or at least a large part of their contents are written—either in the third person (pseudohistorical narratives or fictions whose authors have not tried to hide the fact that they are fictional) or in the first person (simulacra of autobiographical narratives or fictions that are, properly speaking, lyric). *La Modification*, however, with the exception of a few rare passages, is written in the second person plural: it is you yourself, reader, whom the novelist seems to be politely challenging, and it requires only a few brief glances at the printed lines as you wield the paper-knife for you to feel you are being confronted with an invitation, if not a summons. This uncommon device incites you to wonder (let us hazard) what particular type of reading you are being invited to do, and your curiosity (I presume) is aroused even before you have finished cutting the pages. You therefore embark (without further delay, I hope) upon reading these 236 large-format pages, which alone can reveal to you what sort of attention the author was expecting from a public that you alone represent, why he proceeded as though it were a question of explicitly establishing a personal re-

This review of *La Modification* by Michel Butor (Paris: Editions de Minuit, 1957) was first published in *Critique* 2, no. 129 (1958).

lationship between him and you, and what he wanted to lead you into by using this method that you will perhaps feel to be artificial, even though he has already indicated in a public conversation the purely logical reasons he felt it was necessary.[1]

The central and almost the only character in the book—an already middle-aged husband and father with whom both male and female readers, caught in the toils of the *you* and the present indicative, cannot help more or less identifying—chooses, on his own initiative, to board the Paris-Rome express one morning as a third-class passenger, thus modifying his habit of making the trip in first class on the evening train whenever he is obliged, at his employers' expense, to visit the Rome headquarters of the typewriter company of which he is the manager for France. His intention is that once in Rome—a city he has been in love with since he was a schoolboy—he will surprise the mistress he visits every time he makes a business trip and to whom this time he will announce that he has found a position (in response to a desire she had expressed) that will allow her to move to Paris, where they will henceforth be able to live together because he intends to separate from his wife and children and thus make a great modification in his own life, tedious and gloomy except for the few rays of light that fall on it from Rome. In the course of his trip, this potential escapee is prey to a host of reminiscences, including (just after the Mont Cenis tunnel) the painful memory of what should have been a festive time for his lover and him, a vacation she spent in Paris. He also gives himself up to a number of reflections and imaginary constructions, the latter at first taking the form of pure and simple daydreams (species of small novels he builds around the strangers traveling with him), then reveries, and a dream whose

[1]In an interview with Paul Guth (*Figaro littéraire*, no. 607, December 7, 1957): "The story absolutely had to be told from a character's point of view. Since what it involved was a dawning awareness, the character could not say *I*. I needed an interior monologue beneath the level of the language of the character himself, in a form intermediate to the first and third persons. This *you* allows me to describe the character's situation and the way in which language is born in him."

general sense, connected to the dreamer's anxiety and the rather un-
comfortable conditions in which he is traveling, is of a descent into
hell, with a last sequence consisting of the hostile appearance of
gods and Roman emperors. At the end of the trip the character's
state of mind has modified to such an extent that he decides against
making the very change in view of which he had left on this trip: he
will spend three days at his destination without going to see his girlfriend, whom he loves, as he now knows, because she is "the face of
Rome," which means that to separate her from this lofty place would
result in failure. He will opt for keeping things as they are and will
promise himself that later he will give his wife the pleasure of a trip
to Rome, their third visit together to this city, which enchanted
them the first time (when they were newlyweds) but disappointed
them the second, when the deterioration of their life together was already evident. When he first boarded the train, the character was
holding in his hand a book he had bought at the station bookstore
without bothering about its title or its author, merely trusting in the
name of the series. Getting off the train at the Stazione Termini, he
is still holding the book, which he has not read after all, having used
it only to save his seat when he left the compartment for one reason
or another. The way out that is so impossible to find, whether he turn
to his mistress or to his wife, to Rome (which, he has discovered, is a
myth for him) or to Paris (whose grayness ravages him), will be provided him by a book physically similar to that one: the work he decides to write "in order to attempt to allow that crucial episode in
your adventure to be relived" by you, the reader, whom the use of
second-person plural in this book has induced to enter, to some degree, the skin of the character who is allegedly responsible for the
very pages you have read.

This book, in which dry notations alternate with sentences whose
often extreme length would be rather irritating if it were not for their
very clear construction and the certainty, soon acquired, that in their
unfolding—supremely ample, in truth—they are simply the con-

densed expression of an abundant and diverse subject, this book, filled with poetry as much in its flights toward historic times or toward myth as in the objectivity of its descriptions (rigorously realistic, because if the whole is to be believed and in some measure experienced, it is indispensable that one see and feel everything that can be seen and felt inside and outside that compartment, the theater at once fixed and moving of the solitary traveler's meditation), this book, which can be called *perfect* in the sense that it closes back on itself and is in fact the story of its own genesis, the summary, schematic as it may be, of what can be described as its manifest content, immediately shows that it operates on several different levels. By this very fact, it avoids unity of action, whereas unity of time (the duration of the Paris-Rome trip by rail) and unity of place (the compartment that the hero does not leave except to go, during breaks in the story, into the corridor of the car, onto a station platform, or to the dining car) are apparently as strictly respected as in a seventeenth-century French tragedy.

Of course the events narrated by Michel Butor take place in an interval of time amounting to not even twenty-four hours and in a confined space that undergoes only infinitesimal modifications (of which the most notable are the changes in lighting, the substitutions of one set of luggage for another when travelers come and go, as well as the stain on the heated floor and the variations whose composition and arrangement affect the elements of that stain). This narrowly dated and situated novel, then, contains both unity of time and unity of place, yet here these unities assume a form completely different from that in the plays of our classical theater. The hero is making not one journey but several, in different periods and in different directions: in fragments that appear out of chronological order, he remembers (among other facts having to do with the problem that obsesses him) other trips he has made from Paris to Rome or Rome to Paris, and he even thinks of his return trip in the near future and what will follow that return. Thus, several different time frames mingle, and the time of the current trip from Paris to Rome is simply the one in which the meditation of the character comes into being and develops. The unity of place, when all is said and done, is treated no better: this almost immutable container in which everything is localized is, in truth, a moving body whose displacement one follows from station to station between Paris and Rome; in the traveler's reminiscences and plans the place du Panthéon, his Paris neighborhood, and various Roman monuments or sites occupy a large place; fictional locations appear, evoked by works of art (such as the two galleries of paintings, one devoted to ancient Rome and the other to modern Rome, portrayed in two pictures by Pannini in which "there is no perceptible material difference between the objects represented as real and those represented as painted"); at moments the thoughts of the traveler (who is at these times a pure gaze) turn on the places shown in the advertising photos decorating the walls of the compartment; last, great panels of a set for some preliminary piece to a mystery play (a desert landscape, the Sibyl's grotto, a river with a gloomy boatman, a Piranesian series opening with a rocky ravine and ending with a field of ruins) appear in his dream. On top of the interweaving of times, there is an interweaving of places, and it turns out that the third-class compartment presently on its way from Paris to Rome is not much more than a stage device that remains fixed through the succession of backdrops and flats.

The story of a crisis that does not last even twenty-four hours and whose theater is this railway car where during the last twelve hours you will find yourself "on your own pillory," Michel Butor's novel appears in a certain sense constructed like a classical tragedy. Yet the time and place that contain this crisis—which here is attributed to a single character—are not an abstract framework but very special elements in a twofold interweaving, and as for the argument (the abandonment of a plan that a man had made to renew his love life, then the replacement of this plan by another, to write a book whose theme will be this abandonment), to see it thus from an anecdotal point of view would be to concentrate on only the most visible aspect of a crisis in which several actions overlap, each operating on its own level. If there is classicism in the formal structure of *La Modification*, it seems that this structure is constantly shaken, if not threatened with explosion, and that the very fragility of the severe limits imposed (a greatly restricted time and place, a plot that at first seems banal) confers on the work as such its peculiar tragedy by apparently endowing with an explosive force the subject that is thus so extremely compressed.

Feeling that to live with his mistress instead of with his wife would be, to use the familiar expression, six of one, half a dozen of the other, a married man decides against the rejuvenation such a change would bring him and will console himself for it by writing a book: a subject which, padded out with a few more twists, could be that of a comedy of manners if not a vaudeville of misunderstandings (the two women interchangeable after a few years, the enormous slip consisting of the character's substituting his mistress's first name for the word "book" designating what he in fact will bring back). Realist that he is, Michel Butor does not hesitate to deal with the subject in depth. His character is situated socially (in the middle class) and his personality traits are clearly indicated. While preserving a facade almost intact, he is beginning to experience the erosion of time. There is no question that he was once in love with his wife, but he has seen the bonds of affection that tied him to her loosen (without either one being at fault). Now he has become bogged down in family life and a job that is no more than a means of livelihood for him, and he has only these few escapes: linked to the passion that, as a man of a certain cultivation, he nurtures for everything to do with Rome, his love for the young woman he met during one of his business trips in that place of so many experiences (since one is away from one's accustomed setting there and in direct contact with strangers), the train. This businessman is what is called a dreamer: ever since Rome assumed the guise of a woman for him, hasn't he systematically sought out the monuments and cafés of Paris that contain a particle of Rome? He is sensitive to the sight of beautiful things (as is evidenced by his curiosity about Rome's artistic riches and the memories of works of art and ancient ruins that crop up in his dream). His opinions are those of a liberal untouched by chauvinism or by any sort of blind faith in religion, opposed to the "frightful foolishness of arms" as well as to police fascism. His weak point is certainly a lack, as they say, of spunk: toward the beginning of this trip, which is the result of an important decision on his part, he reveals himself to be so timorous that he cannot ask for his seat back from someone who took it from him when he had left without marking it; his wife behaves toward him with condescending pity and he has very little prestige in his children's eyes; when his girlfriend from Rome came to Paris for her vacation and he invited her to his house, a sort of complicity sprang up between the two women to his detriment and he could do nothing to gain control of the situation; in Rome he is very cautious, because he fears his affair will hurt his relations with his directors. There is nothing surprising in the fact that a man of this sort, disturbed by the unusual conditions in which he is once again making a trip that has become a habit for him, assailed by thoughts that become more anguishing as he approaches his goal, and finally dead tired from the long hours he has spent in the third-class compartment, should change his mind, before even arriving in Rome, about the decision that had made him leave Paris and, having come up against reasons that seem decisive to him but are perhaps only covering up reasons that are even more crucial though less far-reaching, fall back on an idea that is clearly attractive to the impulsive and dilettantish side of him: to create a literary compensation for his incapacity to produce a positive change in his life, a work whose substance will be provided him by the tale of his failure.

Michel Butor has therefore built his novel along a perfectly coherent psychological thread (and it is not the least merit of this writer, who is barely over thirty, to have so easily and convincingly donned the clothing of a man past his prime). We must point out, however, that it is nothing but a thread and that other subjects are inextricably mingled with the psychological subject.

Placed between two women, one who is part of his growing older day by day and one who seemed to him, before his night of torment on the train, "like his youth preserved," the character is also placed between two cities, Paris and Rome, one he lives in and one he leaves only to dream of. By way of his reminiscences, his reflections, and the dream that expresses the character's fascination with Rome, we arrive at another subject, which is no longer that of a psychological novel. Rome, which is identified with this woman whom he will not bring to Paris because there she would be deromanticized (so to speak) at the same time that Rome would lose much of its attraction for him, is obviously the poetry that illuminates his life—but what is Rome, really, and what is the meaning of the myth it seems intended to illustrate?

It is apparent quite early on that there is more than one Rome in Rome: ancient Rome is distinct from the Rome of modern Christianity (an idea expressed by Pannini's paired pictures that the character saw at the Louvre), and in contrast to Rome properly speaking there is Vatican City. Before he makes the crucial change by abandoning his plan, the two women—his illicit and his licit spouses—are associated one with pagan Rome and the other with Christian Rome, since he recalls the repugnance that the former always showed for the Sistine Chapel in particular and the day she said to him, laughing, that he was "rotten to the core with Christianity," whereas the latter, during her second trip, when she felt that Rome was a place from which her companion was excluding her, wanted "at all costs to see the pope." As for him, he who has among the books on his bedside table not only the *Aeneid* (the story, as we know, of the adventures of Aeneas, son of Venus and founder of Rome) but also the *Letters* of Julian the Apostate (the emperor who rejected the

Christian faith in order to restore the old polytheism and who is remembered in Paris by the baths attributed to him), he strives to carry
out a "systematic exploration of Roman subjects" and pursues Rome
by attaching himself to its avatars from different periods. For him,
it is the "Eternal City" (in which he periodically immerses himself
as though in a fountain of youth), the "place of authenticity" (where
he is no longer alienated, as he is in Paris by a job whose only satisfaction is financial), the city that from the first seemed associated
with beauty and love, since during their honeymoon his wife and he
visited the temple of Venus and Rome, and as she sat next to him on
a bench "on that exhilarating evening" she asked him why the cult
of the goddess and the cult of the city were thus joined (a scene that
will come back to him, along with other details from the honeymoon, as an implicit sign of the fact that he and his wife had a relationship of mutual understanding very different from the close-
mouthed relationship that exists now). What is revealed to him
about this "City of Cities"—which he thought he would be able to
enter fully through his lover, after having only touched upon its surface—by the dream at the end of which, arrested after a scandal on a
public street and having encountered only mistrust or a vague commiseration on the part of the Romans, he is judged and condemned
by the Catholic powers (the cardinals, the pope, and the "King of
Judgment" himself), then feels his body sinking into the mud after
the startling appearance of the emperors, gods, and goddesses ("a
crowd of faces approaching, huge and hateful, as though you were an
insect on its back, flashes of lightning casting stripes over their faces
and their skin falling from them in patches"), is that one aspect of
Rome remains the same through its changes: the cardinals declare
that they, too, are Romans, and as for the pope, he calls himself "the
ghost of the emperors, for centuries haunting the capital of their
abolished, regretted world."

If this vision—at once awe-inspiring and terrible—ends in a syncretic affirmation, since any break between Roman paganism and

Christianity disappears here, it is in their unanimous reprobation that the opposed figures unite, their reprobation of this man who has not been able to understand Rome, and in a sort of Götterdämmerung in which they are no longer anything more than specters. When the meditation of the character (now rescued from his uneasy sleep, freshly shaved and on the point of arrival) has led him to recognize that the malady from which he is suffering is not his alone and that "this gaping fissure . . . connects with an immense fissure in history," Rome, with his memory of the *pax romana*, will appear to him as a token of the time now past "in which the world had a center," a focal point "that sought to shift to Byzantium after the collapse of Rome, then much later to imperial Paris," and the lack of which is felt today. As a myth with evasive and ambiguous aspects whose roots plunge very deep, Rome will remain for the character an enigma he cannot answer. As a city, it will retain its special quality even though he has become aware of precisely what is mythical about it, so that it has become demystified: he will return there with his wife, who will no longer have cause to be jealous of it now that the wave of illusions has subsided, and he will continue to go there and visit his mistress even though he knows that her powers would not have withstood the "ravages" of Paris and that this love will not resist the passage of time any more than the first one. As a parallel is made between the two Romes and Paris, so are the two female characters likened to each other, but in a negative way, since what they seem to have in common is the fact that in the end, any love will run aground in the aging of the two partners.

Such is the pattern one can trace in the traveler's meditation, at least in its specifically Roman component, and insofar as one can, without falsifying too much, thus reduce to a few very general lines a meditation that becomes more and more chaotic (its rhythm accelerated by the traveler's growing fatigue), while the fragments of a dream—interrupted by frequent wakings and deriving many of its elements as much from the appearance of the other travelers or certain details of the setting as from incidents along the way or the situation of the dreamer, who is sitting in a railway car jolting on its rails—overlap with scraps of memories and erratic reflections that mesh with one another according to the laws of an essentially emotional mechanism.

At the end of the twenty-one or so hours occupied by the trip from the Gare de Lyon to the Stazione Termini, the character has certainly not lifted the last veil, but at least he has learned a certain number of things, if only about his own feelings toward the girlfriend he went off to surprise in Rome and about the city itself. On another level, different from that of psychology or historical panorama, Michel Butor's novel, in which a physical itinerary and a mental itinerary are meticulously described in a parallel fashion, assumes the guise of the tale of an initiatory pilgrimage. Not only does a Roman mythology—introduced by the traveler's cogitation—emerge within the context of an everyday reality, but the entire narration is situated on the level of myth, without ever straining its *realism*, as I would be tempted to call it inasmuch as it is so very down-to-earth.

In this compartment marked with the "set of initials SNCF," which (whether or not the author intended this) is not unlike the Roman inscription SPQR, the traveler will find himself in the presence of various specimens of human beings, to certain of whom, as he daydreams, he will assign a name and a biography, so that a semblance of a link will thus be created between him and them, though not a reciprocal one. People who are very different in age, nationality, condition: a young couple on their honeymoon trip (reminding the character of the trip he and his wife, armed, like them, with a Guide Bleu and a Méthode Assimil, had made a number of years before), a clergyman, a professor, a soldier, a businessman, a middle-aged woman with her child, workers and lower-middle-class Italians (including an old man and an old woman), an Englishman at the very beginning, and toward the end a very beautiful woman who could be Italian or French. Like the men of all colors whom Herman

Melville brought together in the boat that sank while chasing the monster Moby Dick, these traveling companions together compose a summary of humanity. Even though he has no other relations with them except for his proximity to them in space and what he imagines about them, the pilgrim to the Eternal City is not strictly alone, and his adventure, part of which is the "crucial" episode he is experiencing, is only one adventure among many others of many other people. The change from day to night, the variations in the weather, the memories of other trips in other seasons, even during another period of history (the honeymoon trip at the time of the reign of the Blackshirts), also contribute to the *universalization*, if one can call it that, of the story's perspective.

Well before the meditation explicitly becomes a descent into hell through a dream, a strange note sounds indicating that this trip is not an ordinary one. In one of those collisions of times and places that make one believe that one is both on a Paris-Rome express train on a certain calendar day and outside space and time, there occurs— on page 97 of the book—the phantasmagoric apparition of the Master of the Royal Hunt, the legendary horseman who haunts the forest of Fontainebleau and whose spectral image crosses a double screen to come to the mind of the character: between two stations in Burgundy he in fact remembers the return from one of his trips to Rome and how, when the train was passing through the forest of Fontainebleau, he thought of the Master of the Royal Hunt galloping on his skeletal horse and wailing: "Do you hear me?" On the outskirts of Genoa—his plan discarded, so that he knows henceforth that he is committed to a family life he no longer wanted—he will recall that it was when they were going to Rome together for their honeymoon that his wife spoke to him of the Master of the Royal Hunt, whom she had feared when she was a child, because she thought he would carry her off when darkness fell during her walks in the Fontainebleau forest. This disquieting apparition, which comes to the traveler from a happy time but one long past and which for his wife emerged from an even more distant past, is the first message he receives from the world of anguish into which he will soon descend, and the lament of the Master of the Royal Hunt is the first indication of what will be a sort of leitmotiv of questioning through the rest of the novel: in his dream the character will be subjected to many questions that in truth will be echoes of his own question.

The apparition of the Master of the Royal Hunt between the stations of Sennecey and Sénozan is—except for its strangeness—of the same sort as the apparitions of vehicles (cars, trucks, motorcycles) that, seen on the road at various points in the journey, seem momentarily to coordinate their motion with the motion of the express train. In the same way the dream, which will gradually change into a vision or a revelation in which the sleeper will be directly implicated, at first assumes an almost impersonal appearance: it is not *you* who hear the Sibyl ask why you do not pose the questions to her that must have motivated your "so very dangerous escapade," then reproach you for being a stranger to your own desires when you tell her that what you want is simply "to get out of here"; it is not you who encounter the boatman of the dead and the customs officer with two faces (one hostile and the other welcoming) who guards the gate of Rome, but it is a *he* still situated in a sort of mythical distance. The beginning of the dream—whose very first image is that of a man walking through an uninhabited countryside, like the wanderer the traveler had imagined to be somewhere in the unread book, a man whom one could therefore call *literarily* imagined, in a certain sense—the beginning of the dream is actually told in the third-person singular, and the return of the second-person plural occurs only when the dreamer—having reached the topographical goal of his personal quest, since he has entered Rome—finds himself in a small square, suffering from a parching thirst, and can drink only "an atrocious wine that burns your throat and gullet with such fury that you howl, hurl the glass against a housefront where it shatters a window, an enormous spot beginning to corrode the plaster and bricks." The legendary or mythical components of the traveler's reflection apparently would come to him, in short, from the outside and as cultural facts (things that are read or things that are told) before being integrated into his lived reality, and the abandonment of the rather impersonal form of discourse, at the moment when the wanderer becomes a thirsty man who will search in vain to quench his thirst and will allow his rage to explode, would be in keeping with the almost physical nature of the revelation that will come to the man who has just now walked a short distance on the platform of the Stazione Principe of Genoa: the discovery not of an abstract truth veiled by a proliferation of myths but of what the harassing realities of his own life actually are, which have a very definite, if enigmatic, affinity with the phenomenon of Rome.

It therefore seems that among the greater organizing principles of this narrative of a trip from Paris to Rome, from which no prosaic detail is omitted (station names, ticket checks, the border crossing), is the idea of a *spiritual pursuit* carried out according to traditional norms: the site of the pursuit is labeled with a phrase of warning aimed at the incautious ("It is dangerous to lean out"); many of the travelers gathered in the compartment have their signs or their attributes (the new luggage of the young married couple, the soldier's plywood trunk, the workers' knapsacks, the priest's soutane, the Englishman's umbrella, the black-and-white pointed shoes of one of the Italians, etc.); the railway station names of Roma Trastevere, Roma Ostiense, Roma Tuscolana, and Roma Termini are mentioned insistently as though they designated the holy places through which the pilgrim must ritually pass; the customs officers or passport inspectors assume the guise of entrance guards; the Guide Bleu becomes the "guide bleu of wanderers" (or something similar to the work of the Jewish philosopher Maimonides, the *Guide of the Perplexed*, generally called the "guide of Wanderers"), and the Méthode Assimil seems to derive its special power from the fact that it is a tool for mutual understanding and therefore a remedy for the confusion of languages; a tingling between his vertebrae and a stiffness in his legs give the drowsy traveler the impression he is wrestling with a "spiny serpent" (namely the sort of dragon encountered by fairy-tale heroes). Furthermore, the confined space of the compartment and the relatively brief duration of the journey expand in the way ceremonial space and time can expand when a series of events whose theater was supposedly the mythical world are reproduced in a ritual subjected to narrow limits of site and duration. In any case, is it not true that when the traveler goes periodically to Rome, called there on business, he is making what is commonly known as a "pilgrimage"? Yet what is happening here is not that symbols—whose not immediately perceptible truth is the most important thing—are being ground down but that polyvalent elements operating on several levels are being brought into play (through a very delicate and very diverse spatial and temporal network), elements none of which could claim to take precedence.[2] Thus, the tourist's vade mecum is at once an appurtenance of the realistic setting, a key to Rome, a guide for seeking the Promised Land, and also one of several books the character handles or sees in the course of this journey, which will diverge in the direction of a book even though his aspiration to live like "a free and sincere man" had originally impelled him toward a city and a woman.

Before boarding the train, the typewriter salesman (who will finally decide to *write* in the absolute sense of the word) has bought a book for himself almost automatically. Throughout the trip this book, which at one moment he is about to open—yet cannot bring himself to do it—will remain for him an object that sometimes

---

[2]The complexity of this structure is clear from a statement the author made to Paul Guth, to whom he had shown the graphs he had used to help him work out his previous novel, *L'Emploi du temps*: "For *La Modification*, I did not manage to make a graphic diagram. I adopted a system of letters, a sort of algebra" (interview, *Figaro littéraire*). If there was symbolism in this, its structure would obviously be simplified, for the elements would arrange themselves as though of their own accord around the diagram furnished by this symbolism.

serves to save his seat, sometimes is stowed away in the luggage rack, sometimes rests on his knees, then is wedged under him while he sleeps and dreams. If in Michel Butor's work there is a leitmotiv of questioning, there is also the theme of reading in its various forms:[3] several of his traveling companions (the young couple with their guide and their Italian handbook, the priest with his breviary, the professor with his black-bound volumes) are carrying books, which they use as such, but in the same way they would use tools of their trades; other travelers are carrying unidentified newspapers or magazines; various billboards and placards are visible here and there, as pure documents, in the stations, in the railway car itself, or by the side of the tracks; last, several holy books (including one that the Sibyl is looking at in her grotto) appear in the character's dream. Already deep in his meditation, he asks himself why he is not reading the book that was supposed to help him kill time: by now you have forgotten the title and the author's name, but a moment ago they "reminded you of something"; you know that in this novel "there are characters who are rather like the people who have come and gone in this compartment throughout the trip"; yet "during this particular trip you would like for once to be completely inside what you are doing," and this is why you have not read and will not read this story, which would separate you from what you are determined not to be distracted from or, inversely, would turn out to be so consistent with your present concern that it could only precipitate a catastrophe. Ignored because it is assumed to be unequal (being either too little or too much) to what the character proposes to do, the book neverthe-

[3] In his contribution to the debate "Why and How Do You Read?" organized by *Cercle ouvert* on October 9, 1956, Michel Butor contrasted "informational reading (which includes reading newspapers, for instance) and artistic reading (which includes reading novels and poems). . . . The words on the page of a novel are only markers on a road the reader himself is traveling. It is he who summons to his imagination the characters, objects, landscapes indicated by the author." As a result, artistic reading "mobilizes a much larger part of our mind than informational reading" and is not without danger, "bad books being those that plunge the mind into pernicious habits, mystify it and obscure it instead of developing it, nourishing it."

less exists, and this theme will attain its full amplitude in the wanderer's search in his dream, a search that briefly takes the traditional form of the quest for the lost book, that is, the compendium of supreme wisdom. To the two-faced watchman who asks him where he is, what he is doing, and what he wants, the character indicates the true goal of his quest, "the search for the book I lost because I did not even know it was in my possession, because I had not even taken care to make out its title, though it was the only real baggage I took away with me on my adventure"; to which the watchman answers that it is not impossible that the searcher will find sufficiently well-preserved Italian versions of it but that perhaps he does not know Italian well enough to be able to read them. Once in Rome (where in fact he will not be offered any book), the dreamer undergoes the difficult experience of finding that he is almost totally incapable of making himself understood (as though there were a wall between him and others similar to the wall that has grown up gradually between his wife and him), and the dream as a whole will appear marked by the idea of the obstacles standing in the way of communication, here represented by the character's language deficiency, then his inability even to articulate. In parallel fashion, his reflections in his waking state lead him to think that it will be impossible for him to explain to his mistress, without there being a misunderstanding about his real motives, why he has decided not to help her move to Paris and that the best thing to do, if he does not want to say anything to her about this plan he has just barely begun to carry out, would be not to go see her. This recognition of the practical impossibility of being understood, obliging him to say nothing in important circumstances, necessarily causes him to react by resolving to express himself in such a way that he can be understood by other people, so that the traveler will make the decision to write this book, the outcome of a journey that will not have corresponded to what he was expecting but will have enlightened him as to the more profound nature of the goal he was pursuing, a goal of which Rome is an image whose outlines remain unclear, whether one examines it with the naked eye or pushes one's scholarly knowledge of it as far as possible.

"I cannot hope to save myself alone," the character says to himself as the train approaches the station of Roma Trastevere. "Therefore, to prepare, to allow this future freedom that is beyond our reach to come into being, for instance by means of a book, to allow it to establish itself to some degree, no matter how infinitesimal that may be, is the only possibility I have of enjoying at least its very admirable and poignant glimmer." Thus the book mythically lost, sought, then found again by the character is actually *his own* book, the one he was holding in his hand from the beginning without knowing it and which, as the guarantee of a freedom that is inaccessible in the present circumstances but cannot remain completely so, for that would be unacceptable, will be a way out for him and will also be a hand reaching out toward another, since to write is to offer oneself to be read and, by definition, to interrupt one's solitude by communicating with others and making available to them what one has been able to discover. If the character's final choice, where his affections are concerned, is to reconcile himself with the real woman (the one whose childhood memory has come back to haunt him) and leave the matter of the mythological woman up to time, not breaking off anything, either, as regards the two cities (between which he will continue to go back and forth), he chooses, by becoming a writer, to exercise a *real* activity, unlike either his chimerical search for Rome or the typewriter business.

Isn't it true that what this character was seeking, he who in his dream experiences a thirst similar to that which the mystics speak of, what he was seeking through his loves as through his pilgrimages to Rome—the capital of the ancient world, then of the Catholic world, a paradise where a Fountain of the Four Rivers flows in the Piazza Navona, the mythic home of the "father" (that father you are seeking, says the Sibyl, "so that he may teach you the future of your race") and the actual home of the woman whom the character calls "Gateway to Rome," perhaps not knowing that this epithet, so like "Gateway to Heaven" in the litanies of the Virgin, expressly posits her as the image of the Eternal Feminine—was something equivalent to the absolute designated by the mysterious figure of the *central point* or supreme point that appears in hermetic literature: the place where contraries merge and paradoxes are resolved, fulcrum of universal life, core that is immutable despite the succession of modifications?[4]

The typewriter salesman cannot penetrate the secret of Rome anymore than Kafka's surveyor could enter the castle; but he nevertheless discovers that "this principal focus of marvels and obscurities" by nature eludes any attempt at even an approximate description, and by writing a book (which amounts to preparing the way for, or throwing the dice for, a possible freedom) he will be vindicated, like the surveyor, whose place in the village is acknowledged in extremis. The book that he will write, conceived to be read and therefore *literary*, will contain the very thing that could have drawn him to the other book "in which there must be somewhere, however briefly, however falsely, however badly expressed, a man in difficulty who would like to save himself, who is taking a trip and who sees that the road he has taken does not lead where he thought it did." After contemplating making it a work of the imagination showing "the role Rome might play in the life of a man in Paris," he rejects this plan as inadequate and resolves to write not exactly a confession (which would make him remain a failure by limiting himself to confirming that failure) but a narrative in which the experience he has undergone will come to life again for others—the very same narrative you have read and of which (if you follow to the end the impetus provided by the use of the second person) you will discover that there could be no other author but yourself, since you were its main actor.

Now the fact is that you are, as it happens, neither an author nor

[4]See Michel Butor's article, already old now, entitled "Le Point suprême et l'âge d'or," *Arts et lettres* 4, no. 15 (1950) (an issue devoted to Jules Verne).

an actor but a simple reader of a novel, one in which nothing seems to result from whim or chance, neither the haunting presence of the trompe l'oeil setting nor the use of the second person (which the novelist has explained elsewhere), a novel that supposedly corresponds, as though to be even more rigorous, to its hero's apparently imperious need to write. Then where is your correct place in all this, you who have allowed yourself to be caught in the trap of a process that seemed inclined, if not to identify you with the character, at least to implicate you in the story?

In the case of this novel, so scrupulously realistic (since even those of its elements associated with the marvelous are connected to the character's physical situation or state of mind), in the case of this novel whose architecture, at once classical and luxuriant (like that of a baroque monument), has as its cornerstone a dawning awareness, what takes place—between the writer and you, the reader—is that here the threatening use of *you* seems to be an actual incitement for you, too, to become aware and to enter the action in such a way that the story of this Parisian bourgeois who has been enlightened about his true desires by some twenty hours in a railway car becomes (if it is not already) an equivalent of your own story and, in its strictly photographic modernity, the myth through which the mediocrity of your existence may assume the lofty appearance of a destiny.

"Who are you? Where are you going? What are you looking for? Whom do you love? What do you want? What are you waiting for? What are you feeling? Can you see me? Can you hear me?" These questions, which are heralded by the lament of the Master of the Royal Hunt and which seem, like that lament, to be hurled at everyone indiscriminately, are asked by a stranger ("who wears the same clothes as you, but undamaged, and carries in his hand a suitcase of the same model as yours and seems a little older than you") in the dream, when the character, arrested and brought before a police commissioner, has changed from wanderer to accused. These questions, asked in the second-person plural, as though there were some secret similarity between the narrative you are reading and the questions the character hears, remain unanswered in the book, just as the enigma of Rome remains unsolved. But this book, which for the alleged author is a fragment of autobiography and for the real author a fiction whose *authenticity* (in the absence of any veracity) could not be in doubt and which must therefore more or less retrace (in transposed terms) the experience that led to its development, this book that is the achievement of both the real author and the alleged author and that could only have helped them—both—to know who they are, is a step toward an answer and a solution.

The second person is not only the person of the imperative mood par excellence, it can also be regarded as the person most illustrative of questioning, since a question, whatever grammatical form it takes, is always directly addressed to someone (either someone else, or an imaginary being, or the one asking the question). Isn't the second-person plural also the person employed in school when formulating subjects for expository themes or problems, those other forms of interrogation? Wondering if the priest in his compartment might not be a teacher, the character tirelessly invents fantastic subjects this educator might dictate to his students: "Imagine that you want to separate from your wife; write to her explaining the situation"; "Imagine that you are a Jesuit father; write your superior to tell him you are going to leave the society." Challenged by these subjects, the student would have only to turn himself into a husband or a Jesuit father in his imagination and look into himself to grasp his reasons and formulate them exactly.

The use of the second-person plural throughout a narrative that, viewed in this light, appears a vast subject for an expository theme or a detailed outline for a meditation or an examination of conscience seems, therefore—whatever might be the compositional motives that determined this choice—to be a way of referring back to you (to this anonymous *you* that could be pronounced *everyone*) the question whose announcement or reminder it is, in page after page where so many different genres, from the impressionistic to the didactic, overlap, inspired by an anecdote so ordinary that one is tempted to see it as a snare when, the more attentively one scrutinizes the book, the more layers one discovers.[5] It goes without saying that this questioning—which starts off prejudicially with the Master of the Royal Hunt's "Can you hear me?" and of which a precise account is given in a "marvelously intelligible" voice by the stranger who resembles the character, and consequently you too, like a brother—can have no general answer and that the one who hears it can only enter in a positive spirit the labyrinth, a model of which is proposed by this novel in which everything, of course, happens twice over in a closed circuit, since the character comes back to his point of departure in his private life and since, with the book closing at the moment he prepares to write it, the end joins the beginning—this novel which only appears to be placed under the negative sign of eternal repetition, because the character who will write will no longer be what he was when he took the Paris-Rome train and will therefore have gone from one point to another while the compartment was moving through space, the compartment where this substitute for yourself who had nothing of the metaphysician about him was gradually confronted with this extremely dizzying problem: the agreement of one consciousness with another or with something other than itself.

Make your descent into hell. It is your turn to make the pilgrimage, now that you have made it "through reading," thanks to this work, which will not only have allowed there to be a communication between you and the author but which also contains a lesson. You, to whom the word will have been transmitted by way of this novel, may now attain what will be *your* book (without necessarily being a book) and will perhaps turn out to be very different from what you origi-

[5] So much so that the task of reviewing a book like this is as discouraging as it is exciting: each time one looks at it closely, one sees new prospects opening out and new relationships forming among its various elements. In the end one must resign oneself to suspending the investigation, if one does not want to become involved in composing yet another book.

nally believed you were looking for, because for you the itinerary can change as it changed for the character, who found his truth somewhere quite different from where his train was taking him and won the match when he seemed to have lost it irretrievably, as though the game he had taken part in (through the effect of some act of mercy or inadvertently) had been a game of whoever-loses-wins.

Reverdy, Everyday Poet

*E*ver since the romantic era, it has been hard to conceive of the poet in any other way than as a creature not quite of this world. We see clairvoyance in one, madness in another, and the numerous ways in which, by vocation or destiny, a person may prove himself to be on the fringes of society—through suicide or some other tragic end, through giving way to some kind of poison, through rebellion, through the deliberate adoption of dandyism or humor, through a quasi-mystical devotion to the exercise of his art (which was what we saw in Mallarmé, the peaceful English teacher), if not through pure and simple excess (as in the case of Whitman)—demonstrating, it seems, that any great poet of our time is inhabited by a demon that varies according to the individual but always, either directly or insidiously, leaves the mark of its claw on the life it has victimized.

A contemporary of Apollinaire (a brilliant mind prematurely and treacherously annihilated by an epidemic) and of Max Jacob (who fell victim to a pestilent racism after living a profoundly divided life), Pierre Reverdy was made of the wood that authentic poets are carved from, the wood that—in an earlier century—had already been about to change into a gallows for one François Villon. Yet there is nothing spectacular about the character in which death has frozen him: no vice, no irrationality, no unhappiness greater (or hardly greater) than falls to the lot of anyone else, and except for his impetuousness and touchiness, no trait in his character or in the events of his life that would provide material for legend. Certainly that char-

First published in *Le Mercure de France*, no. 1181 (1960) (memorial issue, "Pierre Reverdy [1889–1960]," ed. Maurice Saillet).

acter was a rough one and that life contained some difficult times, disappointments, and turbulent periods, but his poetry—whose tone was generally mezza voce and which did not tend to burst out in broad lyrical effusions or crystallize into diamonds except at rare moments—depicted this faithfully. Such as he was, and with a life story whose most striking highlights were his conversion to Catholicism and the semiretreat that followed it, then his loss of faith, Reverdy will nevertheless remain an exemplary poet. Not only did he make the image the flesh and blood of the poem, but, because he did not provide fodder for lovers of myths, he forced respect by the frankness of his game as well as by the distance he was able to take without posing, live, for his future statue.

A hotheaded and passionate man, a man who was absolutely open but subject to so many rages that association with him, despite his lofty good-heartedness, was sometimes difficult, a poet whose work obviously shows that for him poetry was something on the order of daily bread or the air one breathes (so completely incorporated that a healthy radiance emanated from his whole being even in his blackest moments)—this was what Pierre Reverdy was. If he did not have as wide an audience as he deserved, wasn't it because of this very authenticity, which eliminated all brio from his work and led him, in his relations with literary circles, to choose to behave like a peasant from the Danube or even an Iroquois? But the side of his poetry having to do with everyday experiences, in which the realities of outside and inside speak to each other without sparkling vocabulary or syntax, the aspect it assumes, being the point of view from which the world is perceived once and for all, rather than a form in which one chooses to recast it, or a gloss for which it is a pretext, or a reflection on what its progress has caused us to suffer, has been a lesson for many poets of the generation that followed him and is still bearing fruit for some of them, though they may not know it.

So that in Pierre Reverdy, one finds oneself confronting this paradox: that here was someone who, equally untouched by malediction and renown, was in the strict sense of the word misunderstood and who suffered this not only as an injustice but also as an affront to poetry; someone who, because of his inability to deceive, proposed a vision of things sharp enough and new enough to exert, through the narrow channel of writings that were most often subdued and not very apt to cause a loud stir, an influence as revolutionary as that of his friends the cubist painters on the poetic sensibility of our century.

On Raymond Queneau

The first time I met Raymond Queneau was in 1924; I did not yet belong to the surrealists, and neither did he. I was vacationing in Nemours, where I have had family for a long time. With me were André Masson, Armand Salacrou (both of my generation), and the cubist painter Juan Gris. One day, our friend Roland Tual came to see us, accompanied by a young man he had met on the train from Le Havre and with whom he had struck up a conversation. It was Raymond Queneau. I remember him quite well. He was much thinner than he is today, very pale (he still is a little, in fact), and seemed very shy. During the several hours he spent with us, he barely spoke more than a few words. At the time I was twenty-three years old, and he was perhaps twenty or twenty-one. At that age, a few years more or less mattered! As he told me later, he considered us "older," as people already part of the literary and artistic world, whereas he felt he was still on the fringes. I must confess that during that meeting he did not make a big impression on us.

A year or two later, I saw him again at a meeting of the surrealists at the Certa bar (which no longer exists). The subject of the Orient—one that preoccupied many of the surrealists at that time—was being discussed. Queneau spoke up and, without dropping his reserved attitude, talked about Asian philosophies and civilizations as a man who obviously knew the subject better than any of us. At that point a few of us realized that behind his silence and self-

Interview with Jacques Bens published in *Queneau* (Paris: Gallimard, La Bibliothèque Idéale, 1962).

effacement, Queneau was concealing an extremely acute mind and a broad education.

His attitude did not change during the whole time he associated with the surrealists: he was always someone in the background, whose behavior made it hard to predict that he would become the great writer he has become. This seems to me worth pointing out. Certainly he was a conscientious, even scrupulous, surrealist, but probably more by nature than through any real conviction: the way he did everything he set out to do, like a good technician. In fact, it was only after he left that he assumed his true role. *Le Chiendent*, his first book, seemed to represent a sudden, marvelous blossoming.

After he left surrealism, he was a contributor to *Documents*, of which Georges Bataille was the moving spirit and which, during a certain period, was the organ of surrealist dissidence. I contributed to it too, and I believe it was at about that time that we actually became friends. Later, we both—along with Bataille—were part of the Cercle Communiste Démocratique, which published a journal, *La Critique sociale*, edited by Boris Souvarine. As he had in the days of *La Révolution surréaliste*, Queneau here proved to be rather withdrawn; probably no group activity really suited him.

In his works, as we know, Raymond Queneau has always attached a good deal of importance to structure. Perhaps this stems from his love of mathematics? I can tell you an anecdote that seems significant to me. Sometime in the thirties, we went to the Salle Pleyel together to hear a concert in which *Art of the Fugue* was played. I recall that we followed this with great excitement and said to each other as we were leaving that it would be very interesting to do something like it in a literary way (regarding Bach's work not as counterpoint and fugue but as the construction of a work by means of variations proliferating almost infinitely around a rather meager theme). In my opinion, Queneau succeeded in doing this with his *Exercices de style*, which it would be a mistake to regard as simply humorous.

Another characteristic in him that strikes me is his horror of the exotic. As you doubtless are aware, he does not much like to travel, and this may seem surprising, since we know he has a tireless curiosity about all things. He probably looks upon exoticism—that mythicizing of what is *foreign*—as mystification pure and simple. I remember that he and I went on holiday together to Ibiza, in the Balearic Islands, just before the outbreak of the Spanish Civil War. Neither Queneau nor his wife knew Spain, whereas I was a fervent admirer of it. In Barcelona I took them all over. We saw churches, museums, nightclubs, markets. We attended a bullfight, one of the most mediocre I had ever seen. It was all a little like the stories about table turning, in which as long as one person is present who does not believe in it, nothing will happen. I sensed fairly soon that Raymond was not in the same mood I was in, that he was closing himself off more and more. I think he was positively disturbed by my obstinate enthusiasm. Frankly disappointed, he refused to allow himself to be enticed by the showiness of the picturesque. I think he is still exactly the same about this. When he travels, it is not so much to discover something new as to rediscover, in another place, his own familiar folklore—that entirely personal folklore that the half-serious, half-ironic use of one or several rhetorics allows him to transform, masterfully, into a highly singular and effective poetry.

Alberto Giacometti
(on a Postage Stamp
or Medallion)

Placed at life's limit, at art's boundary, Justin
Prérogue was a painter.

APOLLINAIRE, *L'Hérésiarque et Cie*

*I*n 1914 a schoolboy named Alberto Giacometti, son of a respected painter, sculpted a bust from life: this was his real beginning
as an artist, after the period of childhood drawings, of which the oldest he can recall illustrated an episode from a fairy tale—Snow
White in a little coffin, surrounded by the seven dwarves. One being
a copy of a flesh-and-blood creature while the other was a representation of imaginary beings, might not the bust and the illustration
correspond to two desires that existed side by side for a long time but
finally merged, two desires that have ceaselessly burned in the life
and art of their author: to give an account of what exists and to express an inner amazement?

To study the immense mass of the unknown offered by the outside
world, to give form to a few particles of the fairyland one bears
within oneself—it seems clear that this twofold desire is the desire
of every painter and sculptor worthy of the name. Painting and

Written on the occasion of Giacometti's being awarded the Grand Prix de Sculpture
at the Venice Biennial Exhibition. It appeared in Italian (with no translator's name)
in *La Biennale di Venezia* 48 (1962), then in French in *L'Arc* 5, no. 20 (1962), from
Aix-en-Provence.

sculpture, in fact, when they are not entirely divorced from representation, pose this basic problem: how to create an image or an object that will be both a reality, convincing by its structure alone, the faithful transcription of the remembered or invented motif, and the expression of an essentially fleeting moment of subjectivity? What is admirable is that Giacometti has explicitly posed himself this problem, implicit for most people; that he has so completely accepted its simple but implacable terms; that with such stubbornness he has played his game without ever trying to deceive; and that he has obstinately avoided false solutions, such as cutting the Gordian knot when one should really untangle it.

Until the end of the last war, Giacometti devoted himself almost solely to the arts that use space as their theater of operations, whether he executed sculptures sometimes reduced to no more than barely modeled plaques (responding to the little he was truly *certain* he remembered of a figure perceived) or endowed with an organization that was more complex but still closely tied to lived experience, or whether he composed varieties of elementary machine constructions or curious little groupings that drew their life from their capacity— real or fictive—to work, or whether he fabricated precious moving objects that were just as much living presences as they were fragments of life's setting.

Yet these were still only fumbling explorations, reconnaissances, and skirmishes before the hand-to-hand combat with a truth that was not to reveal itself completely until 1945, as stupefying as it was dazzling. In two interviews, one for radio and the other for a Paris weekly, Giacometti told the story of this event, which could without exaggeration be described as an illumination, even though it remained within the bounds of what anyone might possibly observe any day (but then wasn't this also true of the philosopher's cogito?).

In a newsreel cinema he realized suddenly that the people projected on the screen were only "ill-defined, moving black spots" and looking at the people next to him, he discovered that they "looked completely unfamiliar." As he left the cinema, the boulevard appeared to him in a way he had never seen it before ("the beauty of the *Thousand and One Nights*" in "a sort of incredible silence"), and from that day on, he began to feel "a sort of continual wonder at everything, no matter what it was." Little by little, there was a "transformation in my vision of everything . . . as though movement had become a succession of points of immobility." The isolation and inertia of things, frozen in their pure identity, touched him to the point of anguish. Thenceforth he was to fix his attention exclusively on the most ordinary reality: what he found in it was a "marvelous unknown," which can only point the artist toward a Danaidean task, for, the moment one accedes to this unknown by looking into it without the screens of culture interposed between one's eye and what one is seeing, to try to fill the emptiness left by this fleeting sensation through one's work amounts to trying to fill something that has no bottom. Today Giacometti would believe he had been successful if he managed simply to form a nose in a suitable way: once this modest miracle was accomplished, no doubt the rest would come too.

The reduction of figures to the size of pins, or the reverse, their prodigious elongation. The emaciation of these figures or the budding of their aggressive protuberances. Nervous touches of the paintbrush, at once color and drawing, composing a sort of scrawl from which the figure emerges (looming out suddenly but not torn from its context). Strokes broadly slashed (almost always more than one, as though a single stroke could be only a partial account) or lines bending in an infinity of turns and returns (as though the stroke were now looking for itself). Such are the marks left—varying according to the period and the technique chosen—by the fight to the death that Giacometti wages with reality in order to penetrate it more effectively, now using almost indiscriminately all the professional skills of which he is past master, though he cannot recognize this because of his horror of overestimating himself and also because the loftiness of his ambition demands the relentless application of a new sort of *methodical doubt*: sculpture, painting, drawing, engraving, which he has come to the point of practicing almost simultaneously.

As though he accepted literally the assertion of one of the very great poets of our century, according to whom it is most essential that every work of art be *situated*, Giacometti attaches a major importance to the question of the relationship of the figures with their surrounding space and to distancing them correctly, an extremely tricky question, since several radically distinct distances come into play: that between the artist and the being or thing that has aroused his emotion, that at which the viewer must in his imagination place the substitute for that being or that thing so that the original emotion is recreated, a distance different from that which physically separates him from the work as such. A question whose complexity is indefinitely multiplied by the fact that it is posed not only for the work as a whole but for each of the parts into which the subject is infinitely divisible (so that if one contemplates it carefully one soon drowns in it), parts that—whatever the case—must be treated as a function of the relations that connect them to the viewer and the relations that unite them among themselves (without any preestablished relation allowing one to deduce their respective proportions and their interconnections within the work).

Determined to resolve problems that are perhaps the ABC of art but that, because of their very fundamental nature, cannot honestly be broached without a total questioning, Giacometti seems to have been dedicated for some years now to perpetually renewing the attempt that, if he felt it was successful, would still be for him only a beginning of beginnings: for instance, to make a good likeness that would not be a false pretense.

Giacometti's greatness can be measured not only by the beauty— always so extraordinarily in suspense—of those results that he is willing to save among all that he undertakes (at the same time denying that they are any more than simple trials), but also by the greatness of a venture that is probably unprecedented: without rejecting what artists of all periods and in all places have produced that is exciting, to approach art as though it had not yet been invented and, as much a stranger to feigned naïveté as to deliberate primitivism, to recreate, day after day, the immemorial invention that will always remain to be created.

A Look at Alfred Métraux

The following speech, delivered at the UNESCO House gathering in honor of Alfred Métraux, was only a token of friendship, in no way indicating what I owe the deceased.

I believe it was in 1934 that Alfred Métraux and I first met. He was returning from a long stay in South America and I had just made my first trip to sub-Saharan Africa. I did not yet have my degree, and I was still a novice ethnographer, even something of an isolated case, since I had become interested in these studies through poetry and the desire to shake off the yoke of our culture rather than a taste for science as such. Though he was already a recognized ethnologist, Métraux still treated me like a colleague. At the Ecole des Chartes he had formed a friendship with Georges Bataille that was to remain strong even after one became a great scholar and the other a great writer, and he must have been happy to become acquainted with one of the closest companions of his old schoolmate and no less happy to be able to talk with a neophyte whose essentially "surrealist" training differed profoundly enough from his own so that he could find it complementary. For my part, I was drawn by this expert's open spirit, by his inclination to roam, which incited him to leave home intellectually as well as physically, by his intensely alive curiosity, by his sharp sense of the burlesque, and by the sudden gestures that showed how deceptive was his rather puritan appearance, that of a correct civil servant.

Within the profession, where he was my elder by qualification even though a little younger in age, I always benefited from his support—close at hand or

Speech delivered June 17, 1963, at UNESCO House and subsequently published in *Le Mercure de France*, no. 1200 (1963). Reprinted in 1964 (preceded by the note included here) in *L'Homme* 4, no. 2.

from a distance—and from the lessons I was able to draw from his multi-faceted experience. Moreover, I am grateful to this ethnologist totally devoted to his profession for having in no way tried—quite the contrary—to induce me to sacrifice literature to science. There is no doubt that for him the two fields were related and that he brought to bear, beyond the distinctions of the two disciplines, a passionate interest in everything that could help men understand things better and understand themselves better too.

When, after long years of an affectionate sympathy, we actually came to work together, it was on the level of a rigorously informed, active humanism for the cause of opposing racism, a cause for which Métraux was a stubborn militant. Thence the publication, under the imprint of UNESCO, of Race et civilisation, *which he had requested from me as part of the series "La Question raciale devant la science moderne," and then, with a preface by him,* Contacts de civilisations en Martinique et en Guadeloupe, *resulting from a mission he had assigned me to examine the problem of relations between Whites and people of color in the two Antilles, which he himself would later visit, purely for pleasure.*

The many professional and semiprofessional conversations I had with him, in Paris as well as in Haiti, where we happened to be together in 1948, were certainly a great help to me in gaining insight into a subject that was one of our shared preoccupations, scientifically and humanly: cults based on possession, two fine examples of which had been offered us by Ethiopian zâr and Haitian voodoo. A few years before he chose to cut short his sufferings with a fatal dose of a drug, I was pleased to accept for the series "L'Espèce humaine"—in which his Ile de Pâques *had already appeared—the work Métraux had written on voodooism. But I owed this pleasure not only to the prejudicial fact that he was the author of the book; for along with Dr. Paul Rivet and Georges-Henri Rivière, it was Métraux who, before the last war, had founded the series I was now editing, and it was essentially he who had established its early program and determined its character.*

Yet all of this is very little compared to what Métraux gave me, not only through the extent and diversity of his knowledge, never encumbered by pedantry, but through personal contact with him. Let me simply say that he and

*his old friend Bataille are among the few who have taught me that nothing
is worth more than the combination of qualities so few people exhibit: a fierce
ardor for life joined to a relentless awareness of the absurdity of this ardor.*

As I reread the few books I own by Alfred Métraux so as to pay
tribute to him more effectively, I came upon a dedication in the front
of my copy of *Vaudou haïtien*. I confess I had forgotten this dedication, but since I reread it, it has haunted me to such an extent that I
am now astonished that I had not immediately perceived all its resonance: "To Michel, in memory of our wanderings, these naive devilries which console us."

In 1948 I had met my old friend Métraux in Haiti when I was
making a brief visit there, and in fact our wanderings had been extensive in Port-au-Prince and its surroundings, not to mention the
side trip we made to Tortue Island, lair of the old-time pirates. Over
several weeks Métraux took me to voodoo sanctuaries, either to visit
the friends he had made among the voodooists or to attend séances in
which we were the interested and enchanted witnesses of scenes of
possession. These "naive devilries," which appeared as such to us for
the simple reason that we did not believe in them, were nevertheless
exciting spectacles. Not only was this rich material for research, but
it was moving to see people forget their generally miserable condition for a few hours by incarnating the gods they revered. For Westerners like us, who remained rather constrained, it was also com-
forting to see ceremonies like these, which were admirably well
organized but in which the mythological drunkenness of the trance
played the largest part.

What strikes me now about the few lines that Alfred Métraux
wrote for me in a copy of that great book, *Vaudou haïtien*, is their extreme melancholy.

"Our wanderings." In this way he qualified as a sort of vagabondage the comings and goings that were actually justified by the demands of our profession. As though the theme of wandering or the impossibility of settling down peacefully had been a major theme for him, a theme representing the need to be elsewhere that, quite apart from his scholarly curiosity, drove him to make so many trips and to choose as fields for his observations so many different terrains: South America, Polynesia, the Antilles, Africa.

"These naive devilries." Clearly, the words express a regret, something like a nostalgia for what Baudelaire called "the green paradise of our childish loves." If rationalism forbids any attitude other than that of disbelief when one is confronted with cults based on possession, isn't that a shame, and wouldn't it be better, more naive, to enter fully into these transparent marvels?

Devilries "which console us." Since we lack a system by which we could live a mythology, is it not somewhat consoling to know that in other climates there are men hospitable enough—as the Haitian voodooists ordinarily are—to allow us to take part in their rituals, rituals whose beauty and the serious or clownish acts for which they are the occasion compensate us (on a level that is for us, admittedly, only that of a game) for what is often too stifling about our daily lives?

A wanderer, a man who knows what it's all about but is none the prouder for it, someone in whose depths dwells a sorrow for which he must be consoled, such is the man who—in ten words or so and very probably without thinking about it—revealed himself in so extraordinary a way.

Returning to what I felt when I reread Alfred Métraux, I realize that what makes his writings valuable, besides their high merit as documents, is the *emotional* relation one always perceives between him and what he is studying: places as well as people, never confined to the simple role of subjects of observation; the past as well as the present, when Métraux examines the legends or the tragic acts with which certain lands are associated, then follows them to their wretched present-day conditions.

In the best known of these works, the object of study is viewed in the broadest of perspectives, one that embraces at once all the diversity of the object itself, history with a capital *H* as well as historiography, and even Alfred Métraux's own history and judgment, which he is not above including, as though he had always been convinced—intuitively, even before he learned it—that every observation is a relationship between someone looking and something looked at.

For him, Peru is inseparable from the myth of El Dorado and all the cruel scenes that were enacted there both at the time the Incas ruled and during the period of the conquistadores; but these marvels of the past fascinate him, so that he cannot resign himself to leaving them behind and ends the book he has devoted to the ancient Andean empire by imagining a possible rebirth of Inca power.

Easter Island is the island Métraux had heard about when he was twelve years old, the island where travelers who visited it before him had had their own adventures or misadventures, the island where he himself encountered a number of people, natives and others, who were for him the means of acquiring information—as was appropriate—but also more than mere means: living beings whom he depicts as such, giving us the illusion that we have known them ourselves.

The same is true when he speaks of the initiates of Haitian voodoo who were his informants and of their meeting places, described as places where he was a constant visitor and, in the end, felt at home.

A personal anecdote—which I will take the liberty of telling— seems to me to show clearly the care Alfred Métraux took to go beyond purely scientific description to attain something tangible and alive. When we were in Port-au-Prince together, spending most of our time attending voodoo séances in the working-class districts from which we generally came back on foot fairly late at night, Métraux once asked me—like someone who is searching for the answer to a secret and counts on the other person to reveal it to him—how one could find a way to give an exact account of the character of these streets we walked through so often and the appearance of their houses. I think I disappointed him a little by answering that I was as puzzled as he was about this and that I, too, could not see what description would help one make these streets and houses truly perceptible and present for someone who had never seen them. Such concern on Métraux's part was not just the concern of the specialist, avid for precision, but a truly *poetic* concern: not to be content with describing things but, having grasped them in all their singular reality, to make them come alive in the eyes of the person reading what he had written.

What I admire in Alfred Métraux, therefore, is that he was not only a scrupulous observer and a man whose vast culture did not fail to have its picturesque corners, as well as an ethnologist conscious of all the human obligations implied by his science, but also what I call a poet. What I mean by this is not so much someone who writes poems, but someone who strives for an absolute understanding of that in which he lives and who breaks through his isolation by communicating this understanding. Perhaps, paradoxically, Alfred Métraux attained this sort of fullness when he drifted off to sleep, all alone, in a secluded spot in the Chevreuse valley.

From the Impossible Bataille
to the Impossible Documents

*I*t was through his colleague at the Bibliothèque Nationale, Jacques Lavaud, like him a former student at the Ecole des Chartes and the author of a thesis on Philippe Desportes, that I first met Georges Bataille. Sometime during 1924, the year I also became a surrealist, Lavaud—whom I had known for some time and who, quite a bit older than I, had introduced me to modern literature—brought us together, partly (as he told me later) to see, as a detached observer, what strange precipitate might result from the meeting. This meeting took place one evening in a very peaceful, bourgeois spot close to the Elysée Palace, at Café Marigny, at a time of year I no longer remember (though it was probably not summer, because I believe Bataille was wearing not only a gray felt hat but a black and white herringbone town overcoat).

I very quickly became friends with Georges Bataille, who was slightly older than I. I admired not only his education, which was much more extensive and diverse than mine, but also his nonconformist spirit and his "black humor," though people did not yet call it that. I was also conscious of the appearance of this person, who, rather thin and looking at once modern and romantic, possessed (in

First printed in *Critique* 15, nos. 195–196 (1963) ("Hommage à Georges Bataille"). Here I revert to the definition of "impossible" in my manuscript, which differs from that printed in *Critique* (p. 690), an obscure formulation that furthermore was disfigured by a misprint: "That which evades the limits established for listening to [*écouter*, 'to listen' instead of *écarter*, 'to avoid'] every threat against the use of the possible."

a more youthful form, of course, and with less discretion) the elegance he would always retain, even when his heavier bearing gave him the almost peasantlike air that most people were familiar with, an elegance that went very deep and that manifested itself without any vain ostentation in his clothing. His eyes were rather close together and deepset, rich in all the *blue of noon*, and his teeth curiously resembled those of a wild animal, often bared by a laugh which (perhaps wrongly) I felt was sarcastic.

Paul Valéry, whom Bataille regarded as the most perfect representative of academicism, was for him—because of this very perfection—a number-one enemy. The dada spirit did not meet with his approval either, and he spoke of the opportunity there might be to launch a *Yes* movement, which would imply a perpetual acquiescence to all things and would be superior to the *No* movement of dada in that it would avoid the childishness of a systematic, provocative negation. A plan we mulled over for some time, but that never came to anything, was the plan we had of starting a magazine, like so many young intellectuals who have recently come to be friends and have discovered that they share a number of views about literature and other things. The most notable singularity of this plan was that we decided to make the headquarters of our periodical, if we could, a brothel in the old quarter of Saint-Denis, an establishment our nightly strolls had led us to and whose rather sordid decrepitude had charmed us. We would have tried, of course, to involve the female personnel in the editing of the magazine, and on December 24 I noted down—with eventual publication in mind—several dreams that two of the girls had described to us. From Gaby: "I had made a piece of embroidery for a slip. I soaked it in the wash basin to clean it; the current carried it off. I jumped in to retrieve it, but instead of water I saw stairs, endless stairs." Also from Gaby: "I buy a revolver to kill my little sister's friend. The more I saw blood, the more I wanted to shoot." From Marinette: "I was walking with a group of little dogs and a little white cat. I was holding the dogs on a leash, but not the cat. They changed into a cloud."

At that time, Bataille had not yet revealed himself as a writer. His *Histoire de l'œil* had not yet appeared, nor had the article on the Aztecs that he wrote on the occasion of a very official exhibition of pre-Columbian art and that gave some idea of the half-objective, half-passionate style he was to develop so brilliantly. Yet we could not have known each other long when he talked to me about a novel in which he was including himself in the guise of the famous murderer Georges Tropmann (his partial namesake) but which later took the form of a narrative in the first person. Maybe this was *W.C.*, the manuscript he destroyed in the end? One episode of this novel has survived, the story of "Dirty" (evidently the deliberate soiling of the first name "Dorothy"), first published separately—headed by an epigraph taken from Hegel and a short note but barely altered at all—then republished as the introduction to *Le Bleu du ciel*. As far as I can remember, this story, set in the London Savoy, was—in the state in which I originally knew it—a first chapter (the one we privately called the "Savoy chapter") followed by an episode in Belgium where one saw the young, beautiful, rich Englishwoman Dirty abandon herself, in company with the narrator, to an orgy with fish-wives in the fish market itself. A certain Mylord L'Arsouille aspect (which disappeared later, when Bataille got rid of all surface romanticism, though he continued to be ardent under his quiet exterior) appears in the sequence of these two chapters, where everything takes place between the two extremes of an aristocratic luxury and a literally fishwife vulgarity.

I am not sure, but it was perhaps during this first period of our friendship that Bataille had me read a work he felt was essential: Dostoyevski's *Notes from Underground*, a book whose hero and alleged writer is, as we know, fascinating for his stubborn determination to be what one familiarly calls an "impossible" man, outrageously ridiculous and hateful. However that may be, Bataille—at the time a habitué of gambling dens and the company of prostitutes, like so many heroes in Russian literature—thought enough of Dostoyevski that an allusion to the great novelist appears in the story of Dirty: "The preceding scene was, in short, worthy of Dostoyevski," he announces when he comes to describe—as a flashback—the scene of drunkenness and ignominious eroticism that unfolds in the grand London hotel.

Shortly after becoming friends with him, I brought Bataille into the group that had been a source of sustenance for me in art and poetry for about two years. This little group met at 45, rue Blomet, in the studio—very Dostoyevskian in its dilapidation—of the painter André Masson, who had already done some marvelous, vivid drawings whose sexual abandonment called to mind a return to the beginnings of the world and who was to be Bataille's great illustrator not only for *L'Histoire de l'œil* but also for texts in which eroticism, cosmogonic lyricism, and the philosophy of the sacred converged.

When I joined the surrealist movement, after Masson and a little before his neighbor Joan Miró, Bataille kept his distance from it. His only contribution to *La Révolution surréaliste* consisted of an introduction to a selection of *fatrasies*, published in issue number 6 with a note by him bearing no signature, not even his initials. It was owing to his erudition as a former student at the Ecole des Chartes that he knew these little thirteenth-century French poems, which one could consider masterpieces of nonsense; he had already spoken to me about them and it was to me that he sent them.

Mistrustful at first, then resolutely hostile (when, at the time he was the editor in chief of the magazine *Documents*, namely 1929 to 1930, he became the principal figure of the dissidence), Bataille—who, attacking like a wild boar, had addressed the refusal "Too many idealistic pests" to a surrealist invitation to discuss the "Trotsky case" in a rather broad colloquium—later became friends with Breton and also Eluard, drawn to them by mutual respect, and he even collaborated with them, literarily in *Minotaure* and politically when he initiated the antifascist movement *Contre-Attaque*, but he nevertheless remained alien to the group.

It was with *Documents* that Bataille found himself in the position of leader for the first time. Even though he in no sense exercised an unchecked power there, the magazine seems now to have been made in his image: a Janus publication turning one of its faces toward the higher spheres of culture (of which Bataille was willy-nilly a native through his vocation as well as his training) and the other toward a wild place into which one ventured without any sort of geographical map or passport.

Documents was published by the picture dealer Georges Wildenstein, who also put out *La Gazette des beaux-arts*, and the moving spirits behind it were, besides Bataille himself, Georges-Henri Rivière, then assistant director of the Musée d'Ethnographie du Trocadéro, and the German poet and aesthetician Carl Einstein, an expert in modern Western art and the author of the first work on Negro art. The contributors represented the most varied outlooks, since alongside some extremist writers—most of them defectors from surrealism who had rallied around Bataille—were representatives of widely different disciplines (art history, musicology, archaeology, ethnology, etc.), some of them members of the Institute or senior staff of museums or libraries. A truly "impossible" mixture, less because of the diversity of the disciplines—and lack of disciplines—than because of the disparity among the men themselves, some being frankly conservative or at the very least inclined (like Einstein) to speak as art historians or critics and nothing more, whereas others (like Bataille, whom Rivière supported and whom I assisted for some months as managing editor, succeeding a poet, Georges Limbour, and preceding an ethnologist, Marcel Griaule) did their best to use the magazine as a weapon to fight established ideas.

In the text of the advertisement circulated at the time the magazine was launched, certain paragraphs seem expressly to bear Bataille's mark: "The most irritating works of art, as yet unclassified, and certain incongruous productions, neglected until now, will be the subjects of studies as rigorous, as scientific, as those of the archaeologists. . . . What we envisage here, in general, are the most disturbing phenomena, those whose consequences have not yet been defined. In these different investigations, the sometimes absurd nature of the results or methods, far from being concealed, as always happens in conformity with the rules of seemliness, will deliberately be stressed, as much through a hatred of platitude as through a sense of the comic." One has only to leaf through the collection of *Documents* in chronological order to see that after its cautious beginnings, the stress was put on those articles of the program that in the beginning seemed simply to indicate the open spirit in which a periodical that essentially would not disappoint the expectations one would normally have of an art magazine was to be created. Under Bataille's direction, items that were irritating, incongruous, even troubling, soon ceased to be mere objects of study and became inherent features of the publication itself, a strange amalgam whose composition included many elements that were nonsensical, if only because of their proximity to certain texts that continued to reflect a most austerely scientific approach or to reproductions of old or modern works whose value was beyond question.

Bataille's first publications in *Documents* consisted of two articles that appeared to be fully worthy of him as an attaché to the Cabinet des Médailles and a graduate of the Ecole des Chartes: "Le Cheval académique," in which he discussed Gallic currency, and "L'Apocalypse de Saint-Sever," a description of a medieval manuscript. Yet themes that Bataille was to develop later are already clearly evident here: hairy forms (in this case, those of the Celtic figurations of the horse) representing "a response on the part of human darkness, burlesque and frightful, to the platitudes and arrogance of the idealists"; the invigorating role of "dirty or bloody deeds" (such as those described in the chansons de geste or in miniatures like those of Saint-Sever).

In issue number 3, under the paradoxically romantic title "Le Langage des fleurs," Bataille gives a first rough outline of the aggressively anti-idealist philosophy he was to embrace in different forms until, after having pondered at length the notion of the sacred, he would begin to work out that mystique of the "impossible" (namely that which goes beyond the limits of the possible and whose pursuit is therefore a pure act of despoiling) and that doctrine—or rather antidoctrine—of "not knowing" with which, in his middle age, he would go beyond the iconoclastic fury of his youthful revolts and be able to dispense to those who wanted to hear him an instruction all the more effective because it was fed by more experience and more knowledge and at the same time was more controlled. This article, which could be called inaugural, gave its author the chance to show some reproductions of plant forms that were quite improper (as though the impropriety were not a matter of one's judgment but inherent in nature itself) and to refer, in conclusion, to the famous gesture of the Marquis de Sade plucking petals off roses over a ditch of liquid manure. Yet it was not until issue number 4 that Bataille— the obstinate peasant, who could appear as though he were not up to anything, yet not let go of his idea—decided to put his cards squarely on the table.

Illustrated with photographs, one of which, taken in 1905, shows a lower-middle-class wedding with impossible embellishments, the others theater people and other characters dating from the turn of the century at the very latest, but with incredibly antiquated clothing, poses, or physiognomies, "Figure humaine" is a real outrage that Bataille, in presenting this clownish gallery of creatures with "madly improbable" appearances, actually men and women who could be our fathers and mothers, is perpetrating against the reassuring idea of a human nature whose continuity would imply "the permanence of certain conspicuous qualities" and against the very idea of "inserting nature into the order of reason." Soon after came "Le Gros Orteil," with which Bataille took a firm stand (so to speak): full-page reproductions of friendly big toes and a commentary setting out to argue that if the foot is laden with taboos and is an object of erotic fetishism, this is because it reminds man, whose feet are planted in the mud and whose head is raised toward heaven, that his life is no more than a "back-and-forth movement from ordure to ideal and ideal back to ordure." This anti-idealist passion was to find its most perfect expression in "Le Bas Matérialisme et la gnose," a text of Manichaean inspiration devoted, in principle, to Gnostic intaglios: dismissing both "God as abstraction (or simply idea) and abstract matter, the head warden and the prison walls," Bataille sees the monstrous deities represented on these stones—one of which is acephalous, a motif on which he will place great emblematic importance at a later time—as "the figuration of forms in which it is possible to see the image of this base matter, which alone, through its impropriety and a staggering lack of consideration, allows the intelligence to escape the constraint of idealism."

As an art magazine, *Documents* did not fail to carry out its program. Actual "documents" (such as those relating to the scandal caused by Courbet and Manet in their time or the unpublished text by the cubist Juan Gris) occupied their proper places in it. The current work of famous or already almost-recognized artists was observed from new points of view compared to those generally adopted by art critics, and that inexhaustible theme, Picasso, furnished the material for a special issue to which the great sociologist Marcel Mauss was not above contributing. In addition, it turned out, for example, that *Documents* was the first magazine, at least in France, to pay tribute to the genius of a man like Antoine Caron—among other older artists who were at that time almost completely ignored—as well as to pay attention to artists who were then unknown because they were just starting out, such as Alberto Giacometti and Gaston-Louis Roux, not to mention Salvador Dalí (who would soon join the surrealists, to Bataille's great displeasure). The fact that it dealt with phenomena that were often very marginal but more or less immediately involving aesthetics and entering into the field of ethnography or folklore was not a departure from the projected theoretical line, and as for his participation in the writing, Bataille himself—whatever conclusions he would come to—played the game, all told, by taking the analysis of forms or iconographic analysis as the point of departure for most of his articles. It is clear, nevertheless, that the art-loving public for whom the magazine was primarily intended was disconcerted not only by the tenor of Bataille's texts and those of his closest friends but also by what was, for an art magazine, a shocking break with custom in those years, the twenties: the lively interest taken in Afro-American or even Parisian vaudeville, in jazz, in talking movies, which were then stammering into existence, in beautiful movie stars from across the ocean, in one or another cabaret singer, in popular imagery in the style of the covers of *Fantômes* or illustrated news items, and in other peripheral subjects (anachronistic monuments in gardens and public squares, children's books, Mardi Gras masks); and along with this, the presence of photographs that Bataille—not without some mischievousness—inserted simply because they were unusual, even grotesque or dreadful.

Lodged on the premises of a business where we seemed a harebrained enclave, badly organized by ourselves and divided into different factions (which was a result of the composite nature of our team and explains in part the motley aspect of a magazine that brought together sharply incongruous elements rather than being merely eclectic), incapable of making sure our issues had the brilliant layout that would have softened their edges, we were in the end abandoned by our publisher, who was to a certain extent amused by the nonconformism of the magazine he was financing (as flattered, perhaps, as he was dismayed) but would nevertheless have liked it to be more profitable.

In the last issue Bataille devoted a long article to van Gogh that established a connection between the business of the cut ear and the theme of the sun, which is present in the painter's work sometimes directly and sometimes obliquely. We are aware of how heavily the theme of the blinding sun, associated with sacrifice as projection out of oneself into ecstasy or into death, bore on the entire work of the writer who, giving way on certain points but intractable when it came to confronting the reader with something confusing, was the leader of the game during that strange match of whoever-loses-wins, the *Documents* venture.

This periodical, most of whose steady contributors (Bataille and his acolytes with their baroque writings, almost always insolent in one way or another; Einstein too, with his difficult and almost untranslatable language) seemed paid to give it an "impossible" style, each according to his nature, proved it was impossible in the strict sense of the word by not continuing beyond the fifteenth issue.

Is it really playing on words to define in this way the course followed by Georges Bataille over the more than thirty years of a literary life that was still in gestation when I first knew him: after having been the impossible man, fascinated by what he could discover that was most unacceptable, who created *Documents* while destroying it, he broadened his views (in accordance with his old idea of going beyond the *no* of the stamping child) and, aware that a man is not completely a man unless he seeks his measure in this excess, made himself the man of the Impossible, determined to reach the point where—in this Dionysiac vertigo—high and low merge and the distance between everything and nothing vanishes.

But it is probably ridiculous, where Bataille is concerned, to try to define the course he took as though his thinking had been so feebly linear that it started from one point and arrived at another. By placing himself under the sign of the impossible from the very beginning, Bataille created around himself a margin that could not be crossed and in particular made it impossible for the friend who is writing these lines to make them convey anything but a very pale and very uncertain reflection of his departed friend.

The Imaginary World of
André Masson

Sharp senses, a quick hand, and the resources of a culture in which his imagination, always at work, reactivates itself—these are André Masson's weapons in the enterprise he has been carrying on, in various forms, for some forty years now: to create images each of which will be a *capture*, an immediate response to a *shock* and a capture of that shock, one might say, the artist sometimes capturing the dazzlement his eyes have experienced in a crucial moment in the face of a certain fragment of the vast panorama of the three kingdoms, sometimes a completely interior illumination in which nature had a part, certainly, but as primary source and not as direct cause.

Imaginary since, whether sensation or thought, it is always an imponderable that he attempts to arrest and nail down on canvas or paper, the world of André Masson nevertheless proves to be closely tied to the physical environment, the purveyor of sudden amazements or the object of a meditation that also proceeds by lightning-fast leaps.

A nature that knows no rest, whether antagonistic forces confront each other (in love as well as in war) or whether the equivocal play of metamorphoses mingles identities, a nature so fleeting and so secret that one can catch certain of its motions only by surprise and one must resort to myth to untangle its weave: these are the depths—

Preface to the exhibition "The Imaginary World of André Masson, etchings and lithographs, 1934–1963," at Galerie Gérald Cramer in Geneva, October 28–December 6, 1963.

changing in their detail but immutable overall—into which André Masson keeps delving, except for rare departures, as often toward subjects derived from his readings, from theater, or from the street and relations with people close to him as toward the expression of states of mind pertaining to the passions properly speaking.

An inventor in the strict sense of the word (his art being essentially the formulation of happy discoveries in the realm of the intelligible as well as in that of the tangible), André Masson is not only an artist who knows how to see and make others see in a new way but even more a visionary artist. The infinity that a moment of complete opening reveals to him in the veins of a leaf, the limbs of an insect, or the folds of a woman's body he encloses within the limits of the work, yet without limiting it. Whether he sets about recreating the shock received from a living presence or whether his quest for a world returned to a primitive purity carries him back to man's origins or even *within* nature, it is as though he challenges all perspectives except that of the cosmogonies and that for him nothing is worth anything if it does not seem to be a blossoming or revelation: the birth of the creatures and things that make up our surroundings, the looming of figures and ideas in the cavern of our minds.

Using widely differing registers (from notation in cursive writing to recording in absolute ideograms), depending on his mood and the momentary demands of the capture, acting as painter, drawer, or engraver whose many resources are not gratuitous demonstrations of virtuosity but varied approaches to giving the beautiful word "imager" its most profound signification, André Masson builds, piece by piece, with sudden flashes, a sort of legend of his moments, traversed from end to end by a breath of *La Légende des siècles*.

Who Is Aimé Césaire?

Translated by A. James Arnold

> "My mouth shall be the mouth of those calamities
> that have no mouth, my voice, the freedom of those
> who break down in the solitary confinement of
> despair."
>
> *Cahier d'un retour au pays natal*

*A*ndré Breton has the distinction of having been the first to point out, in his epoch-making article "Un Grand Poète noir," the importance of Aimé Césaire's appearance on the scene of French-language poetry and of poetry in general.

In April 1941 Breton, who was in Fort-de-France on his way to the United States and had just been subjected to police harassment by representatives of the pseudogovernment in Vichy, discovered an issue of the magazine *Tropiques* and then met Césaire, the principal force behind that publication whose contents proved that in spite of the horrible blows recently dealt to freedom there were still voices independent, timely, and resounding enough that their very existence was a pledge against despair for the fate of mankind. In Césaire, Breton recognized a magnificent spokesman for surrealism's enduring and essential claim: that instead of being put down and divided against himself, as he is in all parts of the globe where rationalistic and mechanistic Western civilization is dominant, man

First published in *Critique* 16, no. 216 (1965), this essay is based on a talk given in the Teatro La Fenice in Venice on the occasion of performances of Aimé Césaire's *La Tragédie du roi Christophe*, directed by Jean-Marie Serreau and presented on September 26 and 27, 1964.

should finally come into possession of his total humanity, which is out of the question as long as internal and external chains are imposed on him in the name of fallacious utilitarian pretexts. But does the convergence of the views of the *Tropiques* team with those of the group Breton had founded more than fifteen years earlier mean that the exceptional caliber of the "great Black poet" must be measured by the yardstick of surrealism alone?

Of course Césaire owes much to this movement and to some writers of the second half of the last century from whom the surrealists claimed descent, notably Rimbaud (in whom Césaire discovered the "rebel" that he himself had been from childhood) and Lautréamont (from whom he borrowed some turns of phrase, as several of his early writings testify). This took place in the hubbub of adolescent reading that also allowed him, as a boy casting about for the elements of a new language, to taste Claudel's "rustic" quality, over and above his catholicity, and Freud and Marx as well, whose joint influence acted upon his thought as it had acted upon the surrealists'. Moreover, it was in Paris, and thanks to a young Senegalese, Léopold Sédar Senghor, who like himself was a student there, that he discovered the beauty of Negro-African civilizations in the ethnographic works of Leo Frobenius and Maurice Delafosse, a decisive event.

As for his principal ideas, Césaire found in surrealism a way of looking at the world that had to appeal to him. Wasn't surrealism in open revolt against the entire framework of Western rationalism, which the European intellectuals assembled around Breton rejected as an intolerable tyranny, less tolerable still for a Black Antillean since that framework is, historically, the one the Whites *superimposed*, so to speak, on the slaves they imported from Africa and on their descendants?

Poetically, surrealism has appeared to a few Martinicans of Césaire's generation as a way out of the academic formalism their elders had subscribed to, guided as they were by a desire to demonstrate their cultural refinement by pure and simple imitation of the models imported from Europe. It was naive to try to use the Creole idiom as a literary vehicle of opposition, since that not only meant conforming to a superficial exoticism and locking oneself inside the narrow bounds of an outdated folklore, it also meant giving in to an idiom that had been forged in the humiliating conditions of slavery and has remained marked by them. Like Parnassianism, which had had a good many disciples abroad, surrealism was certainly a product of Europe, so that it was a simple matter to claim that the attitude of those Martinicans who were passionately interested in surrealism differed from the attitude of their predecessors only in the feeble extent to which Europe this time brought them the teaching of a different school. But contrary to Parnassianism, this European phenomenon was truly an instrument of warfare aimed against the ideas imported from Europe, and on top of that, by founding its method on automatic writing as a means of forgetting all that had been learned by descending into the deepest recesses of the self, this instrument furnished Césaire and his friends with a method that, first of all, would provide a tabula rasa and, without creating any ruts in advance, would permit them to get rid of their Antillean alienation (whereas they were Africans by reason of part of their ancestry at least, their culture was essentially French) and so to rediscover the authenticity that had been denied them.

This is approximately the amount of the Martinican Césaire's debt to modern European literature and thought that, not so long ago, evolved in a part of the world that today has lost many of its privileges. But hasn't this Martinican given back to world culture a truly irreplaceable contribution?

European surrealism, which provided a basis other than indiscriminate negation for the total subversion of arts and letters undertaken by dada, expressed the revolt of a certain number of intellectuals who could no longer take satisfaction in any of the goals that bourgeois society offered its members and who were indignant at the general state of affairs around them: the accountant mentality that regarded any exaltation of feeling or of the senses as a threat to law and order, a pervasive industrialization, the exploitation of practically everybody by a pretentious, silly minority who held all the important positions, colonial wars in which violence bordering on extreme barbarity was perpetrated against peoples whose only crime was to refuse a Western takeover. The officially recognized philosophy of rationalism not only was undermined in theory by progress in the physical and social sciences, it also appeared in practice to function as the tool and the cover for the most inhumane undertakings of a civilization centered on technology and profit. From all this derived the high value attached to the irrational (automatic writing and dreams), to the hyperrational (Alfred Jarry's pataphysics), even to the paralogical (occultism) as snubs to the Cartesian tradition and as a means for partially recuperating that which mankind is necessarily cut off from in a technological, profit-oriented society—that essential part that will be won or lost on a plane other than that of the intellect.

The surrealists were certainly sincere in embracing the proletarian cause, the only factor of positive upheaval they could count on. But their revolt—at the outset it was a mental revolt, a protest and a disavowal deriving from value judgments that lay claim to a higher morality—was not motivated by a sense of belonging objectively to a disadvantaged class. On the other hand, Césaire's revolt, though it was linked to similar high aims, sprang from his daily experience of injustice against the group with which he was aligned, a group that the Martinican ruling class, supported by the mother country, allows almost in its entirety to stagnate in poverty and, to top it off, despises for its physical features as well. That is why it should not be surprising that Césaire's surrealism takes on an especially harsh and dense quality: something like a volcanic explosion that had no need to place itself "in the service of the Revolution" since it was already of the same nature, having been born of the direct pressure of those harsh realities that open the way to revolutionary movements.

However disconcerting Césaire's poetry may sometimes be with its unbridled lyricism, its wild exuberance, and its willfully sibylline form, it is never far from concrete expression and has, moreover, gradually become more essential and clear and gotten rid of some baroque excrescences. Real scenes, sensations, and feelings are far more important than imaginary constructions, however much an extraordinary freedom of expression and a frequently apocalyptical tenor might induce one to believe that the poet puts little stock in the real world he lives in or in the precise way he lives in that world.

Yearnings of the heart, the evocation of his native land, or more generally, the exaltation of the tropics (as the antithesis of Western measure) through an explicit appeal to material details or a kind of mimetic savagery negating the very order of his utterance, references to the fate of Blacks, to Africa, which virtually haunts him, to the urgency of instituting a free and just society, to the overgrown and rocky terrain to be crossed in order to reach that society, these constitute the warp and woof—sometimes manifest, sometimes latent—of poems whose rhythm is almost always torrential and choppy, rich in unusual images and in odd turns wherein the frequent strangeness of the words (names of vegetable and animal species that Césaire intends to designate precisely so as to better react against Antillean "vagueness" and to make the thing itself stand out better, rare terms or neologisms that his solid training in French and Latin allows him to form easily) testifies neither to some preciosity nor to a desire to surprise the reader but simply to his will to extend the vocabulary of poetry and to take advantage of all the resources of the word as a prodigious human instrument.

Among the themes on which Césaire's poetry is constructed (not as a discourse on elevated subjects but as the natural expression of what is most meaningful to him), the central theme is certainly that of "negritude." He and his friend Senghor put forward this idea when, along with another future anticolonialist poet, the Guyanese Léon Damas, they published a paper called *L'Etudiant noir*, which aimed at enlightening their comrades from Africa and the New World concerning the common bond of their ancestry and their common condition as well: their belonging to a category of people not only whom the industrialized society of the West, and the imperialism deriving from it, exploits but who, in the eyes of Whites, are condemned as inferiors by the color of their skin. One must accept one's negritude positively, no longer shameful at being Black, and proudly lay claim to one's African roots; this is the substance of the message Césaire has struggled to communicate from his student days on and that has broadened and deepened with its proponent's increasing maturity.

It is necessary to insist a bit, since the idea has lent itself to numerous misunderstandings: "negritude" in Césaire's conception of it is not a synonym for "Blackness first" and in no way corresponds to what some have called a racism in reverse. The Black race is no more the chosen people than any other, and if it has one sovereign privilege, it is that of having for centuries, because of the slave trade and the enslavement of nearly all of Africa, undergone material and moral attacks that make of Blacks the "humiliated and offended" par excellence. It goes without saying that one could not truly and wholly live one's negritude without affirming the value of Black African cultures. If what Blacks have been able to create with a rudimentary technology were unworthy of our attention, the injustice would be less flagrant, and the wisest policy would be to endure ill fortune with a stout heart. Therefore it is imperative for all to know that, in many respects, these cultures can teach us precious lessons. For all that, can one consider oneself thoroughly Black without giving them the benefit of one's affection? This does not mean, however, that African cultures are decreed to be superior: what must be obtained for them is finally the right to equality or, most precisely, the right to be what they are and to remain *different*.

For Césaire to be conscious of his negritude and to be conscious of it as a Martinican requires that he pursue from the start two objectives: politically, to free his country of forms of economic exploitation that condemn the masses to pauperism; culturally, to bring the specifically Antillean element into proper relief, which implies that without underestimating the role of Western civilization one must turn toward the African heritage that is so often forgotten or denied by Antilleans of color who want only to be first-class Frenchmen. But thanks to an intelligence that finds a footing in his knowledge of Marxism, Césaire does not remain on that level alone: no salvation is possible for a people (or for an individual) in isolation and no one can claim to be free in a world where freedom is held up to ridicule by the oppression of others. Césaire, humiliated and offended, will therefore take up the cause of all the humiliated and offended, whatever race they may belong to, and his grand design will be to work toward a completely free world order in which henceforth no one should be obliged to endure the ordeals endured by the Black race. He was to commit himself in this direction not only as a writer but more actively as well, which is why he was to become mayor and deputy from Fort-de-France, first as a Communist leader and later as the leader of the Parti Progressiste Martiniquais, working for his constituents, of course, but in such a way as to work for all Blacks and for all humanity as well.

Throughout his various stages, which represent a deepening rather than an evolution of his thought, Césaire has on all occasions shown himself to be a humanist and a universalist in the grand tradition. The thirst for liberation that drives him and that knows neither ethnic nor geographic boundaries has always expressed itself in two areas, the one social and the other psychological. To finally bring about a world order such that no group or individual should be oppressed or despoiled by it and in which none of mankind's inner resources should be stifled, as they are in a civilization posited on technological excess, such are the ultimate goals toward which Césaire directs his labors, not as a utopian but as a man who knows that noth-

ing worthwhile can be realized without a constant effort to surpass
the present, without a vast enough vision to take in everything.

This elevation of vision and this passion for humanity are manifest, expressly or on reading between the lines, in all of Césaire's
writings: the poetic and dramatic works, those of the political man
who is capable of functioning as a historian, and the speeches of the
orator (which unfortunately have nearly all disappeared). Is this not
the quality that gives them all an equal density and resonance, whatever the genre in which Césaire expresses himself: opening up to the
song or the cry of pure poetry, formulating trenchant criticism, objectively reporting facts, or employing a Shakespearean sort of hybrid of various modes, as demonstrated so brilliantly in his recent *La
Tragédie du roi Christophe*. Throughout this diversity of accents one
discovers, in the Césaire of today as in the young poet, what Breton
had recognized at once: that invariably *major* tonal quality that is
close to what Baudelaire meant in his reference to Chateaubriand,
Alphonse Rabbe, and Edgar Allan Poe in *Fusées*: "the eternal note,
the eternal and cosmopolitan style."

A great Black poet according to Breton and according to those Africans who consider him one of their own, it happens that Césaire is
a Martinican poet, born on an island that is not only a racial and cultural melting pot but that possesses a still more significant characteristic: this tiny and presently overpopulated territory constitutes
the grudging support for a civilization of transplants. In Martinique
today no one can claim to be indigenous, since the Indians who were
the first inhabitants were wiped out by immigrants from Europe a
little over three centuries ago and since the White settlers made use
of Africa to furnish them with manpower; so that the present population essentially includes a small number of White descendants of
those settlers or of more recent ones, Black descendants of former
slaves, and a large number of people of color sprung from the mixing
of the two races.

If the poet is essentially someone who has to construct another world because he finds in this world no place to really put down roots, one is tempted to think that Césaire, more uprooted than anybody else because he is conscious of being the product of a disparate and narrow society that was formed not only in violence and iniquity but under the sign of a general transplantation as well, was in the most favorable situation to become more a poet than anybody else. Doubtless these conditions go some way toward explaining why the quest for authenticity, the reason behind all great poetry (to achieve one's own truth by creating one's own view of things) but in this case responding to the brutality of the real situation, was for Césaire all the more powerful as a motivation, since the stakes were of immediate importance both for him and for a multitude of other uprooted people; why, too, the freedom of expression he owed to surrealist practice led him to write so many poems whose jagged and torn aspect expresses, over and above their content, his profound state of division and disturbance at the same time that it reflects the practically unresolvable contradiction between the use of French (the mother tongue that he handles like a classical writer) and his urgent desire to become as African as possible. However, these are finally only conditions that others have reacted to differently, and if the analysis of this substratum can help one understand the sense of Césaire's vocation in terms of the precise range of his main themes and some of the characteristics of his poetry, it is vain to expect it to shed any light on the original cause of the presence in him of such verbal power. To try to explain the poetic genius of Césaire as a function of his Martinican origins would be as absurd as looking for the key to Lautréamont in the sociology of Montevideo or for the reasons behind Rimbaud's sudden appearance in the sociology of Charleville.

If there can be no further doubt that Césaire is not only a great Black poet but a great poet of decolonization, it is nonetheless necessary to forget his "negritude" and to listen to his voice as that of a great poet, period. For that, no better preparation than to place one-self in that perfectly unencumbered state that he talks about in his *Cahier d'un retour au pays natal*, concerning those men who have sprung from the land of Africa, for him the object of ardent nostalgia:

> they yield, captivated, to the essence of all things
> ignorant of surfaces but captivated by the motion of all things
> indifferent to conquering, but playing the game of the world
> truly the eldest sons of the world
> porous to all the breathing of the world
> fraternal locus for all the breathing of the world
> drainless channel for all the water of the world
> spark of the sacred fire of the world
> flesh of the world's flesh pulsating with the very motion of the
> world!

Opera: Music in Action

For René and Mary-Jo Leibowitz

One opera scene that never fails to move me, when it is performed tolerably well, is the famous "Miserere" in the last act of *Il Trovatore*: the touching lament of the soprano downstage is joined—in an astonishing mosaic of styles—by the brilliant song of the tenor who, supposedly locked within prison walls, is standing in the wings, and by the clamors or buzzings of a religious chorus, which also emanate from a hidden source, though this one is impossible to locate exactly. Our ears, therefore, are struck by sounds divided into distinct levels, two voices that can be clearly situated (one belonging to the woman we see lamenting and one, a little farther back, emitted by an invisible person) as well as a diffuse choral mass—the drone of a miserere—of which we know only that the place where it originates, masked by the stage set, is farther away from us than the pit in which the orchestra is playing its part as the fourth element in this musical and spatial constellation.

Those who hold that any debased work is vulgar (and this is the case of *Il Trovatore*, so well known that one of the oldest pieces of jazz is an adaptation of the "Miserere," and the Marx Brothers later would construct a marvelously burlesque film around a performance of that opera, in addition to which there is the startling parody of the "Miserere" that a London troupe, the Crazy Gang, presented in a show at Victoria Palace about ten years ago), those obsessed by the

First published in *L'Arc*, no. 27 (1965) (special issue "L'Opéra comme théâtre," ed. Bernard Dort), from Aix-en-Provence.

fear of seeming too much like a "good audience," will feel that here Verdi's methods are, as often, too obvious: a melodramatic situation handled in a way that strives for effect by the use of contrasting styles all the more marked because this diversity is illustrated by the respective relations of the performers with the stage, as it happens: a protagonist who is acting at the same time as she sings; a voice "off," as they say in movie language; and last, a group of voices thrown into the background as much by their lack of personality as by the invisibility of the choristers emitting them. With all due respect to the fastidious dilettantes, it seems we must recognize that these obvious methods are the methods of opera par excellence, opera being not only theater in music but also music in a theatrical space.

What is immediately striking, in fact, is how consistently composers of opera have used this procedure from the beginning of the last century to the present day. Both before and after Verdi, in whose work one sees an extreme case of the musical division corresponding to the division of the stage set (a vertical division for the quartet in *Rigoletto*, with the duke and the wench frolicking inside the inn, while outside the jester and his daughter exchange bitter words; a horizontal division in the last scene of *Aïda*, with, below, the tender duet of the lovers dying in a vault of the temple and, above, the sacred songs and dances of the priestesses, then the prayer of the pharaoh's daughter), the Italians have made ample use of it: not only does Bellini sometimes have the chorus sing in the wings in *Norma* and *I Puritani* but in the same way, in the latter, he has us hear the sound of horns and then shows us, in the third act, the hero venting his sorrow while the mad heroine walks and sings behind a window; in *The Barber of Seville*, Figaro begins his famous aria offstage, and in *Lucia di Lammermoor*, the distant sound of a festival comes from behind the theater during the scene that precedes that of the solemn signing of the marriage contract; closer to us, in *Tosca*, the procedure is used several times (in the second act, what one hears from the apartment of the baron Scarpia of the royal evening party where the beautiful Floria is singing, then the questioning of the patriot at the mercy of torturers, and, at the beginning of the third act, which takes place on a terrace of the Castle Sant' Angelo, the song of the shepherd walking by the base of the fortress). The case is exactly the same for German as well as Austrian opera: Weber employs it in the diabolical episode of *Der Freischütz* (demonic voices mingling with the yelping of dogs and cracking of a whip); in Wagner it appears most notably in *The Flying Dutchman* and in *Tristan* with the choruses of sailors, in *Siegfried* with the bird whose warbling the monster's vanquisher understands, and in *Parsifal* with the "children's voices singing under the cupola" of which Paul Verlaine has spoken; finally, Richard Strauss uses it in *Salome* (Iokanaan prophesying from the bottom of his well), and Alban Berg, who in *Wozzeck* puts the orchestra back on stage (a classical device: Mozart opted for it in *Don Giovanni*), derives a powerfully dramatic effect from the moaning of Wozzeck, who has disappeared in the pond. Nor could one forget the role of the chorus, sometimes visible and sometimes invisible, in *Boris Godunov* and, where French opera is concerned, the din from the *plaza de toros* in the last act of *Carmen*, the aria sung in the wings by the young peasant woman in Chabrier's *Le Roi malgré lui*, as well as the chorus of sailors that, in the second act of *Pelléas*, proves even Debussy was not above resorting to this method, though his intention was much more to create a musical atmosphere than to give musical emphasis to the vicissitudes of the drama (despite the fact that the closing of the heavy park gates on the innocently guilty Pelléas and Mélisande are expressed by the orchestra).

These are only examples, cited almost at random as they come to mind, and no doubt a somewhat systematic search would allow one to add more. But it is, in truth, much less important to demonstrate the consistency of this method than to figure out its significance. Now, this significance is more evident if one considers that another device, different but, as we shall see, aimed at a similar effect, is also in common use.

The fact that at the end of the first act as well as in the last scene of *Don Giovanni* Mozart places the musicians on stage, that in the second act of *Tristan* one hears hunting fanfares from offstage, or that in *Aïda* the trumpets are in the hands of musicians who appear in the procession of victorious Egyptian troops represents an integration (visible or not) of the orchestra into the action; whereas in the "Miserere" it is on the contrary the singers who, with one exception, find themselves if not withdrawn from the action and attached to the orchestra, then at least put between parentheses. Although each of these devices appears in some sense as the negative of the other, in both cases is it not a matter of substituting a more complex organization for the simple division between singers and instrumentalists, the first on the stage, the second at their music stands? It is as though the composer used voices and instruments with primary stress on their physical distribution, conceived not as a function of hearing only, but with the understanding that opera music assumes its true meaning in relation to the imagined realities of which a special portion is set within the space of the stage—sometimes lavishly furnished; sometimes abandoned to the protagonists alone, even a single protagonist; sometimes promoted to the rank of the only visible fragment of a vaster region in which other beings breathe whose presence one can only divine. Within the actual limits of the stage and beyond these limits, a living space is established, which is modulated by many types of division—auditory or almost palpable— and which is the site of a constant traffic not only for the characters (entering, exiting, moving about) but also for the instrumental music itself, whether the performers become involved in the action or whether the circumstances of the action find their direct expression—another variety of osmosis—in the orchestra, as when Puccini introduces into the prelude to the last act of *Tosca* the noise of the bells of Rome, which (they say) he had noted with the greatest concern for realism and which, combining it with other themes, he used for a sort of musical *collage*. Of course, these devices are not the prerogative of operatic theater (since the other sort of theater is also capable of having actors speak from the wings or sound invisible fanfares, among other offstage noises). But it is in the opera house that their use, ceasing to be purely occasional, gives rise to developments of a certain amplitude; and this, no doubt, is a result of the very nature of opera.

Far from being the simple outcome of the addition of a dramatic action and a musical composition, an opera is music in action and, beyond its emotive value (serious or farcical), literally takes the theater as a *theater of operations*. Here singing—a highly stylized variety of speech—proves to be organically linked to the immediately "theatrical" elements that are the respective positions of the characters, their movements, their appearances and disappearances, in an interaction in which the music remains supreme and the orchestra therefore cannot have the passive role of a background of sound but (to different degrees, naturally, depending on the periods and the composers) finds itself involved in the plot, whether it remains in its pit or doubles up to invade the stage and possibly penetrate even behind the set. In this theater, the very special reason for the work's existence seems to be that it should cause an intensely palpable space to blossom forth, a space that will differ from the neutral space in which, too often in spoken theater, a text is simply delivered and scenically illustrated. One would say it was a sort of *sonorous space*, suggested not only by the organization of sounds in an imaginary architecture but by the striking plurality of their sources, the mobility of at least a few of these sources, the attribution of clearly distinct vocal parts to variously situated singers, and the exchanges that take place between music emanating from this side of the footlights and the singing (if not music) produced on the other side by performers whose

number and mutual relations manifestly vary. At least in its traditional forms, doesn't opera include, besides the orchestral overture
that presents the essential themes, a series of recitatives, arias,
duets, or ensembles of greater or lesser numbers whose alternation
alone, on the stage, already outlines the frameworks that will be
filled by the argument and the staging? Musical invention and dramatic movement are therefore interdependent, to the point of perfect overlapping for the major part of the work, the action then being
simply music in images and the music being action that has become
an insidious or urgent resonance. To see music caught in the toils of
a space affirmed in a new way each time by the workings of the stage
mechanics and yet feel that it escapes this web to create the vibrant
space in which one finds oneself plunged is the miracle of opera.
And on the faith of the correct executions one may have heard (difficult performances given the many factors involved), one is tempted
to suggest, paraphrasing Charles Baudelaire, according to whom
"music carves out the sky," that, as it happens, it carves out and
sculpts the space of the theater in the way that the inner arrangement
of a baroque building animates its geometry and opens up perspectives within it.

That a chorus of underground demons threatens Don Giovanni as
he is about to descend into hell, that Verdi for the "Miserere" locks
his tenor in a tower whose front is the only part shown, that he also
exploits musically the dichotomy of a set seen in section, that the instruments gathered in a group just in front of our seats mingle with
Roman bells, or that certain of them leave their pit either with great
ceremony or surreptitiously—these distensions of the normal
framework of the stage, these manifest intrusions of the drama into
the orchestra or the doublings of the latter to create another plane of
sound and establish a "music within the music" in the same way that
there exists a "theater within the theater" (illustrations of which are
offered by Shakespeare's *Hamlet*, Corneille's *Illusion comique*, and
many other works), these devices finally appear as nothing more than

paroxysmal applications of what I believe is opera's golden rule: a close alliance of the music not only with the fictive world of the dramatic situations and the personalities assigned to the various characters but with that concrete reality, the spatial situation of the performers. Whether they fall within our visual field or not, their arrangement and their proximity, separation, solitary wandering, formation into larger or smaller and more or less homogeneous groups for alternating or simultaneous songs are fundamental elements in the amazing combination of sounds, articulated words, rhythms, gestures, postures, and images that make opera a total theater, not only because the different arts work together but because the conjunction of opposites that occurs here may impel the spectacle to the most extreme point of tension. In opera, in fact, lyric expansion (in the fullest sense of the phrase) joins with a clockwork rigorousness of movement, and music lifts into the realm of the unlimited a closed space in the heart of which, one may say, the maneuvers of a chess game take place.

Design by David Bullen
Typeset in Mergenthaler Garamond #3
by Wilsted & Taylor
Printed by Maple-Vail
on acid-free paper